ORGANIZATIONAL STRUCTURE
IN AMERICAN POLICE AGENCIES

SUNY series in New Directions
in Crime and Justice Studies

Austin T. Turk, editor

ORGANIZATIONAL STRUCTURE IN AMERICAN POLICE AGENCIES

Context, Complexity, and Control

Edward R. Maguire

State University of New York Press

Published by
State University of New York Press, Albany

For information, address State University of New York Press,
90 State Street, Suite 700, Albany, NY 12207

Production by Diane Ganeles
Marketing by Patrick Durocher

Cover photo: courtesy of the National Archives, photo no. 412-DA-4154

Library of Congress Cataloging-in-Publication Data

Maguire, Edward R.
   Organizational structure in American police agencies : context, complexity, and control
/ Edward R. Maguire.
      p. cm. — (SUNY series in new directions in crime and justice studies)
   Includes index.
   ISBN 0-7914-5511-4 (alk. paper) — ISBN 0-7914-5512-2 (pbk. : alk. paper)
      1. Police administration—United States. I. Title. II. Series
HV8141 .M24 2003
353.3'6'0973—dc21

                                                                    2002021817

10 9 8 7 6 5 4 3 2 1

For Meme,

for Mom and Dad,

and for my little buddy Alexander,

the Sunshine of my life.

Contents

Tables

Figures

Foreword

The way in which police forces are organized is thought to be important in determining how they perform. Whenever problems occur, such as dramatic rises in crime rates, incidents of misconduct, violations of human rights, or inability to meet community expectations, the first response is to reorganize the police by eliminating units, changing lines of command, abolishing or creating new positions, changing rank structures, revising codes of conduct, intensifying supervision, and developing new operating policies. As I observed several years ago, "Changing organizational boxes is to policing what curriculum reform is to universities—a fractious exercise periodically repeated whenever the institution is challenged" (Bayley, 1992).

The problem with this solution, so popular with the public as well as the police, is that it assumes that the organizational structure of police forces is manipulable, that it can be changed by human decision. What if this is not the case? What if the structure of police organizations is shaped by factors beyond easy human contrivance, such as the size and age of the force, the degree of stability in the political environment, the complexity of governmental regulation, the geographical dispersion of the population, or the nature of police work itself? What if would-be reformers aren't given a free shot in changing police organizations?

Ed Maguire tries to answer this question in this insightful and readable book. Doing so requires considerable courage because in order to answer the question it is necessary, first, to develop a way of describing variations in police organizations and, second, to specify a short list of factors that are most likely to play a powerful role in shaping police organizations. Maguire rises to both challenges brilliantly by systematically reviewing with enormous insight the entire field of organizational studies. Indeed, his distillation of the major empirically supported theoretical propositions about the environmental determinants of organizational change is a major contribution of the book.

By developing and testing a parsimonious theory, Maguire rescues police organizations from the intellectual limbo of being considered unique. He provides evidence that allows us to determine scientifically whether police organizations are different in their genesis and organizational dynamics from other organizations, both public and private. In short, Maguire places the police in the intellectual domain of public administration and organizational sociology.

This book should also revive interest in a topic that, although recognized as important, has received scant scholarly attention. Other than James Q. Wilson's attempt in *Varieties of Police Behavior* (1968) to develop a theory of police service based on governmental determinants, there has been only one other previous scholarly study that took up the challenge of explaining the organization of the police: Robert H. Langworthy's *The Structure of Police Organizations* (1986). Interestingly, Langworthy's study, like Maguire's, began as a doctoral dissertation at the School of Criminal Justice, State University of New York at Albany. What accounts, one wonders, for the growth of this tenuous tradition at Albany? Perhaps it's the water. More seriously, perhaps good work inspires good work.

This book represents the leading edge of theorizing about the diversity of American police organizations. It covers a wide swath of American policing; it develops a concise and elegant theory; it draws inclusively on studies of complex organizations from other realms of public and private endeavor; and it presents its findings in clear, straightforward language. Most important of all, it should hearten reformers who sometimes despair about producing significant change in police organizations. There may be impediments to reform, but they do not lie primarily in the external environment of policing.

David H. Bayley

Acknowledgments

Because this study has benefitted from conversations with dozens of police practitioners, scholars, researchers, conference attendees, and colleagues from around the country, it is impossible to personally thank all of those whose thoughts, words, and ideas have in one way or another influenced this work. There are a number of people, however, whose influence was more direct, and I would like to acknowledge their various contributions personally.

This book is a revised version of my doctoral dissertation from the School of Criminal Justice at the University at Albany, SUNY. The cochairs of the dissertation committee were David Bayley and Rob Worden. Both were responsive and helpful and share the credit for making this a better work. Graeme Newman, David Duffee, and David McDowall rounded out the committee, each lending a unique form of expertise. I owe Graeme a personal thank you for all of his help during the Ph.D. program. Joe Kuhns and Jeff Snipes were fellow doctoral students when I was writing the dissertation that preceded this book, and both contributed to my general notions about what it means to be a good scholar.

Bob Langworthy's 1983 doctoral dissertation at SUNY kindled my interest in police organizations and laid the foundation for this study. Bob was the first person in police research to go this route, and he made the way a lot simpler for those of us who followed. My thinking on police organizations has benefitted from many conversations with him, and his influence is woven throughout this book.

Thanks to Langworthy and others, organizational scholarship in policing is now growing. The thoughts and ideas expressed in this book have benefitted from my intellectual kinship with a number of police organizational scholars. Dick Ritti and Steve Mastrofski both read earlier versions of the manuscript, contributing their insights about both police and organizations. Chuck Katz's work on specialized units influenced my discussion of functional differentiation and institutional theory. William King's application of a life-course perspective to police organizations influenced my discussion of organizational age. As these scholars and others continue to generate theoretically compelling ideas, I grow more optimistic about the future of organizational scholarship in policing.

The first half of this book was written when I was working for the U.S. Justice Department's Office of Community Oriented Policing Services (COPS). My exposure to police agencies around the nation gave me a more tangible appreciation for the extent to which police organizations vary. Several COPS interns assisted with the literature review and data collection, including Tom Donnelly, Will Keyser, Matt Hickman, Jen Beadle, and Carlo Arquillano. They made the otherwise tedious work of original data collection fun. I especially thank Craig Uchida for making it possible to collect the data and for providing a fascinating firsthand experience with criminal justice policy at the national level.

The second half of the book was completed while I was an Assistant Professor at the University of Nebraska at Omaha (UNO). Dennis Roncek provided expert assistance with questions that arose during the statistical analyses. Samuel Walker contributed to my thinking about the role of organization age and the extent to which organizations are influenced by their own history. Jihong Zhao served as my partner in several research projects on police organizations and also influenced my thinking in these areas. Finally, while at UNO I was also fortunate to have had a dream team of research assistants, especially Kimberly Hassell and Hank Robinson.

No author can responsibly claim complete ownership of all the ideas expressed in a book. I thank all those who have influenced my thinking about police organizations and take credit for whatever else, however good or bad, remains.

CHAPTER 1

Introduction

Formal organizations surround us and pervade almost every facet of our lives. We work in them, shop in them, pay our bills to them; we become angry with them and enamored by them; we are educated and nursed to health in them; we earn credentials from them, seek justice from them, fight against them, and wait in line in them; we are treated fairly and unfairly by them; we are both victimized and protected by them; and, although we might want to, we can almost never escape them. Because formal organizations are such a basic element of modern life, social scientists from a variety of disciplines have strived for many decades to understand them.

In the beginning, research usually focused on particular organizations or types of organizations. Factories were studied as factories, prisons as prisons, and government agencies as government agencies—not as organizations. Early researchers rarely made an effort to draw generalizations beyond the particular types of organizations under study (Scott, 1992). By the early 1950s, scholars began to recognize that although there are many differences between collectivities like factories, prisons, and government agencies, they share one important thing in common: they are all organizations. Many of the classics in organizational studies emerged around this period, including Weber's (trans. 1947) writings on bureaucracy and leadership, Selznick's (1949) analysis of the Tennessee Valley Authority, and Merton's collection of readings on organizations (Merton et al., 1952).

Early organizational scholars emerged from a variety of disciplines, including political science, public administration, sociology, and psychology. Most specialized in various approaches to studying organizations; these specialties often reflected the academic background of the individual. For instance, many focused on social-psychological processes among workers, managers, and other key actors, others on economic aspects of the organization, and others on sociological processes (Scott, 1992). By the late 1950s, organizational specialists from a variety of disciplines began to form schools specializing in organizational studies. A journal, *Administrative Science Quarterly*, was born in 1956 to publish

1

the growing number of research studies in organizational science. Several classic texts appeared, organizing the collected knowledge of the new field of study (Blau, 1955, 1956; March and Simon, 1958). Since that time, dozens of new schools and journals and hundreds of books have emerged in the organizational studies arena. Today, organizational science is a well-developed field of study, with doctoral programs around the country, annual conferences, and a specialized literature that continues to grow each year. Nearly every conceivable type of organization has been studied using a variety of methodologies. Chapter 2 will expand on this brief history of organizational studies.

One type of organization that has not been frequently subjected to rigorous analysis by organizational scholars is police agencies. Given their role in promoting public safety, responding to emergency situations, maintaining order, and fighting crime, it is surprising that organizational scholars would pay so little attention to the police. Nevertheless, a number of scholars within the policing field have applied organizational theory concepts to the police. Peter Manning's *Police Work: The Social Organization of Policing* and James Q. Wilson's *Varieties of Police Behavior* are classic books on the police that employ an organizational approach. Although these two books contributed lasting insights to the policing literature, theoretically oriented studies of police agencies as organizations are rare.

Social scientists have studied the police for nearly four decades. Yet, the majority of these studies have focused on police officers and police work, rather than police organizations. This is not surprising, given the frequently heard sentiment that it is not the organization that matters, but the people within it. In a chapter entitled "Organizations Matter," Wilson (1989) argues that although people and tasks are important, we cannot fully understand either until we understand their organizational context. The almost exclusive focus on people and tasks has left a large gap in our systematic knowledge of the police. Although reformers have described numerous schemes for reorganizing the police, scholars have echoed well-worn complaints about the paramilitary nature of the police "bureaucracy," and many have outlined the flaws of the police rank structure, there have been few empirical studies describing and explaining police organizations and their features. Duffee's (1990) advice to criminal justice scholars seems particularly appropriate—we should focus on describing and explaining what criminal justice organizations do, rather than on what they should be doing.

Unlike other Western nations, the United States has an extremely fragmented and localized "system" of policing, with a confusing array of overlapping jurisdictions and responsibilities (Bayley, 1985; Maguire et al., 1997b). Under the American federal system of government, thousands of local governments created their own police forces (Bayley, 1992). Each of these forces is separate, distinct, and under autonomous command. Though most police agencies have informal or formal mutual aid agreements (in case of emergency) with those in neighboring communities, they are independent entities with their own unique structures, cultures, policies, and procedures (Ostrom et al., 1978a). The result of the fragmented and localized evolution of American policing is that: (1) there is a huge number of police agencies, and (2) these agencies exhibit tremendous variety in organizational form.

According to the 1992 Directory Survey of Law Enforcement Agencies conducted by the U.S. Census Bureau (Reaves, 1993), there are 17,344 publicly funded state and local law enforcement agencies in the United States. Of these, 12,444 are classified as municipal police departments. The majority of these are quite small, with over 11,000 (over 90%) serving communities of fewer than 25,000 people, and nearly 12,000 (over 95%) serving communities of fewer than 50,000 people. These smaller municipal agencies employ a mean of 12 full-time sworn officers—half employ 5 or fewer officers. Although the remaining 529 agencies serving populations greater than 50,000 constitute only 4.2% of all municipal police agencies, they employ 58% of the sworn officers—a mean of 383 officers per department.[1]

While small police agencies exhibit less variation in formal organizational structure than larger agencies, there is still some structural variation among smaller agencies (Ostrom, Parks, and Whitaker, 1978b). However, larger agencies have more people, more resources, and more tasks. One method for improving coordination and control as organizations grow is to institute formal structures. The largest municipal police agencies in the country exhibit staggering variety in the way they are organized, both in terms of the complexity of their structural arrangements, and the modes of structural coordination and control that they employ. Some have 4–5 rank levels, whereas others have 10–12; some operate out of a single headquarters facility, whereas others have dozens of precinct houses; some are staffed by generalists who respond to nearly every conceivable situation, whereas others are staffed by specialists in dozens of areas, from missing children to traffic accident reconstruction; some are heavily decentralized administratively, with front-line supervisors empowered to make strategic decisions, whereas others are highly centralized, with decision making authority granted only to the chief or a few selected deputies; some have hundreds of forms, rigid rules, and written policies covering almost every imaginable contingency, whereas others rely on more informal mechanisms for maintaining order; some employ large administrative staffs to keep the organization under control and running smoothly, whereas others maintain lean administrative units to focus their resources "on the streets." What factors explain this tremendous variation in the structure of large American municipal police agencies? That is the focus of this study—to empirically examine the determinants of formal organizational structure in large municipal police agencies.

To do so, I rely extensively on the large body of theory and research which has emerged in the sociology of organizations and structural organization theory over the last four decades. Several hundred studies have examined the factors which influence the structures of nearly every type of organization: manufacturing and service, professional and nonprofessional, public and private, profit and nonprofit, large and small. Police organizations, however, have received very little attention in these studies.

Only one scholar has imported the accumulated knowledge of structural organization theory into policing in a comprehensive fashion. Robert Langworthy examined for the first time the determinants of structure in large municipal police agencies (1983b). He followed the dissertation with several articles (Langworthy, 1983a; 1985a; 1985b), and a book (Langworthy, 1986). What research into the determinants of police organization structure that has been done since has been at least partly based on Langworthy's work.

Langworthy's work forged a new road in the study of the police. Langworthy argued persuasively that nearly all scholarly attention to police organizations as a unit of analysis was based on normative theories and prescriptions, leaving a large empirical gap of unexplored territory. His analysis was the first comparative empirical examination to treat the structure of police organizations as a dependent variable. Since his work appeared, a few empirical articles on the subject have been published, but, in general, the examination of police organizational structures has not progressed in an orderly fashion.

This study will update, expand, and improve upon the prior literature on police organization structures, making four contributions. First, the entire study process—from the development of a theoretical model, to variable selection, measurement issues, and methodology—will be more firmly rooted in the broad sociological literature on organizational structures. Second, the cross-sectional data set used for this analysis contains information from approximately 400 large municipal police agencies, far more than in prior studies. Third, because some of the data used in the analysis were collected specifically for this study, I will be able to measure some concepts (such as centralization of command) that have been unavailable in other data sets. Finally, the statistical analysis that will be used in this study will be more concise, cohesive, and powerful than prior analyses. Most studies have used bivariate correlations and other similar techniques to infer relationships among a dozen or more variables. This study tests a series of multivariate theoretical models using structural equation modeling techniques. With these four contributions, this study picks up where Langworthy and others left off.

The results of this study will be directly applicable to ongoing debates about how police organizations ought to be structured during the community policing era. Despite three decades of normative prescriptions urging police agencies to modify their structures, police administrators may not be entirely free to design their organizations as they see fit. Police organizations exist in certain contexts—they have different histories and traditions, they come in a variety of sizes, they approach the job of policing in different ways, and they are located in different environments. For decades, organizational theorists have studied the impact of these contextual features on how organizations are structured. Put simply, certain organizational forms may simply "go with" certain contexts. Langworthy (1986, p. 2) explored this possibility by examining the "extent to which the structure of police agencies is constrained by factors beyond managerial control, including city size, composition of the population, and agency size, or by more basic decisions, such as how the job of policing is to be done." This study will extend Langworthy's analysis by testing for the possibility that these and other social forces constrain the way that police organizations are structured. Although the primary goal of this study is to develop and test a theoretical model of formal structure in police organizations, the results of this exercise will have implications for policy, reform, and practice in policing.

Outline of the Work

Chapter 2 examines the definition of organizational structure, delineates the various components of structure, and reviews the different strategies for measuring structural variation. Organizational structures have two primary dimensions: complexity and control. Structural complexity is a cluster of attributes that gives the organization its shape. Vertical, functional, and spatial differentiation are the individual components of structural complexity. Structural control and coordination mechanisms are tools that an organization uses to control and coordinate its work and its workers. Formalization, centralization, and administrative density are the individual components of structural control and coordination.

Chapter 3 discusses the "context" of organizational structure. The four broad components that comprise an organization's context are its size, age, technology, and environment. This chapter reviews the various conceptual and methodological issues in each of these four areas, and summarizes the research evidence on the effects of these factors on organizational structures.

Chapter 4 briefly reviews the specific literature on police organizational structure. Although the literature that explicitly examines police structures is quite small, certain empirical and theoretical works have implicitly touched on structural issues. I first discuss the frequent uncritical use of structural concepts and variables in prior theory and research on the police. I then try to extract from the policing literature any works or ideas that may be useful for developing and testing a theoretical model of police organizational structure.

Chapter 5 develops a new contextual theory of police organizational structure. This chapter briefly reviews the role of theory in prior studies of police structure, and then outlines a basic theory that assumes a causal order between context, complexity, and control in large municipal police organizations. Next, this chapter outlines the details of the contextual theory of police organizational structure by expanding the concepts of technology and environment as they pertain to police agencies. In all, this chapter outlines more than fifty hypotheses about the direct effects between individual elements of context, complexity, and control in large municipal police organizations.

Chapter 6 first describes the sample and the various data sources that will be used to test the theory developed in the prior chapter. Next, this chapter describes all of the variables used to measure the theoretical concepts. Finally, this chapter provides descriptive statistics for all of the variables in the model. Since there is a twenty year gap in our descriptive knowledge of how large police organizations are structured, the discussion of structural dimensions provided in this chapter represents the state-of-the-art.

Chapter 7 first describes in detail the methods used to test the theory outlined in chapter 5, and then reports the results. This chapter improves on prior tests that relied on simplistic measures of association by estimating a series of comprehensive multivariate models. Structural equation modeling techniques are used to simultaneously estimate the measurement and structural portions of each model. Following the results of the analysis, this chapter summarizes the evidence for and against a contextual theory of police organizational structure.

Chapter 8 summarizes the findings from the previous two analytical chapters, and then assesses the utility of these results in three areas: (1) implications for future theories of police organizational structure; (2) implications for future research on police organizations, including studies of police behavior that use organizational variables; and finally, (3) implications for policy and reform in large municipal agencies.

CHAPTER 2

What is Organizational Structure?

This chapter introduces the concept of formal organizational structure and the various roles that it has played in theory and research on complex organizations. Structure was initially considered important only for how it might impact other organizational attributes like performance or employee productivity. However, as sociologists began to apply their theoretical perspectives and research methodologies to the study of complex organizations, structure came to be regarded as a dependent as well as an independent variable. Sociologists added much to the growing field of organization theory, and for several decades, structure occupied center stage in sociological research on organizations. As a result, the theories, methods, and concepts used for studying formal organizational structure were refined repeatedly throughout the literature. Today structure no longer occupies center stage in the study of organizations, but it remains an important and well-grounded element of organization theory (Donaldson, 1995; Kalleberg et al., 1996).

Organizations as a Unit of Analysis

Organizations have been the focus of empirical research for several decades. Much of the early research sought to discover organizational correlates of increased performance, in whatever way performance might be measured. In order to make organizations better, early reformers argued, it was necessary to change their leaders, personnel, culture, behavior, policies, and/or structures. Most early studies of organizations sought to confirm or deny normative prescriptions for achieving better organizations. These studies typically examined organizations as independent variables.

In the late 1950s researchers began to conceive of organizations as more than just rationally-derived mechanisms for the production of goods and services, but as entities worthy of understanding for what they are in addition to what they produce. Organizations are greater than the sum of their parts. They expand and contract, rise and fall, and

9

generally take on lives of their own. Organizations, like individuals and social groups, do not only act, but are acted upon as well. They are influenced, shaped and constrained by a complex interaction of political, social, economic, cultural, and institutional forces. Organizations exhibit patterned regularities, and they can (and indeed should) be studied apart from the people within them (Blau et al., 1966; Blau and Schoenherr, 1971). Just as psychologists strive to understand the behavior of individuals, organizational researchers strive to understand the behavior of organizations as "corporate persons" (Coleman, 1974). As Scott (1992, p. 7) argues, organizations are "actors in their own right . . . they can take actions, utilize resources, enter into contracts, and own property." Furthermore, they can commit crimes and cause large-scale accidents (Hall, 1999, pp. 12–14). The general point here is that organizations vary. Explaining this variation is worthwhile. Therefore, organizations have come to be regarded in empirical research as dependent as well as independent variables.

The Sociology of Organizations

In the late 1950s and 1960s, the study of organizations split into two separate but related camps: micro-level organizational behavior and macro-level organizational theory. Doctoral programs in organization studies tend to reflect this split—faculty within programs usually specialize in one or the other. For those focusing on organizational behavior, the attitudes and behaviors of actors within organizations are the primary unit of analysis. Academics from this group emerged primarily from psychology and management backgrounds. For those focusing on organization theory, organizations themselves—their processes, structures, and goals—are the primary unit of analysis. Academics from this group emerged primarily from sociology, public administration and political science backgrounds.

Early organization theorists focused a great deal of attention on the many differences between organizations. They sought to find out how these differences developed, and whether or not they were important. As Scott (1992) argues, "while organizations may possess common generic characteristics, they exhibit staggering variety—in size, in structure, and in operating processes." Organizations are defined by a number of conceptual components, including, but not limited to their structure, size, performance, goals, leadership, professionalism, culture, and identity. All of these components are important features of organizations, and all have received a good deal of research attention. Starting in the early 1960s, however, the formal structures of organizations began to receive a disproportionate amount of attention in the empirical and theoretical literature. This trend continued strongly into the early 1980s, and then tapered off. Although research examining organizational structure continues to appear in popular organizational studies journals, the bulk of the research in this area emerged in the twenty-five year period from approximately 1960 to 1985. By the mid-1990s, however, it began to experience a mild resurgence (Donaldson, 1995; Kalleberg et al., 1996).

Much of this research attention was devoted to defining structure, identifying its distinct components, and seeking valid and reliable methods for measuring structural variables. Over this two-decade period of intense research on organizational structure, researchers and theorists debated the merits of various definitions, theoretical perspectives, measurement schemes, and methodologies. Like many scholarly debates, some of the issues emerging from the search to understand organizational structures were never entirely resolved. Researchers have developed long lists of variables to describe organizational structures, and have suggested a number of methodological and conceptual schemes for grouping these individual dimensions together into meaningful constructs. Yet, for the most part, although researchers continue to squabble over naming conventions and other particulars, a basic consensus has developed about the key generic dimensions of formal structure.

Dimensions of Structure

Organizational structure is the formal apparatus through which organizations accomplish two core activities: the division of labor and the coordination of work (Scott, 1992). Mintzberg's (1979, p. 2) definition of structure eloquently reflects these two dimensions:

> Every organized human activity—from the making of pots to the placing of a man on the moon—gives rise to two fundamental and opposing requirements: the division of labor into various tasks to be performed, and the coordination of these tasks to accomplish the activity. The structure of an organization can be defined simply as the sum total of the ways in which it divides its labor into distinct tasks and then achieves coordination among them.

Organizational theorists and empirical researchers have identified dozens of individual structural variables. Some of these have been widely discussed throughout the literature; others have appeared only briefly. Some have achieved a broad consensus among organizational scholars as core elements of structure; others have been dismissed or ignored altogether. Some overlap conceptually with others, and some are considered conceptually distinct. But nearly all of them relate to how an organization divides, controls, coordinates, organizes and structures its workers and its work. The following list shows a sampling of the more popular structural elements identified in the literature (Blau and Schoenherr, 1971; Robbins, 1987, pp. 54–55).

• Administrative Component	• Integration
• Autonomy	• Occupational Differentiation
• Centralization	• Professionalization
• Complexity	• Segmentation
• Concentration	• Span of Control
• Delegation of Authority	• Spatial Differentiation
• Differentiation	• Specialization
• Formalization	• Standardization
• Functional Differentiation	• Vertical Span

The sheer number of variables that are used to describe organizational structures prompted researchers to seek out ways of organizing the variables into a more parsimonious conceptual model, and/or to combine the individual features into broad constructs.

Just as efforts to identify the features that constitute an organization's structure have prompted decades of debate, the best way to reduce the number of variables necessary to describe the variation in structure has also been problematic. Some researchers have turned to inductive statistical data reduction techniques such as factor analysis (Pugh et al., 1968; Reimann, 1973), cluster analysis (Reimann, 1973), or Q-analysis (Blackburn, 1982) to identify the core dimensions of structure. Others have attempted more deductive approaches, relying on intuition, common sense, or theory to develop parsimonious conceptual schemes for describing organizational structures (e.g., Hsu, Marsh, and Mannari, 1983). Despite the technique used, nearly all of these efforts have resulted in similar two- or three-dimensional descriptions of structure. Hall, Haas, and Johnson (1967) distinguished between complexity and formalization; Hage and Aiken (1967b) distinguished between complexity and centralization; Klatzky (1970) distinguished between complexity and coordination; Blau and Schoenherr (1971) distinguished between differentiation and administration; Child (1973) distinguished between complexity and bureaucratic control; Kriesburg (1976) distinguished between differentiation and centralization; Rushing (1976) distinguished between differentiation and coordination; Ford and Slocum

(1977) distinguished between complexity, formalization, centralization, and administration; Mintzberg (1979) distinguished between division of labor and coordination mechanisms; Dalton and his colleagues (1980) distinguished between structural characteristics and structuring characteristics; Hsu, Marsh and Mannari (1983) distinguished between complexity and control; Robbins (1987) distinguished between complexity, formalization, and centralization; Scott (1992) distinguished between division of labor/structural differentiation and coordination and control of work; and most recently, Glisson (1992) distinguished between complexity, formalization and centralization. This list represents just a sample of efforts to develop parsimonious conceptual schemes for describing the variation in organizational structures.

Reviewing the above list of structural dimensions, one is struck by the conceptual similarities. In fact, there are really only two prominent differences between the various schemes: differences in nomenclature, and differences in indicators. The differences in nomenclature are prominent and are likely to confuse an organizational theory novice wading through the vast literature for the first time. After acquiring some familiarity with the literature, however, it becomes readily apparent that division of labor, differentiation, and complexity are terms that are nearly always used interchangeably to describe the way the organization slots, places, organizes, or locates its work and its workers.[1] Likewise, coordination, administration, control, formalization and centralization are all used to describe mechanisms by which an organization achieves coordination and control among its work and its workers. Hsu, Marsh, and Mannari (1983) and Child (1973) term these two clusters of variables "complexity" and "control." Despite differences in the nomenclature used to describe variation in organizational structures, researchers have essentially settled on two main dimensions: structural complexity and structural control. These naming conventions will be used throughout the rest of this study.

More problematic than differences in nomenclature are differences in the individual variables and/or indicators that are used to measure structural complexity and control. Throughout the literature, organizational scholars mistakenly confuse structural concepts, using complexity variables to measure control, and control variables to measure complexity. Stanfield (1976) argues that this type of error is a serious flaw in the organizational literature, and is based on the tendency of organizational researchers to rely on "unrationalized categorizations." This type of error results when researchers use careless or partial indicators of a construct, when they define a concept poorly, or when they fail to distinguish between two related concepts. Part of the problem can also be attributed to the abstract nature of the prominent concepts in organizational studies. The solution to the problem of unrationalized categorization is to select variables that are clearly indicative of structural complexity and structural control, and to justify their selection based on the bulk of prior research, rather than relying on individual studies to justify variable selection. In the following sections, I define complexity and control, and describe the individual structural variables used to measure each concept.

Structural Complexity

Structural Complexity, according to Robbins (1987, p. 5), is "the extent of differentiation within the organization. This includes the degree of specialization, or division of labor, the number of levels in the organization's hierarchy, and the extent to which the organization's units are dispersed geographically." Thus complexity has three basic components: vertical differentiation, functional differentiation, and spatial differentiation.[2] The more an organization becomes differentiated in any or all of these areas, the more complex its structure. As I will argue many times throughout this book, it is very important for a number of reasons to view the elements of structural complexity as analytically distinct.

Vertical Differentiation

Vertical Differentiation focuses on the nature of the hierarchy within an organization. Organizations with elaborate chains of command are more vertically differentiated than those with simpler command structures. Organizational hierarchies are often described as pyramids, with the width of the pyramid signifying the number of workers, and the distance from the base to apex representing the number of layers. Analysts interested in vertical differentiation have used graphical techniques to compare the shapes, or the "morphology" of different organizations (Kaufman and Seidman, 1970). The pyramid analogy is particularly helpful for understanding vertical differentiation.

The most obvious element of vertical differentiation is the number of command levels, or the segmentation, of an organization. Police departments often measure the number of levels by counting ranks. Previous research has shown that most police agencies in the United States have between six and twelve levels, from patrol officer to chief executive (Bayley, 1992). Departments with fewer ranks would be characterized by a very short pyramid, whereas those with many ranks by a very tall pyramid.

In addition to the number of levels, vertical differentiation also focuses on the degree of concentration within different levels of the hierarchy. Police agencies and other "street-level bureaucracies" tend to have a large percentage of employees at the bottom of the hierarchy, and thus would be characterized by a pyramid with a wide base (Lipsky, 1980). "Top-heavy" organizations, often criticized for having "too many bosses and not enough workers," tend to have a concentration of employees at the top of the hierarchy, and thus would be represented by a thickened point at the peak of the pyramid. The police are often criticized for having "bloated" middle management ranks (Kelling and Bratton, 1993), which would be represented by an odd-shaped pyramid with a wide middle. Organizations vary widely according to these various elements of vertical differentiation.

Langworthy (1986) suggests that in addition to segmentation and concentration, vertical differentiation has a third, more abstract component: height. The height of an organization is the vertical distance, or the amount of social space, between the those at the bottom of an organization and those at the top. Height is typically measured by using a standardized measure of income disparity between the lowest and highest ranking employees (Black, 1976; Langworthy, 1986). Although this measure is not ideal, it is useful as a proxy for the social distance between production workers such as patrol officers, and executives, such as the police chief.

Functional Differentiation

Functional differentiation measures the degree to which tasks are broken down into functionally distinct units. An organization with a sales force, separate production staffs for each product, a planning staff and an engineering group is more functionally differentiated than an organization containing only one department. Police organizations have become more functionally differentiated throughout the twentieth century, adding specialized units to handle new technologies and to respond to newly emerging social problems (Reiss, 1992). Indeed, the police are well-known for dealing with new problems by forming specialized units (Bayley, 1994; Mastrofski, 1994; Moore, 1992). Sparrow, Moore, and Kennedy (1990) quote an appropriate London Metropolitan Police saying: "when in doubt, form a squad and rush about." Although community policing reformers urge police agencies to become less specialized (Cordner, 1997; Mastrofski, 1994; Redlinger, 1994), recent research has demonstrated that police agencies are continuing to become more functionally differentiated (Maguire, 1997).

Spatial Differentiation

Spatial differentiation is the extent to which an organization is distributed geographically (Langworthy, 1986; Bayley, 1992). A single convenience store, for example, is far less spatially differentiated than a chain of convenience stores with sites in several states. Increasing spatial differentiation is becoming common among large corporations, who, in order to tap new markets, are decentralizing their operations spatially, expanding into multidivisional firms with operating sites all over the world. Most researchers measure spatial differentiation by counting the number of separate operating sites, subsidiary organizations, branch offices, or franchises. Langworthy (1986) measured spatial differentiation in police organizations by counting the number of station houses and the number of beats. Since the focus of spatial differentiation is on the spread of an organization, police agencies with a greater number of patrol beats and police stations are more spatially differentiated. Community policing reformers urge police agencies to become more spatially differentiated or geographically decentralized so that they can become closer to their communities (Skolnick and Bayley, 1986).

Structural Control and Coordination Mechanisms

Structural Control refers to the formal administrative apparatuses that an organization institutes in order to achieve coordination and control among its workers and its work. Many scholars suggest that as organizations increase in levels of structural complexity, they must institute administrative mechanisms to coordinate and control the various parts of the organization (Rushing, 1976; Hsu, Marsh, and Mannari, 1983). The three primary mechanisms that organizations use to achieve greater control are administration, formalization, and centralization. Each of these factors will now be explored in more detail.

Administration

Administrative intensity (also known as administrative overhead or administrative density) is the relative size of an organization's administrative component (Langworthy, 1986; Monkkonen, 1981). The administrative component is comprised of all workers who perform tasks related to the maintenance of the organization itself, rather than the core tasks of the organization. Thus, the administrative component of an organization "is not a unitary structural element but rather, . . . a 'heterogeneous category' composed of varying participants performing quite different functional roles" (Scott, 1992, p. 259; Rushing, 1966). Organizations with large administrative components are often considered to be more bureaucratic, and indeed, administrative intensity was sometimes used in early research as an overall proxy for bureaucratization (Scott, 1992).

Formalization

Formalization is the extent to which an organization is governed by formal written rules, policies, standards, and procedures (Hall, Haas, and Johnson, 1967). Some organizations are extremely informal, relying on simple control processes such as word-of-mouth. Others are extremely formalized, with mountains of rules, piles of forms, and rigid standards of conduct. Accounts of overly formalistic organizations are heard frequently. For example, Pennsylvania State Police Troopers tote around a binder several inches thick containing the department's rules and policies (Mastrofski, 1995), and the Kansas City Police Department in Missouri has 356 separate forms for reporting police matters (Reiss, 1992). In addition, a recent audit of the Los Angeles Police Department by a prestigious management consulting firm identified a number of formalized procedures that made little sense. For example, their arrest and booking forms "require the entry of a juvenile drunken-driving suspect's name 70 separate times" (Bailey, 1996). Community policing advocates urge police agencies to become less formalized to produce more efficient and effective service delivery (Mastrofski, 1998).

Centralization

Centralization is the degree to which the decision-making capacity within an organization is concentrated in a single individual or small select group. On one hand, centralization is a popular method for achieving organizational control and internal accountability. On the other hand, centralization slows decision-making and removes discretion from lower-level employees. Most current reform literature on reinventing government and reengineering corporations suggests the need to decentralize management in order to allow front-line workers and local operating sites more discretion in their day-to-day business.

Decentralization can take many forms. Conservative command devolution strategies might only entail pushing decision-making authority down a one or a few notches. More radical decentralization measures might empower managers in local operating sites (e.g., branch offices, or precincts) with the discretion and autonomy to make decisions about local operations.[3] In some organizations, local managers must consult with centralized administrators about all major decisions—in less managerially centralized organizations, site managers have the autonomy to make local-level decisions without consulting headquarters. Fiscal decentralization focuses on the extent to which operating units or local sites have control over budgets. This includes both input into the distribution of the centralized budget, and autonomy over how local budgets are spent. Decentralization schemes run the gamut from simple delegation to radical organizational change strategies.

Chapter Summary

Organizations, like people, are comprised of many components. Each organization differs along a number of dimensions: size, performance, goals, leadership, professionalism, culture, identity, and formal structure. Structure is not necessarily any more or less important than the other components of an organization, but it is important nonetheless. Organizational reformers in both the public and private sectors continually recommend new strategies for restructuring organizations. Often these normative prescriptions treat structure as a one-dimensional phenomenon, in the classic Weberian sense. Bureaucracies have many components however, and it is not helpful analytically to characterize an organization as bureaucratic. This chapter has demonstrated how organizational structures are not one-dimensional. Rather, they are best characterized as having two broad dimensions: complexity and control.

Complexity and control, however, are also multidimensional. Organizations can become more complex by adding hierarchical layers, by creating new functional units, or by expanding their operations spatially. They can achieve control and coordination by increasing the relative size of their administrative core; instituting formal written rules, policies, standards and procedures; or centralizing decision-making authority. Organizations vary in the nature and magnitude of each of these separate dimensions. The "structure" of an organization is a complex mix composed of these separate features. Just as psychologists strive to understand the factors that produce variations among people, organizational sociologists strive to explain variations among organizations. Chapter 3 explores some of these explanations, focusing on the factors that account for variations in organizational structure.

CHAPTER 3

Explaining Organizational Structure

Sociological approaches to the study of organizational structure thrived from the 1960s to the 1980s. As researchers began to define the dimensions of organizational structure, a variety of causal explanations emerged to explain these features. Though based on a number of different theoretical perspectives (Donaldson, 1995), most of these explanations have involved three consistent factors: size, technology, and environment. As Hall (1972, p. 139) argued, "when size (and growth) is taken in conjunction with technological and environmental factors, predictions regarding organizational structures and processes can be made." In addition, the concept of organizational age has been used in several studies to explain the variation in a number of organizational attributes, including formal structure. Though organizational age has not received as much attention in the literature as the other three factors, a substantial body of theory and research has demonstrated that it should be considered as one of the main explanations for organizational structure (King, 1999). This chapter first reviews the literature on the effects of size, technology, environment, and age on formal structure. The chapter concludes with a discussion of other possible explanations for organizational structure.

Size

Organizational size has been conceptualized and measured in a variety of ways. While some researchers have conceived of size as an element of structure, most treat it is a contextual variable which falls on a causal chain between environment and structure. The general assumption in the literature, with some exceptions, is that larger organizations require more complex structures to control employees and coordinate work. Size has been measured in a number of ways, including square footage of floor space, sales volume, and net assets (Kimberly, 1976; Scott, 1992). However, the most widely used measure of organization size is the number of employees. In highly technical production organizations

19

with routinized computer or robotic operations, this may be an inadequate measure, but for human service bureaucracies and other personnel-intensive organizations like the police, the number of employees is an ideal measure of size.

Most studies have found consistent positive relationships between organization size and structural complexity (Blau, 1994; Blau and Schoenherr, 1971; Child, 1972a, 1973; Hsu, Marsh, and Mannari, 1983; Langworthy, 1986; Meyer, 1972; Pugh et al., 1969; Terrien and Mills, 1955; for a comprehensive review, see Kimberly, 1976). However, a handful of others have found the effect of size on complexity to be either weak or insignificant (Beyer and Trice, 1979; Hall, Haas, and Johnson, 1967). In addition, there is limited evidence that the effect may be nonlinear: the marginal effects of size may decrease as size increases (Blau and Schoenherr, 1971; Crank and Wells, 1991; Child, 1973). Blau (1970) is the best known proponent of this hypothesis, suggesting that "increasing organizational size generates differentiation along various lines at decelerating rates." If the effect is indeed nonlinear as Blau and others suggest, then at some unknown level of size, the effect of size on structure would begin to decrease.

Although the size-structure relationship is well supported in the literature, the evidence is not universal. Some researchers have failed to find a consistent positive effect. There are several potential explanations for the mixed findings on the relationship between size and structural complexity. First, as mentioned, size is measured in a variety of ways: it may be that these different indicators are not equally reliable measures of organization size. Second, as Scott (1992) points out, increasing size might sometimes lead to more complex personnel (i.e., the use of autonomous professional or craft workers) rather than more complex structures. Both types of complexity are frequently used means of coordinating and controlling work, and research on the effects of size on complexity needs to account for both. This distinction might only be important, however, in studies that use samples of different organizations with varying occupational groups. Organizations with similar occupational groups would be expected to become more complex, both in personnel and structure, in similar ways.[1]

The research on size and complexity has come under some criticism. Aldrich (1972) suggests that size may be dependent on structure: greater differentiation might lead to increased personnel requirements. If this is so, then several decades of organizational research has depended on mis-specified models of organizational complexity. Aldrich's hypothesis has been criticized on methodological grounds and has not received much support in the literature (Hilton, 1972). On a different note,

Argyris (1972) suggests that although size is correlated with complexity, it may not necessarily cause complexity. Although not addressing Argyris's point specifically, some researchers have suggested that organizational variables like size and structure might be entwined in a complex web of relationships that cannot be untangled using cross-sectional methodologies. Using longitudinal methods however, Meyer (1972b) and Meyer and Brown (1978) have confirmed that size has a causal impact on organizational complexity.

In addition to the size-complexity relationship, researchers have also noted a link between size and centralization, and size and formalization. The bulk of the research shows that larger organizations rely less on centralization, and more on formalization as a mechanism for achieving coordination and control. In fact there is some evidence that in large organizations, the two may be seen as alternative mechanisms for achieving control—formalized rules and procedures may allow larger organizations to decentralize their decision making without losing too much control (Blau and Schoenherr, 1971; Child, 1973; Mansfield, 1973; Scott, 1992). Research confirms a consistent negative relationship between organizational size and centralization (Blau and Schoenherr, 1971; Child, 1972a, 1973; Hsu, Marsh, and Mannari, 1983; Mansfield, 1973), and a consistent positive relationship between size and formalization (Blau and Schoenherr, 1971; Hall, Haas, and Johnson, 1967; Hsu, Marsh, and Mannari, 1983; Pugh et al., 1969).

Unlike other size-structure relationships, the effect of organization size on administrative intensity is somewhat unclear. Early researchers reported a variety of mixed findings, including a positive effect (Terrien and Mills, 1955; Tsouderos, 1955), a negative effect (Anderson and Warkov, 1961; Bendix, 1956; Hall, Haas, and Johnson, 1967; Melman, 1951), and no effect (Baker and Davis, 1954; Haire, 1959). Rushing (1966), as reviewed in chapter 2, suggested that the administrative component is a heterogeneous category, and that the relationship between size and administrative intensity depends on the definition used. The most common usage refers to horizontal administrative intensity, which is the proportion of personnel devoted to administrative support (working outside the technical core). However, some theorists contrast this usage with vertical administrative intensity, which refers to the size of the supervisory component (as with the majority of the literature, this is not the preferred usage in this study). In short, organizational size appears to have a negative effect on vertical administrative intensity (Indik, 1964; Langworthy, 1986; Scott, 1992) and a positive effect on horizontal administrative intensity (Blau and Schoenherr, 1971; Langworthy, 1986; Kasarda, 1974; Rushing, 1966, 1967).

Taken together, the results of research on the effects of organizational size are a collection of mixed findings. In an insightful and thorough review of the literature, Kimberly (1976, p. 573) concluded that the majority of research on the size-structure relationship has emerged from a "theoretical wasteland." Kimberly found that rationales for including size as an independent variable in models of structure ranged from simplistic assumptions that little organizations are different than big ones, to the common argument that size is "something that should be controlled for" (p. 574). Kimberly goes on to point out a number of methodological inconsistencies in the literature, any one of which could produce the inconsistent findings on the relationship between size and structure. He recommends that future researchers should demonstrate a sound theoretical rationale for studying the effects of size, and that theory should also be the driving force behind the selection of a suitable measure for organizational size.

Technology

Among organizational theorists, technology is a broad term that "has come to refer to the work performed by an organization" (Scott, 1992, p. 227), or as Thompson and Bates (1957, p. 325) put it, "a system of techniques" for processing raw materials. Technology, conceived broadly, lies at the heart of functionalist theories of organizations, which assume that what organizations do determines how they are structured. If organizational structures are at all rational, then differences in structure should be associated with differences in technology.

A number of early studies investigated the link between technology and a variety of organizational attributes. However, the first theoretical statement to focus on the link between technology and structure was an article by Thompson and Bates (1957). Shortly thereafter, in a study of 90 British industrial plants, Woodward (1965) reported the first empirical evidence to suggest that technology influences organizational structure. Woodward found that the production systems in most of these organizations could be classified into three levels of technical complexity, including: (1) unit and small batch technologies useful for producing custom, specialized, or made-to-order products; (2) large batch and mass production technologies useful for manufacturing standardized products, such as automobiles, on an assembly line; and (3) continuous process technologies useful for the continuous production of liquids, gases, chemicals, and pharmaceuticals (Gillespie and Mileti, 1977; Pugh and Hickson, 1989). Woodward found that these fundamental differences in operational technology had distinct implications for how organizations were structured. Organizations employing unit and small batch techologies relied on simpler command structures and more informal coordination processes than those employing more complex production systems. Similarly, organizations employing continuous process technologies were characterized by tall hierarchies and more formal control systems. Aside from the many specific findings of her research, Woodward's lasting contribution to the study of organizations was the general notion that technology affects how organizations are structured.

Since Woodward's influential work, organizational researchers have regularly employed measures of technology in models of organization structure and process. The search for the ideal way to measure technology has prompted decades of debate. Early measurement schemes applied only to certain "types" of organizations, such as manufacturing plants, and focused on such peculiar items as the "hardness" of the materials being processed (Rushing, 1968). Other schemes, like the one developed by Perrow (1967), were developed in an effort to construct universal measures of technology that might be useful for all types of organizations. These efforts were based on abstract operational definitions of technology, such as "technical complexity" (Woodward, 1965), "routineness of tasks" (Hage and Aiken, 1969; Perrow, 1967), and "scope of tasks" (Dewar and Hage, 1978). Others have either eschewed the search for universal measures of technology, or have modified standard definitions to fit the particular type of organization under study (Glisson, 1978; Mills and Moberg, 1982). These researchers argue that organizations performing markedly different tasks cannot be compared using the same measures of technology.

The literature on the link between technology and structure is riddled with conceptual and operational inconsistencies. Technology has been measured in a variety of ways by organizational researchers, and indeed the line between technology and environment is often quite narrow. In synthesizing the voluminous literature assessing the effects of technology on structure, Scott (1992) suggests that most of the specific measures of technology used can be encompassed by three general dimensions: complexity and diversity of inputs, uncertainty and unpredictability of work, and interdependence of tasks. The key point to remember is that although these dimensions are found throughout the literature under a variety of names, all of them are subtly different variations on the same idea. The nature of the raw materials that an organization processes, and the methods used to process these materials are what defines an organization's technology.

Theorists have hypothesized that technological differences alone should result in structural differences (Perrow, 1967; Thompson, 1967; Thompson and Bates, 1957; Woodward, 1965). However, research into the effects of technology on organizational structure has yielded mixed results. Several studies have found that technology influences structure independent of controls such as size (Comstock and Scott, 1977; Dewar and Hage, 1978; Hage and Aiken, 1969; Harvey, 1968; Meyer, 1968a; Van de Ven and Delbecq, 1974). However, a number of other researchers have found that technology explains little of the variation in structure (Hickson, Pugh, and Pheysey, 1969; Hsu, Marsh, and Mannari, 1983; Mohr, 1971; Pugh et al., 1969).

Researchers have suggested a number of possibilities for why there is such disparity in the results of technology-structure research. First, a number of reviewers have argued that the conceptualization and measurement of technological variables has often been done haphazardly, with little attention to theory and consistency with prior research. Second, a handful have suggested that technology may be dependent on structure, rather than the other way around (Glisson, 1978,1992; Manning, 1992). This idea, while certainly plausible, has not received much attention in the literature, presumably because none of its proponents have outlined exactly how technology might affect specific structural elements. Third, another possibility that has received some empirical support is the notion that an organization may have more than one technology, and rather than focusing on the organization as a unit of analysis, we should concentrate on the technologies used by subunits, workgroups, or individual workers (Comstock and Scott, 1977; Scott, 1992). This idea has probably not received more widespread support in the literature because researchers are often not interested in the full range of technologies within an organization, but only on the dominant or "core" technology. The fourth possibility, suggested by Mohr (1971, p. 452), explores the alternative possibility that "technology may not actually force structure, but rather that organizations will be effective only insofar as their structures are *consonant* with, or follow the dictates of, their technologies." The consonance hypothesis has received qualitative support over the years from researchers noting how the "fit" between technology and structure is integral to organizational effectiveness (Burns and Stalker, 1961; Woodward, 1965; Mastrofski and Ritti, 1995). If the consonance hypothesis holds, we may only find evidence of a technology-structure relationship in those organizations that are "effective." In public-sector organizations, however, judging effectiveness requires normative judgments about agency goals, therefore measuring effectiveness is difficult (Langworthy, 1986; Ostrom, 1973). The fifth possible reason for the lack of consensus on the technology-structure relationship is the diversity of organizational settings studied. This possibility will now be explored in further detail.

Different types of organizations use very different technologies, and developing universal measures that capture this variation is difficult (Child and Mansfield, 1972). Several researchers have suggested that two broad classes of organizations—manufacturing and service—need to be examined separately when examining technological effects on structure. Unlike manufacturing, most service organizations process people, thus human beings are their "raw material" (Hasenfeld, 1992a). Mills and Moberg (1982) demonstrate how the technologies used to manufacture goods are not comparable to the technologies used to provide services to people: manufacturing organizations tend to be driven by material technologies such as computers and mechanical equipment, whereas service organizations like the police are driven more by social technologies (Glisson, 1978, 1992; Manning, 1992; Mills and Moberg, 1982; Reiss, 1992).[3] In a classic article, Hasenfeld (1972) takes this theme one step further, noting a fundamental difference between service organizations whose function is merely to *process* people, and those whose core task is to *change* people. The technologies used by people-processing organizations, according to Hasenfeld, will be less complex and of a shorter duration than those used by people-changing organizations. The works discussed in this paragraph will be discussed further in chapter 5. The common theme running throughout each is the fundamental notion that different types of organizations and different technologies prompt different types of structural accommodation. Many researchers have argued convincingly that the lack of consensus on the effect of technology on structure can be attributed to inadequate measurement and conceptualization of the technologies used by different types of organizations (Glisson, 1992; Mills and Moberg, 1980).

Not only does the nature of technology vary between different types of organizations, but the magnitude of technological effects on structure may vary as well. While manufacturing organizations can tightly seal their technical cores (where the majority of the organization's work is accomplished) from both their institutional and managerial environments, service organizations are subject to the uncertainty which arises from frequent interactions between workers and clients (Hasenfeld, 1992a; Lipsky, 1980). Public service organizations like the police, who conduct the majority of their work in the public eye, may be far less able to develop structures that are consonant with their core technology, because they must adapt their structures to the uncertainty of their environments (Lipsky, 1980; Reiss and Bordua, 1967). Most organizations, especially public service bureaucracies, attempt to buffer their technical cores from the environmental turbulence that surrounds them, so that their day-to-day work is not affected (Scott, 1992; Thompson, 1967). Where the environment that surrounds an organization prompts some sort of defensive structural accommodations, environment will attenuate the impact of technology on structure. We now turn to a discussion of organizational environments as a potential explanation for structure.

Environment

The greatest advance in organizational studies over the past four decades has been the shift in theory to reflect the important link between organizations and their environments. Early "closed system" approaches focused on workers, tasks, policies, and other internal elements of organizations. Open systems approaches, which began to gain popularity in the mid 1960s, emphasized the importance of the environment in shaping organizational goals, structures, and processes. The open systems perspective recognizes that organizations are not like islands in a lonely sea, but rather, they exist in complex environments with which they must constantly interact. Kimberly captures the essence of the open systems perspective as it pertains to organizational structure:

> As open systems, organizations engage in various transactions with their environments. These transactions are complex, variable across organizations and environments, and reciprocal. At a given time however, there are various environmental constraints which limit the structural form that organizations can adopt. Thus, the etiology of organizational configurations is, at least in part, a function of environmental influences, and variability in these configurations should be predictably related to variability in environmental influences. (1975, p. 1)

Organizational environments are immense in scope, as can easily be seen by a cursory review of the literature. As conceived by organizational scholars, the environment consists of all that is external to an organization. Funding agencies, raw materials, clients, potential employees, the media, politicians, rumors, legislation and employees' unions all reside in an organization's environment. Since the birth of the open systems perspective, organizational scholars have tried to deconstruct, typologize, measure, simplify and otherwise come to grips with the enormity of the environment construct. The bulk of the work in organization theory today continues to explore relationships between organizations and their environments.

Some of the classic works in organization theory emerged from the open systems school. These include dozens of studies employing the broad-ranging and enduring tenets of structural contingency theory, which suggests that no single organizational form is ideal for all circumstances (Donaldson, 1995; Lawrence and Lorsch, 1967). Successful organizations survive by adapting to the contingencies of their specific tasks and environments. James Thompson (1967) showed that in order for organizations to maintain some semblance of technical rationality, they must seal off their technical cores (where the primary work is performed) to protect them from external uncertainties. Focusing on these uncertainties, Meyer and Rowan (1977) argued that organizational structures are not exclusively shaped by rational or technical imperatives, but rather, by powerful myths existing in their institutional environments. Weick (1969) and Duncan (1972) both demonstrated how various elements of the environment contain "pools" of information that are critical to the organization. Organizations process this information in such a way as to decrease "information uncertainty." Pfeffer and Salancik (1978) discussed the merits of resource-dependency theory, namely that organizations are dependent on the environment for strategic resources, and therefore are to some degree "externally controlled." Aldrich (1979) outlined a natural selection (Darwinian) model of organizational forms, in which organizations or their components evolve over time toward a better fit with their environments. The "population-ecology" approach suggests that if organizations do not fit into an environmental niche, they do not survive. This small sampling of classic works in organization theory is meant to show how examinations of organizational environments are based on a wide variety of theoretical perspectives.

Because environmental explanations for organizational structure encompass such a broad theoretical expanse—from resource availability and information uncertainty to environmental turbulence and institutional mythology—scholars have searched for typologies to "reduce" the number of conceptual dimensions in the field. Duncan (1972), Lawrence and Lorsch (1967) and Thompson (1967), all used similar two dimensional typologies to characterize organizational environments. Though they used different terminology, all three of these typologies essentially plotted environmental complexity (high and low) vs. environmental stability (high and low) yielding four cells. Dissatisfied with such simplistic schemes, Jurkovich (1974) created a 64–cell typology to describe organizational environments. However, scholars recognized that although such complex typologies are useful heuristic tools for distinguishing between organizations, they suffer two primary flaws: first, they lack the simplistic elegance, or *parsimony*, of earlier schemes; and second, they are difficult to test or explore empirically without a large sample size, due to the threat of obtaining blank cells. Returning to an earlier level of parsimony, Aldrich (1979) identified six core dimensions that comprise an organization's environment: capacity, homogeneity-heterogeneity, stability-instability, concentration-dispersion, domain consensus-dissensus, and turbulence. Dess and Beard (1984), arguing that some of Aldrich's six dimensions overlapped with one another conceptually, factor analyzed dozens of environmental variables and found that three main factors were useful for distinguishing between organizational task environments: munificence, dynamism, and complexity. Munificence measures an environment's capacity to support growth or change, dynamism measures the turbulence of an environment, and complexity measures heterogeneity. These generic variables are represented under many names throughout the literature on organizational environments. Research on organizational structure continues to feature new environmental typologies as the field advances along a number of different dimensions.

In addition to differences in the flavor of environmental theories, there are also pronounced differences in the basic levels of analysis in which these theories are grounded. One of the most basic decisions in studying any social phenomenon is selecting the level of explanation to be employed. When we examine the effect of environment on organizations, we are implicitly conducting an ecological level analysis. However, Scott (1992) notes that there are at least four sub-levels within the ecological level: the organization set, organizational population, areal organizational field, and functional organization field:

- *Organization Set*: Viewing the environment from the perspective of a particular (focal) organization, an organization set consists of all elements of the environment that affect the focal organization. Langworthy (1986) employed this level of analysis in his cross-sectional examination of police organizational structures.
- *Organizational Population*: This level is used to identify and examine aggregates of like organizations. All of the police departments within the United States, for instance, might be considered as one organizational population. Most population ecologists employ this level of analysis, employing longitudinal methods to examine changes in populations of organizations over time. Bayley (1985) and Virtanen (1979) employ an implicit population ecology approach in their study of the evolution of police organizations cross-nationally, showing how

different forms of policing emerge at the national level. Similarly, Sutton (1988) traces the evolution of the juvenile justice system in the United States from 1640 to 1981. All of these studies share in common their focus on changes in populations of organizations, rather than changes in individual organizations.

- *Areal Organization Field*: This level focuses on the relationships among organizations within a particular geographic area. Hassell (2000) employed this level of analysis when she examined the network of agencies and organizations responsible for dealing with serious, habitual juvenile offenders in one jurisdiction.
- *Functional Organization Field*: This level is similar to areal fields, except it focuses on interdependence of organizations for functional, rather than geographic purposes. The suppliers, producers, wholesalers and retailers in a particular industry might form a functional organizational field. Weiss (1992, 1997) employed this level of analysis when he examined patterns of innovation diffusion and adoption in American police agencies.

Identifying the sub-levels that analysts employ when examining organizational environments is important. This study, and most of the literature it is based upon, analyzes organizations at the "organization set" level.

Another primary area of debate among organizational scholars is whether *objective* features of an environment are most important in shaping organizations, or organizational members' *perceptions* of the environment. Most of the early work employing the open systems perspective focused on objective accounts of the environment. Other researchers, especially those interested in social psychological phenomena, began to expand on objective accounts of the environment by interviewing key organizational actors about their perceptions of the environment. The study of organizational environments thus split into the use of subjective measures and objective measures. Certain analysts suggest that both perspectives are important, arguing that environmental perceptions influence organizational actors, but that certain aspects of the environment affect the organization regardless of whether they are perceived (Pfeffer and Salancik; 1978). Weick (1979) takes this argument one step further when he introduces the concept of an "enacted environment." Organizational managers "enact" their environment when they "construct, rearrange, single out, and demolish many 'objective' features of their surroundings" (164).[4] Burrell and Morgan (1979) suggest that the functionalist (objective) and interpretivist (subjective) perspectives serve as major sources of division within organization science.

Like subjective approaches, institutional theory focuses on the "meaning" of the environment to the organization. For institutionalists, however, the focus is not necessarily on how individuals perceive the environment, but on how the environment contains sources of "symbolic meaning" for the organization.[5] Talcott Parsons (1947) depicted organizations as consisting of three components: technical, managerial and institutional. The technical component is responsible for performing the core work of the organization, for example, the assembly line in the factory. The managerial component is responsible for administering and managing the organization. The institutional component consists of such intangibles as standards, norms, rumors, myths, knowledge and ceremonies. Thompson (1967), considering the institutional component as external to the organization, showed how managerial components buffer the "technical core" from the institutional environment. Building on these classic works, institutional theorists (e.g., Meyer and Rowan, 1977; Scott, 1992) argue that there are really two environments external to any organization. The "technical" or "rational" environment provides raw materials and other tangible goods to the organization, whereas the institutional environment is the primary source of legitimacy. This conception of a dual environment, with an intangible component (containing symbols, myths, and other forms of meaning) and a tangible component (containing clients, resources, and information) is unique enough that institutionalists have formed their own new "branch" of organization theory (Donaldson, 1995). Since elements of the institutional perspective are now starting to emerge in the study of police organizations, institutional theory will be examined more thoroughly in chapter 4.

This brief review of the literature shows how theoretical perspectives on the link between organizations and environments have evolved separately on a number of dimensions. Early typologies focused on simplifying the enormity of the environment construct. As open systems approaches evolved, analysts employed four different sub-levels of analysis: the organization set, the organizational population, the areal organization field, and the functional organization field. Later, theorists debated on which was the most important factor in shaping organizations: the environment itself (objective), or organizational actors' perceptions of environment (subjective). Other theorists focused on which elements of the environment were most important. Resources (dependency), information (complexity) and institutional myths emerged strongly as some of the most important components in an organization's environment. From this debate emerged a new branch of organization theory: the institutional school. Institutional theorists essentially split organizational environments into two components: technical/ rational and institutional. The rational environment is the primary source of tangible components which organizations need to perform their business, and the institutional environment is the primary source of organizational legitimacy. Because studies of organizational environments have varied on so many different dimensions, we still cannot be certain about the effect of the environment on organizational structures.

The concept of organizational environment is the great snafu of organization science. The discovery of its importance was one of the most important achievements in the study of organizations, but conquering its overall complexity remains one of the greatest challenges. Scholars have struggled with the concept of environment for nearly four decades now, tapping numerous dimensions of variation and applying a number of theoretical perspectives. Some scholars are beginning to show how combining these different approaches can yield fruitful results. For example, Tolbert (1985) combined institutional theory and resource-dependency theory, meeting with some empirical success. Similarly, Aldrich (1992), bemoaning the lack of theoretical integration in organizational studies, combined population-ecology and institutional theories. In one of the finest recent sociological studies on organizations, Gupta, Dirsmith, and Fogarty (1994) developed a structural model based on elements of contingency theory and institutional theory. Combining theoretical perspectives is one direction in which organization scholars seem to be heading with greater frequency (and with moderate success), in part to achieve greater unity in the field, and in part to increase explained variance in organizational structure and process (Donaldson, 1995; Hall, 1999, pp. 106–7).

Age

While the literature on organizational age is not nearly as large as that for size, technology and environment, there is some evidence that age may nonetheless be an important factor. Researchers have found evidence of relationships between age and a variety of organizational attributes, including adoption of innovations (Kalleberg and Leicht, 1991), autonomy (Pugh et al., 1969), gender integration (Baron, Mittman, and Newman, 1991), interprofessional cooperation (Kriesburg, 1973), organizational mortality (Carroll and Delacroix, 1982), participation in joint programs with other organizations (Aiken and Hage, 1968), performance (Fowler and Schmidt, 1989), quality and stability of outputs (Heydebrand, 1973a), and revenue growth rates

(Khandwalla, 1977, p. 574). However, many other studies have failed to find an effect of age on a variety of organizational properties (e.g., Hage and Aiken, 1967a). Of more interest for this study is that theorists have generated a variety of propositions about the link between age and formal organizational structure.

According to King (1999), the two most important theoretical perspectives on the nature of the age-structure relationship are those by Stinchcombe (1965) and Downs (1967). Stinchcombe suggests that new organizations of a similar type tend to be formed during the same general period of time, in temporal "spurts." Those organizations founded during the same era are temporally imprinted with similar structural forms, and tend to be structured differently than organizations founded in different eras. Thus, according to Stinchcombe's theory, age has a *cohort effect* on structure (King, 1999). On a slightly different note, Downs suggests that organizations exhibit similar structural transformations as they age. Thus according to Downs's theory, age has a *constant* or *linear effect* on structure (King, 1999).

Based on these theories, researchers have investigated the possibility of a link between age and structural complexity on a variety of organizational types. The theoretical rationale for expecting a relationship between age and complexity is quite simple. As organizations age, they add new structural elements to pre-existing ones, and thus structures should become more elaborated "as a simple product of time" (Kriesburg, 1976, p. 5). Despite Heydebrand's (1973b, p. 15) assertion that "older organizations are internally more differentiated and complex than younger ones," the research has not supported a strong or consistent relationship between organizational age and structural complexity. Mannheim and Moscovits (1979) found that age was not capable of distinguishing between various structural configurations in their empirically derived typology (using multidimensional scaling techniques) of organizations. When Khandwalla (1977) split his sample of Canadian firms into three age categories, he found that younger and older firms relied more heavily on hierarchical structures than middle-aged firms. Several others, including Kriesburg (1976) and Meyer and Brown (1978), have reported that age has an insignificant effect on various measures of structural complexity. In their mixed sample of Canadian and American industrial organizations, Brown and Schneck (1979) found support for Stinchcombe's hypothesis that era of formation affects structure. However, the structural features that they used were not "mainstream" structural variables. In a study of Japanese factories, Marsh and Mannari (1981) found that age has a significant positive effect on vertical differentiation ("number of hierarchic levels") but a negative impact on overall complexity.[6] In addition, correlation coefficients suggest a positive relationship between age and functional specialization, and an insignificant relationship between age and spatial differentiation. Lastly, Epstein, Russell, and Silvern (1988) found that older shelters for battered women were more functionally differentiated, and that age was more important than ideology in predicting organizational structure.[7] Although the literature provides little evidence for a relationship between age and structural complexity, the studies are riddled with conceptual and methodological problems that make it difficult to draw definitive conclusions.

Research on the relationship between age and centralization is equally confusing. The Aston Group (Pugh et al., 1969) found that in their mixed sample of organizational types, older organizations have more autonomy and are more decentralized. Kriesburg (1976), on the other hand, found that older international non-governmental organizations are more centralized than younger INGOs, though his measures of centralization were unique. Correlation coefficients from Marsh and Mannari's (1981) study of Japanese factories suggest a positive relationship between organizational age and centralization (see note 6). Glisson and Martin (1980), in their sample of human service agencies, found a weak but negative effect of age on centralization and formalization.[8] Weed (1982) found that state welfare organizations formed during periods of centralization remained more centralized and that those formed during times of decentralization remained less centralized. Weed's finding may help explain the disparate findings of earlier research—the effect of age on centralization may depend on the degree of industry-wide centralization during the era of founding. Unfortunately, the conceptual and methodological problems in the literature make it difficult to determine the effect, if any, of age on centralization.

Studies examining the effects of age on formalization and administrative intensity have yielded more consistent findings than research on age and other structural dimensions. Three of the four studies on the link between age and formalization have found that older organizations are more formalized. Glisson and Martin (1980) found a weak but negative effect of age on formalization (see note 8), while Meyer and Brown (1978) found a positive effect (their study examined only one aspect of formalization). Correlation coefficients from Marsh and Mannari's (1981) study suggest a weak positive relationship between organizational age and formalization (recall note 6). Lastly, Samuel and Mannheim (1970) found a significant positive relationship between age and organizational "impersonality" which may be related to the concept of formalization. In addition, all three studies examining the effect of age on administrative intensity have found that older organizations have larger administrative components (Marsh and Mannari, 1981; McCurdy, 1991; Rosengren, 1968).

The literature on the link between age and structure is of generally poor quality: variables are defined inconsistently; only partial results are reported, leaving the reader to guess about empirical relationships given limited information; methodological problems inhibit the generalizability of findings; significance levels are not reported for inferential statistics; and conclusions are stretched beyond the reach of the findings (e.g., Kimberly, 1975). The state of the literature is unfortunate given the elegance and parsimony of the theoretical propositions underlying the research. Though these studies suffer a host of conceptual and methodological flaws that limit our ability to draw inferences about age-structure relationships, two results appear consistently: older organizations are more formalized and have higher rates of administrative intensity.

Other

A variety of other explanations for organizational structure have been suggested in addition to size, technology, environment, and age. Many of these explanations can easily be subsumed within one of the four dominant explanations, though some suggest truly unique alternatives. To highlight the ways that explanations of structure either fit or do not fit these dominant dimensions, consider the work of Pugh et al. (1969), who discuss the effects of seven concepts related to organizational "context" on the structure of organizations. These seven concepts are listed in Table 3.1, together with their operational definitions.

The first two explanations, size (1) and technology (2), we have already discussed as two of the four dominant explanations for organizational structure. The next two explanations, ownership and control (3), and dependence (4), are both aspects of the organization's relationship with its environment. Dependence is a concept that some authors have used in building models to explain structure (e.g., Hsu, Marsh, and Mannari, 1983). However, it should not be conceived as a separate concept from environment, but as one of many potential environmental explanations for organizational structure. Though the authors argue that their model is not "a model of organization in an environment" (p. 91), at least two of their indicators are distinctly environmental in nature. The next variable, location (5), is particularly troublesome. In concept, the location of the organization can be thought of as an *environmental variable*. However, as measured (number of operating sites),

Table 3.1
Elements of Organizational "Context" in Pugh et al. (1969)

Contextual Variables	Measures
1) Size	•Size of Organization •Size of Parent Organization
2) Technology	•Workflow Integration •Labor Costs
3) Ownership and Control	•Public Accountability •Concentration of Ownership with Control
4) Dependence	•Dependence •Recognition of Trade Unions
5) Location	•Number of Operating Sites
6) Charter	•Operating Variability •Operating Diversity
7) Origin and History	•Impersonality of Origin •Age •Historical Changes

this variable is not an indication of location (as the authors claim), but is instead a structural variable describing the geographic spread, or *spatial differentiation* of an organization. Langworthy (1986) and numerous others have used this same measure as a structural indicator of spatial differentiation. Thus, with this measure, the authors confuse their independent and dependent variables, using an element of structure to construct a model explaining other structural features.

The next variable, charter (6), is defined by the authors as an organization's "social function, goals, ideology, and value systems" (p. 99). This variable represents one alternative explanation for structure which cannot easily be subsumed by one of the four dominant explanations. There are several reasons why goals have not assumed a more dominant role among explanations for structure. First, this explanation assumes a more rational process of organizational development (i.e., tight coupling between goals and structure) than most structuralists subscribe to. Second, it assumes that there is a consensus on what the goals of an organization are. In many organizations, especially government agencies, goals are unclear and sometimes conflict with one another (Wilson, 1989). Third, organizational researchers may assume that an organization's goals or objectives determine the type of technology that it selects (Woodward, 1965). And as we have seen, technology—the means and methods by which an organization accomplishes its work—is often used as a primary explanation for structure. Similarly, even without the assumption of a link between goals and technology, researchers are often more interested in what an organization does in reality (technology), than its written goals or claims. We will discuss the absence of organizational goals from traditional theories of structure further in chapter 5.

The last variable, origin and history (7), represents another alternative explanation for structure. This area has been explored frequently by historians and researchers employing qualitative methods and case-study approaches, but has appeared rarely in cross-sectional research studies comparing large numbers of individual organizations. The origin and history of organizations are central features in population ecology research, which almost always employs longitudinal methodologies and detailed attention to organizational life-cycles. The reason that historical approaches are so rare in research employing cross-sectional data sources is that origin and history are not amenable to comparative research methodologies. The subtleties of historical variables are difficult to quantify, and might best be employed in longitudinal analyses. The one exception, of course, is organizational age, which is readily quantifiable, and can easily be used in cross-sectional studies. As reviewed in this chapter, a handful of researchers have employed age as a potential explanation for organizational structure.

Another alternative explanation, though not identified by the Aston researchers, is the strategic choice perspective outlined by John Child (Child, 1972b). In a highly influential article, Child criticized the last decade of structural research for not incorporating the notion of "strategic choice" into their explanations for organizational structure. Child argued that theorists who concentrate on the effects of organizational context have succeeded in drawing attention to the constraints on structure, but have failed ". . . to consider the process of choice itself in which economic and administrative exigencies are weighed by the actors concerned against the opportunities to operate a structure of their own and/or other organization members' preferences (1972b, p. 16). Pfeffer (1978, p. 29) also highlights the tendency for organization theorists to neglect the conflicting preferences of organizational members, and the resulting political "contest for control of the organization." These works highlight the need for organizational theorists to account for culture and micro politics within the organizations they study, and how internal strategic choices might impact formal structures.

In his broad review of organizational theory, Scott (1992) repeatedly shows how variables in organizational research are often mis-measured and confused for one another. Measures of structure in one article are measures of technology in another (thereby mixing dependent and independent variables), and measures of technology in one article are measures of environment in another. The only consistent theme noted in the literature is that the primary explanations for organization structure are size, technology, environment, and to a lesser extent, age. The article by Pugh et al. (1969) was included here to show how "other" explanations for structure can sometimes be subsumed within the more dominant explanations, but that there are also exceptions. Organizational goals, the origin and history of an organization, and strategic choice are all plausible "other" explanations. These and other alternative explanations for organizational structure will be revisited at the conclusion to chapter 5.

CHAPTER 4

Police Organizational Structure

The organization of the police is a curious subject. To begin with, it is boring. Everyone in policing has sat through endless briefings about command structures, internal organization, and the ranks of personnel. Police departments hand out charts about these matters as hostesses distribute party favors. Such information is essential in order to find one's way around a police department, but no one pretends it is fun to learn. Nor is it often studied as if it were intrinsically important. Knowledge about police organization is used like a road map—once you get where you are going, you stuff it in the glove compartment. At the same time, police fight their most bitter battles over changes in organization. . . . Proposals to assign detectives, for example, to patrol commands or to base traffic units in police stations can be as controversial as selling condoms in a convent. So what is one to do with a subject that is variously perceived to be boring, basic, inconsequential, fateful, and diversionary?

In this passage, Bayley (1992, pp. 509–510) succinctly describes the plight of organizational research in police scholarship. Researchers have generally neglected studying police organizations in favor of studying police work—including situations, encounters, strategies, and occupational characteristics—and police officers—their attitudes, feelings, beliefs, behaviors, and interactions (Punch, 1983; Reiss, 1992). Although there have been at least 150 empirical studies of police behavior in the past four decades,[1] there have only been 10 studies of police organizational structures. Five of the ten were derived from one doctoral dissertation (Langworthy, 1983a; 1983b; 1985a; 1985b; 1986), and two only treated structure as an intermediate variable in models explaining police performance (Monkkonen, 1981; Slovak, 1986). Interestingly, sixteen studies have treated organizational structures as independent variables in models explaining police attitudes and behaviors (see Table 4.1). Thus, police organizational structures appear to be relatively unimportant areas

39

for scholarly inquiry, except when these variables might be helpful in understanding other phenomena.

Those who do study police organizations are sometimes criticized for not relating their analyses more closely to the world of the street-level police officer. In his review of Manning (1977), Jermier (1979, p. 691) complains that "there is too little discussion of how it *feels* to participate in social control agencies." Ironically, in his review of Langworthy (1986), Manning (1988a) makes a similar point, complaining that Langworthy "conveys to the reader no sense of what police work means." While feelings and meanings are important elements of organizational analysis, they are not crucial elements whose absence necessarily invalidates or weakens a study of police organizations. One is left with the impression that knowledge of police organizations is only of interest when it is linked with the nitty-gritty of policing. Organizational-level phenomena are often abstract, boring, and intangible. They are not the most sordid, entertaining, or fascinating aspects of policing, and they do not garner the respect and attention by scholars that other aspects of policing receive.

Ironically, although organizational structures are not treated as fundamentally important in empirical research on the police, they earn a great deal of attention among reformers. For many years, police administrators have been exhorted to change the structures of their organizations. Reformers have presented dozens of theories of the "best" way to organize in order to achieve greater efficiency, effectiveness, equity, and/or accountability in police organizations (e.g., Angell, 1971, 1975; Archambeault and Wierman, 1983; Franz and Jones, 1987; Stinchcombe, 1980). Langworthy argues that these "normative theories" can be classified into three general categories: bureaucratic, democratic, and contingency theories.[2] Proponents of the professional model, including Bruce Smith and O.W. Wilson, advocated a bureaucratic model of policing in order to centralize administrative control and reduce opportunities for corruption. Democratic theorists, whose arguments are most explicitly outlined by Angell (1971; 1975), advocate an open model of police organizations with flat hierarchies, generalist orientations, and decentralized operations. Contingency theorists like Kuykendall and Roberg (1980) suggest that there is no one "best" structure—that structures should be contingent on the specific task and environment. Normative theories of organizational structure continue to emerge today as reformers suggest optimum strategies for designing organizational structures that are conducive to the implementation of community policing (e.g., Bayley, 1994; Moore, 1992; Roberg, 1994; Skolnick and Bayley, 1986).

As evidenced by the number of publications that have appeared in the literature, empirical studies of policing have treated organizations as less important phenomena than individuals or situations. Occasionally, organizational variables are employed in studies of police attitudes and behavior, suggesting that organizations might only be considered important for how they affect other variables. Reformers have generated a number of normative theories about the way police organizations ought to be structured, but these theories have not helped us to understand why we have the police organizations that we have, and what factors might constrain our ability to change them. The volume and patterns of the literature to date suggests that our knowledge of police organizations is insufficiently developed.

This study is based on the fundamental assumption that the structure of police organizations is important, or as one theorist put it: "organization form matters" (Williamson, 1985, p. 274). There is little specific evidence in the policing literature to support this assumption. As I will show, most of the studies that have assessed the impact of structural variables on either aggregate arrest statistics or the attitudes and behaviors of police officers, have generated mixed results, and have defined and measured structural variables poorly. However, the bulk of empirical and theoretical work in the general organizational theory literature supports the assumption that structure is an important element of organizational performance (Scott, 1992, p. 89). Like Langworthy (1986), I also make the assumption that we must understand the forces that impact organizational structure before we assess the impact of structure on performance. Based on this assumption, the distant goal for those who study police organizations might be envisioned as a model in which structure is endogenous to a variety of contextual forces (such as size, technology, and environment), all of which can be used together to predict or explain organizational performance. This study will only concentrate on the first half of the model: the forces that shape and constrain organizational structures.

In this chapter, I first introduce the few works in policing that might offer theoretical insights into the structure of police organizations. Second, I summarize and critique those studies that have treated police structure as an independent variable. Third, I examine in detail the empirical studies that have examined police structures as a dependent variable. Finally, I summarize and evaluate efforts to explain police organization structures.

Theoretical Review

Although this study will be based primarily on theoretical developments in the sociology of organizations, some theoretical works have emerged within the policing literature that might illuminate our understanding of organizational structures.[3] The first theoretical pieces we examine focus on the link between technology and structure.

Peter Manning (1992) outlines the link between organizations, environments and information-processing technologies such as computer aided dispatch (CAD) systems, centralized call collection mechanisms (911), "expert" systems, management information systems, and other tools designed to increase the organization's capacity to intake and process information. He shows how "technology is embedded in social organization and has social meanings attributed to it; it changes organizations and occupations and is shaped by them" (p. 351). Technology, he argues, might affect organizational structure by altering the distribution of power within the traditional rank-hierarchy, spawning new areas of specialization within the organization, creating new management tools and shifting the balance of information centralization. This theme was first suggested by Reiss and Bordua (1967, p. 49) more than three decades ago, when they wrote: "in the dialectic of dispersion versus centralization of command, every development in the technology for police control of the population is accompanied by changes in the capacity of the organization to control its members." However, Manning believes that the causal sequence between environment, organization and technology is more complex: "technology is molded and shaped by the environment, the organizational structure, and the operational culture of policing more than they are shaped by technology" (p. 388). Manning doesn't hypothesize about the relative lengths of time (lags) by which technology affects structure, and structure affects technology, but he concludes by suggesting that information technologies have "an indeterminate effect on the organizational structure of policing; technology is used to produce and reproduce traditional practices, yet is *slowly* modifying them" (p. 391; emphasis added). The challenge for researchers and theorists is to untangle this cyclical web between technology and structure.

Although technology has received some attention in the literature, the majority of theoretical works on police organizations focus on how elements in the environment shape organizational attributes. However, the environments surrounding police organizations are massive and complex entities, and the theoretical orientations emerging from this perspective focus on very different elements of the environment. The first set of works reviewed here focuses on the *political environment*.

Sociologists Albert Reiss and David Bordua wrote a pair of articles in the mid-1960s outlining a view of police organizations as actors involved in constant transactions with their environments (Reiss and Bordua, 1967; Bordua and Reiss, 1966). They believed that the external environment of the police had a variety of "internal consequences." Two elements of the environment that they deemed most important to the organization are the security of the police chief's tenure and the degree of accountability that the government executive demands from the chief. Cross-classifying these two variables, Reiss and Bordua created a crude taxonomy of four department types that might reflect variation in political interference into police department affairs. Other environmental variables they deemed important to the organization include civil service requirements, type of local government and police employee organizations, which all "structure the effective range of command and control" (p. 49) in municipal police departments.

Like Reiss and Bordua, Mastrofski (1988) also focuses on the political involvement in policing. Mastrofski argues that the various efforts to reform the police over the past 50 years have produced three distinct "ideal-type models of the proper role for local officials' relationship to their police: professional autonomy, team, and political activist—ranging from low to high in the extent to which the involvement of outside officials in police affairs is appropriate." The professional autonomy approach grew out of the good government movement to separate politics from the police (Banfield and Wilson, 1963; Wilson, 1968).[4] The police chief is viewed as an autonomous professional who dictates policy and runs the police department as s/he sees fit. The team approach, Goldstein's (1977) solution to the problems of the professional autonomy model, suggests that police chiefs and local government executives should work together as active partners. Communities adopting the political activist approach grant minimal power to the police chief for setting and guiding department policy. In these communities, the police chief is merely "a minion of the politician"—the politician makes all major policy decisions in the police department. Mastrofski shows how departments vary widely on these levels of external control. However, in addition to these levels of control, local governments differ on the types of control they employ over their police departments. Some restrict their governance to initial policy formulation, whereas others maintain continuous oversight. Mastrofski was unable to explain much of the variance in levels and types of police governance with data from 24 departments, though city-size appeared to be an important variable.

The second set of works reviewed here focuses on the *inter-organizational environment*. Clark, Hall and Hutchinson (1977) conceive of police agencies as existing within a "network" of organizations that includes, at a minimum, the other elements of the criminal justice system. Based on research in twelve cities, they find that "the character of the organizational milieu in which police are embedded is apparently related to their task performance" (p. 191). Though they focus on the link between network context and performance, they acknowledge that their approach would also be valuable for understanding "police department power structure, organizational structure, administrative style, operational characteristics, and the like . . ." (p. 179). In his text on organization theory, Hall (1999, pp. 222–226) uses the police as an example to illustrate the notion of an organization set. In this case, the police are the "focal organization" and they are enmeshed in relationships with numerous other organizations and agencies, from schools and mental health clinics, to the welfare department and the court system. The idea that organizations exist within organizational fields or networks has received increasing attention in the organizational theory literature in the past two decades, but only minimal treatment in the policing literature. Duffee (1990), for example, notes that criminal justice institutions are heavily shaped by their community contexts; Hassell (2000) examines a network of local agencies responsible for dealing with serious, habitual juvenile offenders; Reiss and Bordua (1967) highlight the "boundary transactions" that take place between police officers and actors from other criminal justice agencies (i.e., prosecutors, judges); Snipes and Worden (1993) examine the interaction between police, members of the judiciary and a special interest group Mothers Against Drunk Driving (MADD) in their study of DUI (Driving Under the Influence) enforcement. Although these studies (and probably many others) have touched on inter-organizational (network) relationships, none have explicitly examined the link between network relationships and structural attributes of the organization.

The third set of works focuses on the *institutional environment*. These works are based on a branch of organizational theory known as institutional theory. The best known statement of institutional theory was published by Meyer and Rowan (1977) in the *American Journal of Sociology*. They argued that the formal structures of many organizations "dramatically reflect the myths of their institutional environments instead of the demands of their work activities" (p. 341).[5] Two sets of scholars have applied institutional theory to policing in subtly different ways.[6] Mastrofski, Ritti, and Hoffmaster (1987) were the first scholars to explicitly apply the concepts and language of institutional theory to policing, though elements of the institutional approach were implicit in earlier discussions by Reiss and Bordua (1967) and Manning (1977). They suggest three competing models of the relationship between the formal police administrative apparatus and police officer arrest behavior: rational, constrained rational, and "loosely coupled" (institutional).

Mastrofski and Ritti continue to develop, refine and test their institutional perspective on police organizations in other papers as well. Mastrofski (1999), for example, describes two competing explanations for structural change in police organizations: rational and institutional. The rational model holds that police organizational structures are designed rationally to accomplish the goals of the agency. The institutional model holds that police agencies are structured according to organizational myths which are largely unrelated to the work of the agency. Similarly, Mastrofski and Ritti (1996) compare contingency theory and institutional theory; two competing perspectives on the link between organizations and their environments. They were the first to do an empirical test of institutional theory in policing, examining patterns of DUI enforcement in six Pennsylvania police jurisdictions. Finally, Mastrofski and Ritti (2000) suggest that institutional theory offers an ideal framework for understanding the community policing movement. Mastrofski and Ritti have specifically focused their attention on 1) examining the linkages between institutional environments and arrest behavior, 2) testing institutional theory, and 3) the potential that institutional theory offers for understanding community policing.

The second set of articles focuses on specifying the theoretical parameters of institutional theory as applied to policing. Crank and Langworthy (1992) have written the most in-depth theoretical discussion to date on the potential that institutional theory offers for understanding police organizations. They suggest that American municipal police departments are "highly institutionalized organizations and should be studied in terms of how their formal structure and activities are shaped by powerful myths in their institutional environments" (338). Sources of these myths include professional associations, reformers, professional (crime fighting) images, organized labor, credentialing mechanisms, civil service, and trends in innovation. All of these entities serve as sources of institutional myths, because they are all sources of institutional legitimacy. Crank (1994) specifies two myths that led to the institutionalization of community policing: the myth of police officers as community watchmen, and the myth of community. By adopting elements "of community and watchman into their structures and formalized activities, police organizations ceremonially regain the legitimacy that was ceremonially withdrawn in the 1960's" (p. 347). Crank and Langworthy paint, in broad strokes, a picture of institutional theory that is helpful for understanding how police might incorporate elements of structure, process and policy in order to achieve organizational well-being and legitimacy.

The small body of theory on police organizational structures encompasses many different perspectives. Whether these are (or should be) competing or complementary perspectives is unknown, because until recently, they have not been considered together by any scholar. In 1992, however, Albert Reiss penned the most comprehensive theoretical statement to date on police organizations. Though he did not focus only on structure, but on police organizations as a whole, his work has a number of implications for studying and understanding police organizational structure. Reiss touched, at least implicitly, on all of the theoretical arguments described so far in this section, including others, and serves as a good capstone for the discussion of theoretical perspectives on police organizations.Reiss outlines how police organizations in the twentieth century have evolved historically in response to changes in "the social organization and political governance of urban communities and neighborhoods, and in technology" (p. 55). Each of these explanations— organization and governance of communities, and technology—will be considered separately.

Like his earlier work (Reiss and Bordua, 1967), and that of Mastrofski (1988), Reiss shows how patterns of local governance are instrumental in shaping police organizations. Political control over, and interference into the daily affairs of police organizations is a central topic in most historical analyses of the police (Fogelson, 1977; Lane, 1992; Woods, 1993). Early efforts to reform police organizations, modeled by such influential reformers as O.W. Wilson, were based, in part, on the need to distance policing from the influence of local politics. Reiss suggests that these reforms had two effects on the internal structure of police organizations: first, they centralized policing territorially, and second, they transformed "the quasi-military bureaucracy of police organizations into a legalistic and technocratic bureaucracy whose members are committed to an occupational community with norms of subordination and service that set it apart from the community that it policed" (p. 57). By altering police organizations in this way, reformers sought to hold police accountable to "bureaucratic rather than political authority" (p. 57).

Yet, decades after these reforms, local governance over the police still varies in both nature and magnitude across different departments (Mastrofski, 1988). Like Mastrofski, Reiss discusses the ongoing tension felt by police chiefs who must toe the line between police professionalism and political appeasement. In most jurisdictions, local police chiefs are beholden to politicians for their tenure in office, and therefore they must be responsive to external pressures. In addition, they are sometimes subject to replacement when incumbent government officials are not re-elected. In an effort to reduce their vulnerability to environmental turbulence, such as publicized scandals and externally driven reform efforts, many chiefs rely on a rigid system of centralized internal control.

Where there is little political support for the chief, internal control mechanisms may be a means of reducing the chances of a departmental scandal and preventing the ceremonial de-throning of the police chief. In short, depending on the nature of their political environments, police chiefs must often walk a thin line between internal and external control of their organizations. Organizational structures are presumably designed to reflect this balance.

Like Manning (1992), Reiss also shows how technological inventions such as the two-way radio, the patrol car, 911, and computer-aided dispatch have strengthened the "bureaucratic centralization of command and control" (p. 52) in police organizations, altered the traditional patterns of patrol work, contributed to widespread specialization, and transformed the occupational basis of policing. Neighborhood call-boxes were replaced by long-range two-way radios, thus expanding patrol beats; foot patrol was largely eliminated by automobile patrols, which expanded patrol beats and permitted the emergence of centralization; technological advances led to the proliferation of specialized positions and units for the maintenance and operation of sophisticated technological gadgetry and procedures requiring specialized training (such as accident reconstruction and evidence collection); as new clerical and technical jobs opened up in information processing and other non-enforcement units, departments began to hire civilian employees. By paving the road for the demise of precinct-based policing, technological innovations (of the material sort) led to massive changes in the internal structure of police organizations.

In addition to patterns of governance and technology, Reiss considers a number of other environmental elements as well. For example, Reiss implicitly employs some of the same language and concepts as those theorists, discussed earlier, who focus on the *institutional environment* (Crank and Langworthy, 1992; Mastrofski, 1994; Ritti and Mastrofski, 1995). Specifically, he discusses the ways that police organizations, faced with turbulent environments and rapid social changes, buffer their core technologies to absorb the "perturbations and fluctuations in demands for police service rather than intervene directly in their environment[s]" (p. 85). In addition to these assertions, Reiss shows how police employee associations limit the ability of police chiefs to implement widespread organizational reforms. Civil service restrictions might also affect organizational structure in similar ways, thereby homogenizing organizational structures within a particular jurisdiction (e.g., Crank and Langworthy, 1992; Guyot, 1979; Reiss and Bordua, 1967). Since Reiss refers to these restrictions as "third-party limitations," we might consider them elements of the *third-party environment.*

One last element of the environment that Reiss mentions, but does not discuss in detail, is the *civic environment*. This environment consists of the citizenry, who are the clients and primary source of inputs for the police organization. Langworthy (1986) taps this dimension of the environment when examines the impact of population heterogeneity and mobility on police organizational structure.

Reiss's work is helpful for two main reasons. First, like Langworthy (1986), he integrates size, technology, and environment (among others) as theoretical explanations for organizational structure. Second, he implicitly illustrates some of the ways that we might be able to deconstruct the environment into its different components. The political environment, the interorganizational environment, the institutional environment, the third-party environment, and the civic environment all shape police organizations in different ways. In order to assess the effect of the environment on organizations, it is necessary to understand the ways that these elements overlap and interact in shaping structures.

Police Structure as an Independent Variable

Just as the early trend in the study of organizations was to treat organizational attributes as independent variables, a number of studies in the policing literature have treated police agency characteristics as independent variables as well. These studies are only of importance here for how they measure organizational structure, our dependent variable. Studies using measures of organizational structure as independent variables have typically examined one of two units of analysis: police officers or police organizations. Table 4.1 summarizes both sets of studies.[7] In this section, I examine each set of studies in turn.

Many studies have examined the effect of police organizational structure on individual-level attributes of police officers, such as attitudes or behavior. Wilson's *Varieties of Police Behavior* (1968) is often cited as the classic work to assess organizational effects on police behavior (Crank, 1990; Langworthy, 1985c). Wilson outlined a constrained rational model of organizational effects in which the police are constrained by local political culture to act within a certain "zone of indifference" (Mastrofski, Ritti, and Hoffmaster, 1987). Within these bounds, police administrators are essentially free to make decisions and implement policies as they wish. While administrative influence does shape officers' street-level behavior in some ways, there are a variety of internal limits on the effect of administrative influence. Examining aggregate arrest statistics, Wilson identified a taxonomy of three police department styles, which he labels as Watchman, Legalistic, and Service. Mastrofski, Ritti, and Hoffmaster (1987, p. 388) suggest that Wilson's theory falls in the middle of a continuum "of the extent to which the administrative apparatus is responsible for influencing police officer discretion." At one end, they argue, is the classic Weberian rational-legal model, which assumes a tight coupling between various elements of the organization. At the other end is the "loosely coupled" model described by institutional theorists, in which changes in structure are assumed to have little impact on individual behavior.

Based on their interpretation that Wilson's taxonomy was constructed by cross-classifying "bureaucratization" and "professionalization," Smith and Klein (1983) test the effect of these variables on arrest-decisions using data from the Police Services Study. They find that the probability of arrest is greater in bureaucratized departments, and lesser in professionalized departments. Though he never defines bureaucratization, or defends his strategy for measuring it operationally, Smith uses similar schemes in three other papers as well (Smith, 1984; Smith and Klein, 1984; Smith et al., 1984). Worden (1994) borrows from Smith's measurement scheme in his study of the police use of force. He found that, controlling for individual and situational variables, officers from more bureaucratized departments are more likely to use reasonable force.

Other scholars have used the terms "bureaucracy" and "bureaucratization" liberally in their studies of police behavior without (a) using the concept as a variable in their models, and/or (b) providing a definition of the concept. Brown (1981), for example, found that officers in larger, *more bureaucratized* departments were more willing to make arrests than officers in smaller departments, who were more lenient. In their examination of DUI enforcement in four police departments, Mastrofski, Ritti, and Hoffmaster (1987, p. 398) found that "contrary to Brown's (1981) findings, the willingness to make DUI arrests decreased as *department size and bureaucratization increased.*" Though both studies considered the size of the agency in drawing these conclusions, neither considered bureaucratization as a variable. It appears that both sets of results were based on the assumption that greater department size equals greater bureaucratization.

Other studies are slight variations on the same bureaucratization theme. Harrison (1975) and Harrison and Pelletier (1987) examine the effects of "perceived" bureaucratization on personal role performance and organizational effectiveness as perceived by responding police supervisors. The assumption in these studies, of course, is that bureaucratization is not an objective quality of police organizations, but is instead a perceived reality (Berger and Luckman, 1967). While some

Table 4.1

Studies Employing Measures of Police Organizational Structure as Independent Variables

Study	Structural Components	Measures	Relevant Findings	Unit of Analysis
Harrison (1975)	Bureaucratization (Perceived)	Ten individual measures of bureaucratization as perceived by supervisors in two police departments.	Responses reveal that these two organizations have "strongly bureaucratic characteristics" and are "populated by supervisors at the lower and middle management levels who perceive themselves, for the most part, at a less than high level of role performance and whose view of their organization's effectiveness tends toward the low side in several critical areas" (p. 322).	Individual (Attitude)
Swanson (1978)	Specialization	Percent of force assigned to specialized non-patrol duties.	Rejects the hypothesis that more specialized departments make more arrests.	Organizational
	Centralization	Number of police stations.	Found little support for the hypothesis that centralized departments make more arrests.	
Mastrofski (1981)	Organizational "Scale"	Population of primary assignment area.	"The data analysis does not show dramatic effects for the scale of patrol on officer behavior" (p. 355)	Individual (Behavior)

(continued on next page)

Table 4.1 *(continued)*

Study	Structural Components	Measures	Relevant Findings	Unit of Analysis
Monkkonen (1981)	Bureaucratization	Ratio of non-patrol to patrol officers (a larger ratio indicates greater bureaucratization).	"bureaucratic growth did have some effect on arrests for crimes with victims" (p. 146).	Organizational
Smith and Klein (1983)	Bureaucratization	Additive index composed of four standardized variables: specialization (number of occupational divisions), authority structure (number of ranks), size (number of employees), and civilianization (percentage of civilian employees).	"The probability of arrest varies directly with the level of departmental bureaucratization. . . controlling for other organizational properties" (p. 84).	Individual (Behavior)
	Centralization	Proportion of encounters involving contact between patrol supervisor and patrol officer	Centralization had no significant effect on probability of arrest.	
Smith (1984)	Bureaucratization	Index of unknown type composed of three variables: size, number of occupational titles, and number of ranks.	Effects were not tested independently. Bureaucratization was cross-classified with professionalism to form a taxonomy of department types.	Individual (Behavior)

(continued on next page)

Table 4.1 *(continued)*

Study	Structural Components	Measures	Relevant Findings	Unit of Analysis
Smith and Klein (1984)	Bureaucratization	Additive index composed of three standardized variables: log of department size, number of ranks, and number of occupational titles.	"Results indicate that the probability of arrest increases significantly as departments become more bureaucratic and professional. Neither of these organizational properties independently influenced the likelihood of arrest" (p. 476).	Individual (Behavior)
Smith, Visher, and Davidson (1984)	Bureaucratization	Additive index composed of three standardized variables: "department size, number of ranks, and number of occupational titles in each department. The mean inter-item correlation among the components of this measure is .739" (p. 241).	"This model indicates that... police arrest decisions are not affected by bureaucratization of police agencies" (p. 243).	Individual (Behavior)
Murphy (1986)	Bureaucratization	Additive index composed of five standardized variables: formalization, centralization, specialization, professionalism, and organizational closure.	"Bureaucratic R.C.M.P. detachments produce an aggressive policing style resulting in high arrest rates. Less bureaucratized police departments produce a more informal policing style with low rates of arrest" (abstract).	Organizational

(continued on next page)

Table 4.1 (*continued*)

Study	Structural Components	Measures	Relevant Findings	Unit of Analysis
Slovak (1986)[1]	Span of Control	Number of patrol officers per police sergeant.	Controlling for organizational and environmental effects, span of control was directly proportional to violent crime arrest rates, and had an insignificant effect on property crime arrest rates.	Organizational
	Civilianization	Percent of employees who are civilians.	Controlling for organizational and environmental effects, civilianization was directly proportional to both violent and property crime arrest rates.	
	Patrol Concentration	Percent of sworn officers who are assigned to patrol duty.	Controlling for organizational and environmental effects, patrol concentration had an insignificant effect on both violent and property crime arrest rates.	
Harrison and Pelletier (1987)	Bureaucratization (Perceived)	Nine individual measures of bureaucratization as perceived by supervisors in a single metropolitan police department.	The first of two hypotheses, that perceived bureaucratization is associated with lower perceptions of self-performance, is rejected. The second hypothesis holds: "bureaucratic organizations elicit less than positive views of organizational effectiveness from their members" (p. 267).	Individual (Attitude)

(*continued on next page*)

Table 4.1 *(continued)*

Study	Structural Components	Measures	Relevant Findings	Unit of Analysis
Mastrofski, Ritti and Hoffmaster (1987)	Bureaucratization	Unknown (size?).	"Willingness to make DUI arrests decreased as department size and bureaucratization increased" (p. 398).	Individual (Behavior)
Crank (1990)	Concentration	Ratio of administrative personnel to total number of sworn officers.	Concentration is negatively associated with arrest for four (out of four) property crime categories in urban areas. It is positively associated with two (of four) property crime categories in rural areas.	Organizational
	Segmentation	Number of ranks.	Segmentation is positively associated with arrest for three (of four) property crime categories in urban areas and two of four categories in rural areas.	
	Supervisory Ratio	Ratio of lowest-ranking officers to sergeants.	Supervisory ratio has an insignificant effect on arrest for all property crimes in urban areas, and a positive association with arrest for two of the four property crime categories in rural areas.	

(continued on next page)

Table 4.1 *(continued)*

Study	Structural Components	Measures	Relevant Findings	Unit of Analysis
Wells and Falcone (1992)	Vertical Differentiation	Number of ranks.	"Departments with the tallest bureaucratic structures reported the most elaborate pursuit policy/procedures" (p. 328).	Organizational
	Hierarchical Structure	Index (unspecified type) measured "by a combination of two items indicating: (1) the extent to which interaction and decision-making was restricted by the 'chain-of- command'; and (2) the degree to which the police chief followed an 'open-door-policy' " (p. 321).	"Agencies reporting more adherence to hierarchy and a clear 'chain-of-command' tended to have more extensive and restrictive pursuit policies, along with specific training and record-keeping procedures" (p. 328).	
	Formalization of Mission	"[The] degree to which the department had an explicit formal mission statement intended to shape policy development" (p. 321).	Departments with formalized mission statements exhibited substantially more formalized and restrictive pursuit policies.	

(continued on next page)

Table 4.1 *(continued)*

Study	Structural Components	Measures	Relevant Findings	Unit of Analysis
Maguire (1994)	Bureaucratization	Additive index composed of five standardized variables: functional differentiation (a count of the primary functions which the agency performs), formalization (the number of agency functions guided by written policy directives), specialization (the number of specialized units in the agency), and two elements of vertical differentiation, including administrative intensity (percentage of officers assigned to administration), and pay differential (the difference between the chief's income and the patrolman's income, divided by the patrolman's income).	Bureaucratization significantly decreases the proportion of child sexual abuse cases cleared by arrest.	Organizational
Worden (1994)	Bureaucratization	Additive index composed of four standardized variables: size (number of employees), vertical differentiation (number of ranks), specialization (number of separate units), and civilianization (percentage of civilian employees).	"The likelihood that reasonable force will be used increases with the bureaucratization of the department" (p. 39).	Individual (Behavior)

1. Slovak included the percentage of officers who are black as an element of "innovation," it is clearly not an element of organizational structure, because it is not a means of coordinating or controlling work or workers.

investigators have examined variability in the individual perceptions of actors within organizations, bureaucracy itself is almost always treated as an objective concept. If the degree to which a single organization is bureaucratic can vary depending on who is looking at it, then bureaucratization is not a stable organizational attribute. Although the scale that they use to measure bureaucratization is more complete than any of the other measurement schemes reviewed here, the authors neither address the subjectivity issue, nor define bureaucratization.

Only two individual-level studies of police behavior have employed structural variables other than, or in addition to bureaucratization. Smith and Klein (1983) included both centralization and bureaucratization (and other non-structural elements) as independent variables in a larger model to predict probability of arrest. They measure centralization as the proportion of encounters involving contact between the patrol supervisor and patrol officers, finding no effect on probability of arrest.[8] Mastrofski (1981) examines the impact of "organizational scale," operationalized as the population of the primary assignment area, on arrest behavior. He finds that scale of the patrol area has little effect on officer behavior. This unique variable taps into a fundamentally important element of organization structure: the degree to which an organization divides its work into smaller or larger pieces.

A second set of studies has examined the effect of police organizational structure on organizational-level attributes, such as arrest rates. Like the individual-level studies, some of these works have treated structure as a unidimensional phenomenon, usually conceptualized as bureaucratization. Monkkonen (1981), for example, finds that "bureaucratic growth," operationalized as changes in the ratio of non-patrol to patrol officers, had a limited effect on arrest rates.[9] Monkkonen neither defines bureaucratization, nor makes a case that it can (or should) be measured by a scheme as simplistic as the ratio of non-patrol to patrol officers. In an earlier study, I found that an additive index of bureaucratization was negatively related to the proportion of child sexual abuse cases cleared by arrest (Maguire, 1994). I defined bureaucracy according to the classic Weberian definition,[10] constructing an index composed of five variables representing a variety of structural characteristics, including functional and vertical differentiation, specialization, and formalization. I failed to defend my simplistic assumption that these variables are indicators of a single concept—that they should not be considered as "separate" phenomena.

Other studies at the organizational level have conceived of structure as a multidimensional concept, assessing the effects of different structural variables individually. Swanson (1978), for example, found little support for her hypotheses that arrest rates are positively related to departmental specialization and centralization. Slovak (1986) found mixed results in exploring the effects of patrol concentration, span of control, and civilianization on violent and property crime arrest rates. Crank (1990) also found mixed results in comparing the effects of concentration, segmentation and supervisory ratio on assorted property crime rates in urban and rural areas.[11] As we can clearly see, only a handful of scholars have conceived of structure as a multi-dimensional concept.

This section has traced the use of structural attributes as independent variables in studies of police attitudes and behavior at the individual and organizational levels. The assessment of structural variation in these studies is plagued by both theoretical and methodological problems, all stemming from their universal reliance on simplistic and/or atheoretical measures of organizational structure. Bureaucratization, as first described by Weber, was a unidimensional concept. A spate of studies challenging various elements of Weber's writings on bureaucracies emerged in the late 1950s and early 1960s. Most relevant to this discussion are those challenging the view that bureaucracies are one-dimensional. Pugh et al. (1968, p. 65), for example, used principal components analysis to show the multidimensionality of organization structures, concluding that "the concept of the bureaucratic type is no longer useful." Similarly, Meyer (1968b, p. 227) found that "there are important variations in structure among bureaucratic organizations . . . [o]ne must not distinguish only between bureaucratic and rational types of formal organization, but he [sic] must also consider the different kinds of bureaucratic structures." Reimann (1973, p. 462) found that "a multidimensional model of bureaucracy is superior to the unidimensional Weberian one." Through the years, scholars continued to amass evidence about the multidimensionality of organizational structure. Despite the almost universal agreement among organizational scholars that bureaucracy is not a "monolith" (Wilson, 1989), many of the policing studies discussed in this section have treated it as a unidimensional concept.

Bureaucratization is an imprecise concept that has either not been defined at all or has been defined inadequately almost everywhere that it appears in the policing literature. The implicit assumption by those that employ the term bureaucracy seems to be that "you know one when you see one." We all know that bureaucracies are filled with piles of forms, bumbling bureaucrats, rigid control structures, and mountains of red tape. Frequently the term is used together with size, as if the two concepts naturally go hand-in-hand. There are many references in the literature to large "bureaucratized" police departments (e.g., Monkkonen, 1981; Mastrofski, Ritti, and Hoffmaster, 1987). Even if bureaucratization is a viable concept, the idea that it is synonymous (or highly correlated) with size should be treated as an empirical question rather than an implicit "fact." However, the bulk of social science evidence is clearly against the utility of bureaucracy as a theoretical concept. Langworthy (1994; 1996) refers to the use of the term "bureaucracy" in the policing literature as "the bureaucratic myth in police organizational theory." He virtually ignored the idea of bureaucratization in his 1986 book on police structures because the term is so unclear.

Not all of the studies cited in this section used bureaucratization as a structural variable. As we have already discussed, Swanson (1978), Mastrofski (1981), Slovak (1986), Crank (1990), and Wells and Falcone (1992) all used other (separate) structural attributes to measure variation in organizational structures. While these studies are a clear improvement over the bureaucratization lot, none measures a large range of variation in structures. In most cases, the author is specifically interested in only a subset of structural variables. Swanson (1978) and Mastrofski (1981), for instance, are not interested in measuring general structure, but only certain components of relevance to their particular studies. Similarly, Crank (1990) is only interested in those structural variables of interest to police reformers. Slovak (1986) and Wells and Falcone (1992), on the other hand, do claim an interest in the general structure of organizations, though neither measures a wide range of variation in structure. Slovak (1986) measures span of control, civilianization, and patrol concentration, whereas Wells and Falcone include three vertical measures and a measure of formalization. Both are significant improvements over the bulk of the prior literature, but neither really comes close to measuring the full range of theoretically relevant structural variables.

Police structure has been measured as an independent variable in a number of studies. These studies were reviewed here in order to determine whether the structural measures used might be helpful for defining and measuring structure in this study as a dependent variable. However, the measurement of structure in all of these studies suffers from at least one of several theoretical and/or empirical shortcomings, and other than enabling us to learn from past mistakes, does not offer much promise for guiding future research.

Police Structure as a Dependent Variable

I have argued that studies using police organizational structure as an independent variable have conceptualized and operationalized structure poorly. So the question remains, if we want to explain the formal structures of police organizations, what are the theoretically relevant components of formal organizational structure, and how do we measure them? Structure is the formal apparatus through which organizations accomplish two core activities: the division of labor, and the coordination of work (Mintzberg, 1979; Scott, 1992). As described in chapter 2, organizational theorists have developed a long list of dimensions intended to capture the variation in organizational structures. However, the only comprehensive empirical work applying the literature of structural organizational theory to policing is Robert Langworthy's (1986) book, *The Structure of Police Organizations*. Langworthy's book was the first and most complete comparative examination of police organizational structures.[12] Langworthy (1986, p. 17) defines formal structure as "the framework on which a police organization arranges its resources to conduct its activities." Basing his selection of structural variables on the work of Blau and Schoenherr (1971), Langworthy examines five dimensions of organizational differentiation: administrative overhead, and spatial, occupational, hierarchical, and functional differentiation. These dimensions generally parallel those identified by other organizational theorists. These five dimensions, which constitute Langworthy's dependent variables, are operationalized in Table 4.2. These same variables are also selected as indicators of structure by King (1999), a former graduate student of Langworthy's.

Other scholars have examined police organizational structures as dependent variables as well, defining and measuring structure in a variety of ways. Ostrom, Parks, and Whitaker (1978b), for example, examine the effect of department size on personnel assignments, including patrol, other direct services (such as investigation), auxiliary services (such as dispatching and the crime laboratory), and administration. Monkkonen's (1981) historical analysis examines the correlates of bureaucratization in urban police departments. Arguing that departments hired more specialists as they enlarged and became more bureaucratized, he measures bureaucratization as an increase in the proportion of non-patrol to patrol officers. Slovak (1986), relying on a perceived (though disputable) consensus among organizational theorists about the dimensions of organization structure, examined five structural elements. Only three of these are considered here, because two are not structural variables (see explanation in Table 4.1). Slovak examines the effect of department size on span of control, civilianization, and patrol concentration. Slovak is the only researcher in policing to consider the effects of structural variables on one another in a multivariate causal model. Crank (1989) examines the effect of size and several environmental variables on civilianization, which is one

Table 4.2
Studies Employing Measures of Police Organizational Structure as a Dependent Variable

Study	Structural Components	Measures
Ostrom, Parks and Whitaker (1978)	Personnel Assignments	"Percentage of sworn officers assigned to patrol, other direct services, auxiliary services, and administration" (p. 39).
Monkkonen (1981)	Bureaucratization	Proportion of non-patrol to patrol officers.
Langworthy (1986)	Spatial Differentiation	Number of station houses, and the number of beats.
	Hierarchical Differentiation	Standardized pay differential, a rank count, and the percentage concentration at the lowest ranks.
	Occupational Differentiation	Civilianization rate.
	Functional Differentiation	Number of divisions, and a measure of task differentiation.
	Administrative Overhead	Proportion of employees assigned to administrative duties.
Slovak (1986)	Span of Control	Number of patrol officers per police sergeant.
	Civilianization	Percent of employees who are civilians.
	Patrol Concentration	Percent of sworn officers who are assigned to patrol duty.
Crank (1989)	Civilianization	Changes in the ratio of full-time civilians to full-time sworn officers between 1973 and 1986.
Crank and Wells (1991)	Civilianization	Ratio of civilians to sworn officers.
	Concentration	Proportion of sworn officers ranking below sergeant to all sworn officers.
	Height	Number of Ranks.
	Supervisory Ratio	Ratio of line officers to sergeants.
King (1999)	Same as Langworthy (1986)	Same as Langworthy (1986)

element of structure according to Langworthy (1986) and Slovak (1986). Finally, Crank and Wells (1991) examine four elements of structure which are pertinent to reformers: civilianization, concentration, height, and supervisory ratio. These variables are selected because they are often contained in normative theories of policing, not because they are thought to represent the range of variation in organization structures. However, though they are named differently, they represent a subset of Langworthy's dependent variables, including civilianization (occupational differentiation), concentration (hierarchical differentiation) and height, or rank count (hierarchical differentiation). They also include the ratio of sergeants to line officers, which can be considered yet another element of hierarchical differentiation. Thus, Crank and Wells consider only two of Langworthy's five structural dimensions.

Ostrom, Parks, and Whitaker (1978b) and Monkkonen (1981) were the first scholars to empirically examine police organizational structures as dependent variables. However, their analyses of structure were limited, constituting just one small component of larger studies with other aims. Langworthy was the first scholar to comprehensively examine police organizational structures as dependent variables. His 1983 doctoral dissertation resulted in a book and several journal articles. Other than Langworthy's work, the small amount of research on police organizational structures does not really offer much guidance in selecting dependent variables that capture the variation in organizational structures. For a summary of the structural variables used in these studies, see Table 4.2. We now turn our focus from dependent to independent variables as we discuss those studies that seek to explain or predict organizational structure.

Explaining Police Structure

Efforts to explain police organization structures have drawn from four separate pools of independent variables: size, technology, environment, and history. This list is parallel to the types of independent variables used to explain organization structures in many types of organizations, from factories to welfare offices. Though other explanatory schemes have been suggested in the organization theory literature, this analysis will focus on these four sets of independent variables.

Langworthy (1986) used three general dimensions to explain police organizational structures: size, technology, and environment (See Table 4.3 for operationalizations). To examine the effect of size on structure, Langworthy relied on Blau's theory that an increase in size results in an increase in all aspects of structural differentiation. For his analysis of technology, Langworthy employs Perrow's framework for the comparative analysis of organizations. Perrow's model focuses on the stability and analyzability of raw materials. In short, Perrow's theory is that the more predictable the input, the more standardized the task. He then develops normative prescriptions for which structures are most appropriate for which types of tasks. Langworthy converts Perrow's normative language into empirically testable hypotheses concerning the relationship between task/technology and structure. Langworthy (1986, p. 97) correctly notes that the examination of the relationship between environment and structure "is a virtually infinite analytic problem." He chooses to examine three dimensions of environment: population size (an antecedent to Blau's theory), complexity of input material (an antecedent to the Perrow theory), and following the lead of Wilson (1968), the characteristics of the local political culture.

Others who have examined the correlates of police organization structure, though in far less detail, include Ostrom et al. (1978), Crank (1989), Crank and Wells (1991), Slovak (1986), King (1999), and Monkkonen (1981). Ostrom, Parks, and Whitaker (1978b), assessing the effect of department size on personnel assignments, found that smaller municipal agencies assigned a lower percentage of officers to administration, and a higher percentage to patrol than larger agencies. Crank (1989) focused on size and environment (budgets, crime, and geographic status) in his examination of civilianization, which is Langworthy's proxy for occupational differentiation, one element of structure. Crank and Wells (1991) examined the effects of size and environment (urbanism) on the structure of Illinois police departments.

Slovak (1986) examined the effects of size on several structural dimensions in an effort to link size and structure to an overall model predicting police style, operationalized as aggregate arrest rates. His analysis is unique in the police organization literature because he developed a multivariate causal (path) model, calculating both indirect and direct effects, showing the effects of structural dimensions on one another. However, though he lays out nearly all the groundwork for a fairly sophisticated analysis of the effects of environment on organization structure, he leaves his analysis incomplete. Slovak's main goal was to link environment and organizational structure to organizational style. He develops separate causal models for the effects of environment on style, and the effects of structure on style. He also places all environmental and structural variables simultaneously into a regression model predicting style. In neither case can we infer the effect of the environment on structure. However, Slovak acknowledges that environment

Table 4.3

Independent Variables Used in Studies Explaining Police Organizational Structure

Study	Variable	Measure	Relevant Findings
Ostrom, Parks, and Whitaker (1978)	Size	Number of sworn officers	"Smaller municipal patrol agencies have a lower proportion of their officers assigned to administration and a higher proportion assigned to patrol" (p. 38).
Monkkonen (1981)	Organizational Age	Not measured	Changes in the structure of policing "came about through external demands upon the police . . . and, to a lesser extent, through the 'natural' growth of the police bureaucracy" (p. 147).
Langworthy (1986)	Size	Number of employees (derived from Blau)	Size is strongly related to spatial differentiation, weakly related to other structural variables.
	Technology	One minus the number of personnel assigned to patrol (derived from Perrow)	Technology is strongly related to functional differentiation, and lesser so to occupational differentiation. Other structural variables are either weakly associated with, or independent of agency technology.
	Environment	1) Population Size—Uses SMSA population (derived from Blau)	The effects of population size on structure could not be disentangled from the effects of agency size.
		2) Complexity of inputs—Uses population heterogeneity and mobility (derived from Perrow)	Only civilianization was related to population complexity.
		3) Political Culture—Uses type of government and type of election (derived from James Q. Wilson)	"Good government cities appear to have fewer ranks and a higher proportion of employees who are civilian than do cities that have mayor-council governments or hold partisan elections" (p. 124).

(continued on next page)

Table 4.3 (*continued*)

Study	Variable	Measure	Relevant Findings
Slovak (1986)	Size[1]	Number of full-time police employees	"Organizational size has no discernible effect on internal police agency differentiation; administrative intensity is a negative function of organizational size (recall that span of control, as measured here, is an inverse indicator of intensity) but is not directly related to differentiation; the innovation of civilianization is promoted by administrative intensity (again, recall the caveat about measurement) but is not directly affected by either size or differentiation" (p. 23).
Crank (1989)	Fiscal Health	Changes in police budgets, 1973–1986	"Contrary to the initial expectations, budgetary decline was not found to be most likely to stimulate civilianization. Instead, civilianization occurred at a more rapid pace in communities experiencing substantial budgetary growth. . . . However, departments in budgetary decline also civilianized, though at a slower pace" (p. 176).
	Criminal Environment	Changes in the level of index crimes, 1973–1986	Mixed findings.
	Organizational Size	Changes in the number of employees	"Civilianization experienced its most dramatic growth in agencies that declined in size" (p. 176).
	Geographic Status	Urbanization (rural-intermediate-urban)	"To the extent that civilianization may be thought of as innovative, rural departments were as innovative as their urban counterparts" (p. 176).

(*Continued on next page*)

Table 4.3 (*continued*)

Study	Variable	Measure	Relevant Findings
Crank and Wells (1991)	Size	Number of full-time employees	Variations in size were associated with significant changes in three of the four dimensions of organizational structure examined, including height, concentration, and supervisory ratio.
	Urbanism	Percentage of the county that is classified as urban	Controlling for organizational size, variations in urbanism do not have an independent effect on organizational structure.
King (1999)	Organizational Age	Length of time since organization was founded	Controlling for size, older organizations employ fewer civilians and are more hierarchically differentiated.

1. In a causal model, Slovak also examines the effect of structural variables *on one another*. Unlike the present analysis, Slovak considers size as a structural rather than contextual variable.

may affect structure, calling his models "artificial" because "selected structural characteristics may well be affected by environmental and especially political forces" (p. 23). Despite his concern with these causality issues, he never tests a model with environment exogenous to structure and style, and structure exogenous to style. The result is a helpful but incomplete analysis.

Two scholars have examined a fourth potential explanation for police organizational structures. Based on the age-structure link first discussed by Stinchcombe (1965), King (1999) explored the effect of organizational age on police structure. His primary thesis is that organizations founded during the same era will adopt similar structures, different from those adopted by organizations founded during a different era. He found that older organizations tend to have taller hierarchies and employ fewer civilians. Similarly, Monkkonen (1981, pp. 143–147) devotes a very small portion of his historical analysis of police to the question, "did police departments grow more top-heavy in their bureaucratic structures as they aged [and] expanded . . . ?" However, Monkkonen never measures organizational age, and his analysis is further limited in scope because it is only one small component in a causal chain linking structural changes to performance.

Conclusion

This chapter has examined a number of resources in the policing literature that may be useful in developing a theory to explain police organizational structure. Three types of works were consulted: theoretical works, studies that use structural features as independent variables, and studies that use structural features as dependent variables. The theoretical works that I reviewed, though few, provide a number of insights. The body of literature using structural features as independent variables is generally weak, relying on variables that are convenient rather than conceptually meaningful. These studies are not of much use here. Finally, the body of literature using structural features as dependent variables was reviewed. These studies, though few and somewhat flawed, will serve as a foundation for this study. In the next chapter, I mesh the literatures that I reviewed in chapters 2 through 4 to create a new theory of police organizational structure. The remaining chapters will focus on testing that theory.

CHAPTER 5

A Primitive Theory of
Police Organizational Structure[1]

In *The Moon*, Argentine poet Jorge Luis Borges (trans. 1964) tells of a man who conceived of an "unconscionable plan of making an abridgement of the universe in a single book. . . ." When the book is completed, the man looks up at the sky and is shocked to learn that he has forgotten to include the moon. Social theorists walk a fine line between building theories that are either too abridged or too complex. The best theories are those that are parsimonious; simplistic enough to make intuitive sense, but just complex enough to explain the phenomenon of interest.

This chapter will introduce and develop a new theory of police organizational structure. Building new theories is a fairly simple exercise: the hard part is constructing testable theories.[2] Past theorists were severely constrained in the complexity of the social theories they could develop because methodologies were often not available to test those theories. Fortunately, as Hage (1980, p. 5) notes, a "parallel development in theoretical and analytical methods . . . can aid us in constructing more complex and subtle statements."[3] No matter how sophisticated the methodologies available to social scientists become though, theories remain only simple approximations of a very complex real world. The more complex a theory, the more theorists must wonder if, like Borges' fictional writer, they might have forgotten to include the moon. With every effort to ensure that "the essence" is not completely lost, what follows is a fairly complex, testable theory of police organization structure.

Although readers who are well versed in organizational theory will find a great deal of this material familiar, there is much here that is new as well. Much of the theory has been cobbled together based on bits and pieces of other sociological theories of organizations, including structural-contingency theory, resource-dependency theory, population-ecology theory, institutional theory, and probably pieces and parts of several others. Although portions of each of these theories are present here, the contextual theory of police organizational structure introduced in this chapter is not really true to any one dominant paradigm

69

(e.g., Donaldson, 1995). At the conclusion to this chapter, I will discuss where and how this theory fits in with other basic paradigms in organizational sociology.

Organizational Structure

Organizational structures are multi-dimensional, and though there is some level of basic agreement throughout the literature on the definition of structure, the conceptualization and operationalization of structure has historically been more problematic. The past four decades have seen hundreds of different combinations of several dozen variables for measuring the variation in organizational structures. Fortunately, scholars have tinkered with many different strategies, both conceptually and methodologically, for reducing the number of variables necessary to measure variation in organizational structures. As described in chapter 2, the bulk of this literature can be boiled down into two basic conceptual dimensions: *structural complexity* and *structural coordination and control*.

Structural complexity is the extent to which an organization is differentiated vertically, functionally, and spatially. Organizations become more structurally complex by differentiating in any one or any combination of these areas. Structural coordination and control mechanisms include formalization, centralization, and administration. Organizations achieve greater levels of structural control by enhancing any one or any combination of these separate coordination and control mechanisms. There are many other techniques that an organization can use to achieve coordination and control that do not have implications for the structure of the organization. For example, a supervisor with a strong, demanding personality may serve as an *individual* control mechanism, but personality is an individual feature, not a structural feature (Blau et al., 1966; Van de Ven, Delbecq, and Koenig, 1976). Structural coordination and control mechanisms are built into the very essence of an organization. For stylistic purposes only, throughout the remainder of the book I refer to structural coordination and control mechanisms as simply control mechanisms.

Complexity and control should not be considered as variables, in the sense that their elements can be united into a composite that represents the whole concept.[4] As discussed at length in previous chapters, this was the mistake made by early bureaucratic theorists who assumed that bureaucracy was a unidimensional variable. An organization may be extremely complex in its level of vertical differentiation, but quite simple in its level of functional differentiation. Similarly, an organization may exhibit a high level of centralization as a means of structural control and coordination, but rely very little on the use of formal rules and policies (formalization) or on the level of administration.[5] Consequently, the best way to conceive of complexity and control is as separate "clusters" of related variables. Later in this chapter I will argue that there is an inherent causal order between these separate clusters.

Organizational Context

Perhaps the greatest contribution of organizational theory to the study of actual organizations is the fundamental principle that organizations are shaped by the contexts in which they are embedded.[6] Aside from this simple assertion, researchers have identified hundreds of particular contextual variables that impact organizations in one way or another. The majority of these variables boil down to four dimensions: the size of an organization, the age of an organization, the technology that an organization uses to produce its goods or services, and the environment in which an organization is located. As discussed extensively in chapter 3, these four dimensions—size, age, task/technology[7] and environment—are the basic elements of an organization's "context." These dimensions appear repeatedly throughout the literature, and they have been used individually and in various combinations for several decades to explain organizational structure. Like complexity and control, context should be conceived as a cluster of variables rather than as a single construct.

The Basic Theory: A Simple Causal Order
Among Context, Complexity, and Control

I have now identified three core factors integral to developing a theory of police organizational structure: context, complexity, and control. The basic theoretical framework shown in Figure 5.1 illustrates the causal order between these three factors. This section will describe at a very simplistic level the principles behind the basic theory. The next section will extend this basic framework, laying out a far more complex theory of police organizational structure.

I start by reiterating a basic premise of modern organization theory, that organizations are shaped in many important ways by their contexts. Specifically, organizational context has a direct effect on structural complexity and structural control. Size, age, technology, and environment all comprise an organization's context and all affect how an organization is structured, both in terms of complexity and control. The relationships between context-complexity and context-control have been explored frequently by organizational researchers. Chapter 3 presented a detailed discussion of the literature in this area.

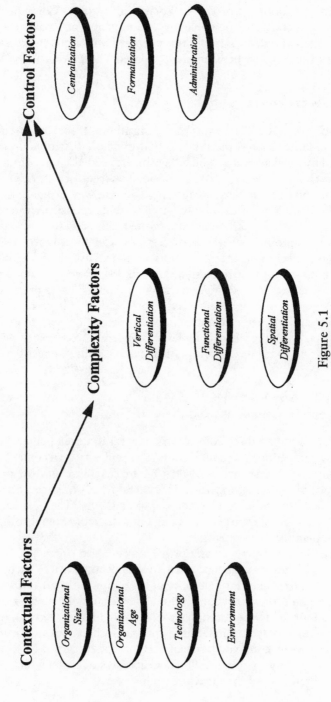

Figure 5.1
Context, Complexity, and Control: Basic Theoretical Model

Having laid out the causal order of theoretical relationships between context-complexity, and context-control, I now address the relationship between the two structural factors: complexity and control. The hypothesized relationship is based on a simple sociological assumption: the more complex a social unit becomes, the greater the need for internal coordination. Rushing (1976) terms this phenomenon the "differentiation-coordination hypothesis," and credits its initial formulation to Durkheim's classic work, *The Division of Labor in Society* (trans. 1949). Rushing (1976, pp. 676, 679) eloquently describes the process by which increasing complexity promotes the development of control and coordination mechanisms like centralization, formalization and administrative density:

> . . . as social systems become increasingly differentiated they tend to develop structures and mechanisms that coordinate the actions of the various parts. . . . An increase in differentiation makes the actions of personnel more difficult to anticipate; conflicting interests emerge and social disorganization is apt to ensue. The resulting strain may lead to a generalized demand throughout the social system for more planning, the development of more well-defined procedures and regulations, and the establishment of agencies to insure that procedures and regulations are adhered to.

In general, previous work by Hsu, Marsh, and Mannari (1983) and Rushing (1976) has found a modest relationship between complexity and control. However, the exact pattern of relationships between individual complexity variables and individual control variables remains relatively unexplored.

At its most simplistic level, the basic theory of police organizational structures introduced here suggests that a single theoretical model can explain the relationships between organizational context, structural complexity, and structural control. As illustrated in Figure 5.1, organizational context has a direct effect on structural complexity and control. In addition, structural complexity has a direct influence on structural control. Therefore, context has an indirect effect on structural control through structural complexity. The exact pattern of these relationships will be explored in further detail in the following section.

The Expanded Theory

Having introduced the basic causal order among the three primary factors in the the theoretical model, we now turn our attention to the individual concepts and dimensions within the three factors and the relationships between them. Two of the concepts described in the basic model are multidimensional. Technology has two dimensions: task scope and task routineness. Environment is a complex concept with four dimensions: capacity, complexity, stability-instability, and concentration-dispersion. The expanded theoretical model containing these additional dimensions is illustrated in Figure 5.2. The exact variables used to measure each of these theoretical concepts will be introduced in chapter 6.

Organizational Size

Chapter 3 discussed in detail the massive literature on the link between organizational size and structure. Although there is some debate about measures and methods in these studies (Kimberly, 1976), and some researchers have noted weak relationships between size and complexity (Beyer and Trice, 1979), the majority of the literature supports the notion that larger organizations have more complex structures (Blau and Schoenherr, 1971; Blau, 1994; Hall, Haas and Johnson, 1967; Hsu, Marsh, and Mannari, 1983; Langworthy, 1986; Meyer, 1972; Pugh et al., 1969). In addition, there is limited evidence that the effect may be nonlinear—that the marginal effects of size may decrease as size increases (Blau and Schoenherr, 1971; Blau, 1994; Crank and Wells, 1991; Child, 1973). If the effect of size on structure is nonlinear, then the larger a police organization, the less important the effect of size on structural complexity. Whether the effect is linear or nonlinear is not known for certain (see Kimberly, 1976), but the bulk of evidence supports the notion that larger police organizations are more vertically, functionally, and spatially differentiated. Larger police organizations, with more personnel to juggle, must implement some degree of structural complexity in order to improve coordination, reduce conflict, and/or achieve tighter organizational control.

In addition to the size-complexity relationship, researchers have also noted a link between size and structural coordination and control mechanisms. As reviewed in chapter 3, research has consistently shown that larger organizations tend to decentralize decision-making and increase their levels of formalization. In fact, there is some evidence that there may be a compensatory relationship between these two forms of control and coordination. Specifically, they may be viewed as alternative mechanisms for achieving control—formalized rules and procedures may permit organizations to decentralize their decision making without a concomitant loss of control (Blau and Schoenherr, 1971; Child, 1973; Mansfield, 1973; Scott, 1992). Among larger police departments, centralized decision-making is not a realistic structural option due to the sheer size of the organization. In order for senior managers in the largest

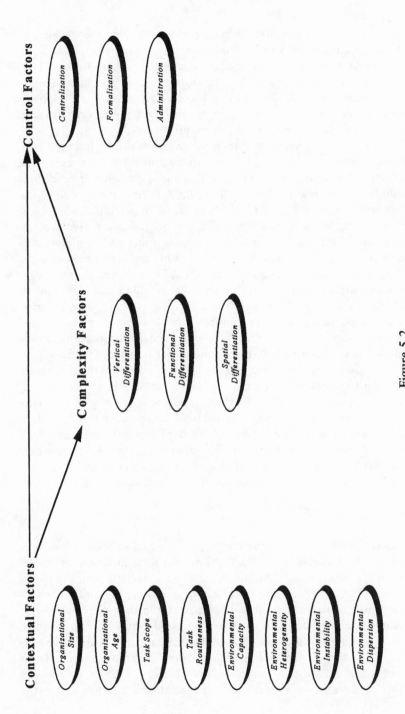

Figure 5.2
Context, Complexity, and Control: Expanded Theoretical Model

police agencies to centralize decision-making like their colleagues in smaller agencies, they would need to access and process inordinate amounts of information about the organization and its operations. Thus decentralization, or delegation to subordinates, is an absolute necessity in large police agencies. On the other hand, formalization is a relatively simple mechanism that senior managers in larger police organizations can implement to achieve coordination and control.[8]

I noted, in chapter 3, that there is some confusion about the relationship between organization size and administrative intensity. The chief source of this confusion was that there are two different definitions of administrative intensity in the literature: (1) the relative size of the supervisory component, and (2) the proportion of personnel assigned to administrative support functions. The second definition is more frequently used, and is the one used in this study. Once these different definitions are taken into account, the relationship between organizational size and administrative intensity is more readily apparent. Larger organizations employ larger administrative staffs (Blau and Schoenherr, 1971; Kasarda, 1974; Rushing, 1966, 1967). Because larger police organizations have a more difficult time achieving coordination and control (like most large social units), they devote a greater proportion of personnel to administrative functions than smaller police organizations.

To summarize the hypothesized effects of size on structure, larger police departments are expected to exhibit greater levels of vertical, functional, and spatial differentiation. In addition, larger police departments are expected to be less centralized, more formalized, and to employ larger administrative staffs. The hypothesized direct effects of size on each structural element are illustrated in Figure 5.3. We now turn to another important relationship between organizations and their contexts: the effect of organizational age on formal structure.

Organizational Age

The effect of age on organizational structure was discussed at length in chapter 3, however it was difficult to extract generalizations from the body of existing research. Although the expected relationships between age and complexity were not observed for a number of studies, the evidence is not sufficient to warrant the conclusion that there is no relationship. Similarly, the link between age and centralization remains unclear, with two studies finding that older organizations are more centralized, and two studies finding the opposite. The relationship between age and centralization, as suggested by Weed's (1982) study of state welfare organizations, may depend on centralization trends within the

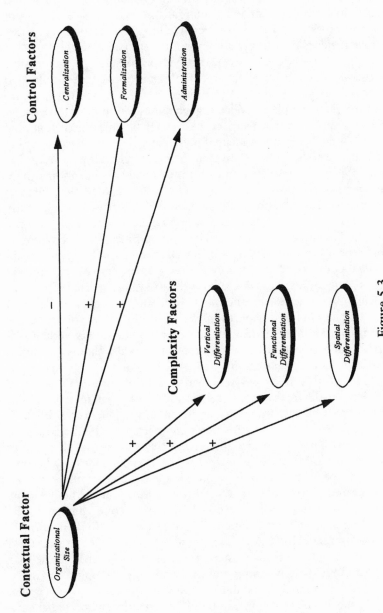

Contextual Factor

Organizational Size

Control Factors

Centralization

Formalization

Administration

Complexity Factors

Vertical Differentiation

Functional Differentiation

Spatial Differentiation

Figure 5.3
Hypothesized Direct Effects of Organizational Size

history of particular organizational types. Despite the ambiguity surrounding other age-structure links, the relationships between age and formalization, and age and administrative intensity, are consistent across a number of studies. Specifically, older organizations are more formalized and employ larger administrative staffs.

Although researchers have examined or commented on possible age-structure linkages in a variety of organizational types, only two studies have explicitly applied and tested theories of an age-structure relationship in a sample of police organizations. In an intriguing analysis, King (1999) collected data on the year of organizational founding from 333 large American municipal police agencies and tested a variety of age-structure hypotheses derived from Stinchcombe (1965) and Downs (1967). Comparing two cohorts of police organizations, those formed before and those formed after World War II, the only structural difference that King found was that the older cohort used significantly fewer civilian employees than the newer cohort. This finding lends little support to Stinchcombe's temporal imprinting proposition. Examining Downs's theory that age exerts a linear effect on structure, King found that older police organizations use fewer civilian employees, and are more vertically differentiated. Downs's theory was supported for two of five structural variables. Furthermore, Katz and his colleagues (2001) found that older police organizations were less likely than younger organizations to have implemented specialized gang units. This finding was robust in the presence of numerous control variables thought to influence the formation of gang units.

Based on this mixed body of evidence, I now propose a series of hypotheses on the age-structure relationship in large municipal police organizations. Older police organizations should exhibit greater levels of vertical differentiation, functional differentiation, formalization, and administrative intensity. Police historians have shown that throughout the twentieth century, large municipal police organizations have become taller, more specialized, more formalized, and have devoted an increasing proportion of personnel to administrative functions. Although some of these changes have been attributed by historians to changes in the size, technology, and environment of police organizations, it is likely that these factors alone cannot explain all of the variance in structural change. Independent of other causal forces, levels of each of these four structural elements may simply increase with age. As police organizations grow older, their personnel become less reliant on impersonal modes of supervisory control, and they develop more elaborated chains-of-command, formalized operations, and larger administrative staffs. Similarly, as new social problems emerge, they develop new specialized units and new divisions to accept responsibility for the new issues (Maguire, 1997). Older police organizations have more complex command structures because they have a longer history of adding new divisions and units, adding new levels of command, adding new formal rules and policies, and enlarging their administrative components.

Of course, one vital question in examining the age-structure relationship is how long police organizations can continue to add new levels, squads, rules, and administrative personnel. Until recently, these structural modifications were consistently endorsed by police reformers throughout the twentieth century as the normative solution for how a police organization should be structured. Vertical differentiation, formalization, and administrative intensity (among other structural features to be discussed later) were explicit elements of the prescriptions endorsed by early police reformers, in an effort to curb the influence of partisan politics and corruption problems. Similarly, functional differentiation—setting up specialized squads—was considered an ideal way of establishing a department's specialized skills and organizational commitment to emerging social problems like juvenile delinquency and family violence. Thus, there is little evidence that police organizations would have interrupted the linear effects of age by restructuring, because police reformers explicitly endorsed the trend toward ongoing structural elaboration over time.

However, the winds of police reform are now blowing in the opposite direction with regard to organizational structure. Arguing that bureaucratic departments are a hindrance to efficient, effective and responsive service delivery, community policing reformers have suggested that police must reverse the trend toward increasingly complex and controlling organizational forms (Cordner, 1997; Mastrofski, 1998; Redlinger, 1994). Specifically, according to scholars and reformers, they must de-formalize, eliminating unnecessary rules and policies (Goldstein, 1990; Mastrofski and Ritti, 2000); they must de-specialize, developing a front-line of "uniformed generalists" (Cordner, 1997; Mastrofski and Ritti, 2000); they must "de-layerize" by shortening or flattening their rank structures (Cordner, 1997; Mastrofski, 1998; Mastrofski and Ritti, 2000; Moore and Stephens, 1992); and they must thin out their administrative components to cut red tape and to focus more resources on the goals of the organization than on maintaining the organization itself. Community policing reformers argue that police departments can serve their communities in a more flexible and responsive manner by altering many of their key administrative arrangements. If departments have responded to this reform movement by reversing the ongoing trend toward structural elaboration, then the effect of age on structure will be attenuated.[9] However, recent research has shown that police organizations have not significantly altered their organizational structures during the community policing movement, and that contrary to reform prescriptions, they have continued to become more functionally differentiated (Maguire, 1997).

Unlike the four structural elements discussed so far, it is difficult to hypothesize the expected effects of organizational age on spatial differentiation and centralization.[10] Historical studies show that during the earliest stages of American policing, police departments were geographically based organizations. Precinct Captains were the main source of power in the organization, each one running essentially a small-scale department. Officers walked beats, rang neighborhood callboxes, and were responsible for particular patches of "turf." Police organizations were decentralized both spatially and administratively. Throughout the twentieth century, a variety of forces—including corruption problems and technological advances such as the automobile, telephone, and two way radio—led to the gradual demise of the geographical model. The station houses, walking beats, and local (neighborhood) command structures of old were replaced by a more centralized model focusing command and operations in a central police headquarters (Reiss, 1992). Thus, spatial differentiation and centralization changed markedly throughout the twentieth century, but unlike other structural elements, it is difficult to attribute any of these changes to organizational age.

All of the hypothesized age-structure effects discussed earlier involved a continuous build-up, or structural elaboration, over time. But unlike vertical differentiation, functional differentiation, formalization, and administrative intensity; spatial differentiation and centralization are not limitless properties amenable to continuous structural elaboration. Spatial differentiation declined throughout the early twentieth century, often probably reaching its lower bound of a single headquarters facility (there cannot reasonably be less than one police facility). Similarly, historical evidence suggests that centralization increased throughout much of the twentieth century, though it too probably has a practical upper bound which it cannot reasonably surpass (the most centralized organization is one in which a single individual makes all decisions). I am not arguing that certain structural elements have no limits, and that age can continue to make organizations more complex until the age of infinity. Rather, I am suggesting that within the history of police reform, for four structural elements, prescribed and actual structural changes in police organizations have gone in one direction—toward increasing levels of complexity and control. Until another reform movement emerges to counter this trend, it is possible that organizational age might continue to affect how police organizations are structured.[11]

To summarize the hypotheses on the age-structure relationship, older police organizations are expected to have more complex structures, with greater levels of vertical differentiation, functional differentiation, formalization, and administrative intensity. No hypotheses are made about the effect of age on centralization or spatial differentiation, since these features are not amenable, in practical terms, to structural elaboration. Although no hypotheses are made about the relationships between age and these two elements of structure, it will still be instructive to examine them empirically for exploratory purposes (Blau, 1994). The direct effects of age on structure that have been hypothesized in this section are illustrated in Figure 5.4. We now turn to another important contextual feature: organizational technology.

Organizational Technology

Technology, as defined in chapter 3, is a generic term that describes how an organization accomplishes its work. Technology focuses on both the nature of the raw materials to be processed by an organization, and the activities, mechanisms, and systems that are used in processing those raw materials. In this section, I describe two distinct components of organizational technology: task scope, and task routineness. Each of these dimensions has distinct implications for how a police organization is structured.

Task Scope. The concept of task scope has been discussed in the organizational literature under a variety of names, including product mix (Van de Ven and Delbecq, 1974), variability of tasks (Perrow, 1967), and functional elaboration (Kriesburg, 1976). In an influential article, Dewar and Hage (1978, p. 115) argue that much of the prior research on technology-structure relationships has missed one crucial dimension of technology, namely the "the variety of inputs or tasks that need to be accomplished," which they term task scope. Organizations performing a wider range of tasks are expected to be more complex. Similarly, as task scope increases, there will be a greater need for the organization to coordinate the increasing technological and structural complexity by adjusting structural coordination mechanisms such as formalization, centralization, and/or administration. Previous research has found a modest causal link between task scope and structure (Dewar and Hage, 1978; Van de Ven and Delbecq, 1974). As Kriesburg (1976) found in his sample of international nongovernmental organizations, "structural elaboration does seem to increase with functional elaboration."

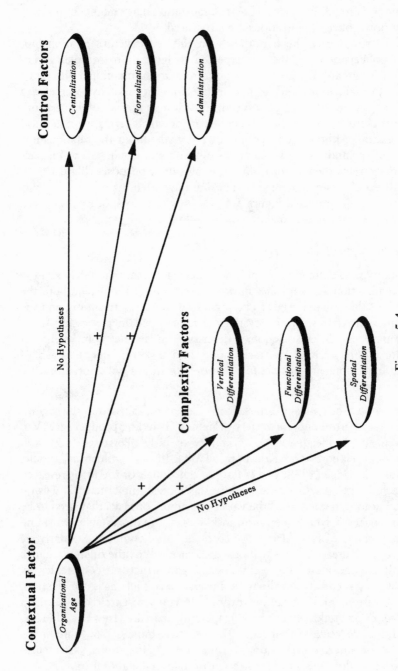

Figure 5.4
Hypothesized Direct Effects of Organizational Age

Dewar and Hage (1978) suggest that the effect of task scope on structure may be even greater among those organizations that perform "people-changing" activities. The raw materials of a people-changing organization are people, and the scope of tasks that is necessary to rehabilitate, train, teach, heal, or otherwise change a human being is presumably complex (Hasenfeld, 1972). The people-processing and people-changing literature has recently been applied to the police by Mastrofski and Ritti (1995), and will play a central role in the following section on technological routineness.

Although large municipal police organizations in the United States perform similar tasks, recent data shows that some agencies are responsible for performing a wider range of duties, or a greater scope of tasks than other agencies (Maguire, 1997). Although all large agencies provide patrol services, not all of them investigate homicides, monitor jails, provide court security, respond to medical emergencies or fires, or perform a number of other tasks. Police organizations that perform a broader scope of tasks should exhibit more complex structures. Similarly, greater task scopes should be related to higher levels of administration and formalization, as the organization takes steps to manage the higher levels of technological complexity. On the other hand, as the scope of tasks increases, decision making in the organization should become less centralized. Greater task scopes will increase the volume and types of information needing to be processed in order to make effective decisions, thereby leading organizations to decentralize decision making.

To summarize, task scope is expected to have a direct positive effect on vertical, functional, and spatial differentiation. In addition, task scope should also have a direct positive effect on formalization and administration, and a direct negative effect on centralization. The direct effects of task scope on structure that have been hypothesized in this section are summarized in Figure 5.5.

Task Routineness. As we discussed in chapter 3, organizational theorists conceive of technology as the means by which work is accomplished, or "the mechanisms or processes by which an organization turns out its products or service" (Harvey, 1968). Although the term "technology" conjures up images of beeps, buzzers, flashing lights, computers, gizmos and other assorted electronic gadgets, organizational scholars define technology more broadly to include more abstract "social" technologies.

This distinction is particularly important for studying police organizations, who rely on both material technologies and social technologies (Manning, 1992). As Reiss (1992, p. 93) argues:

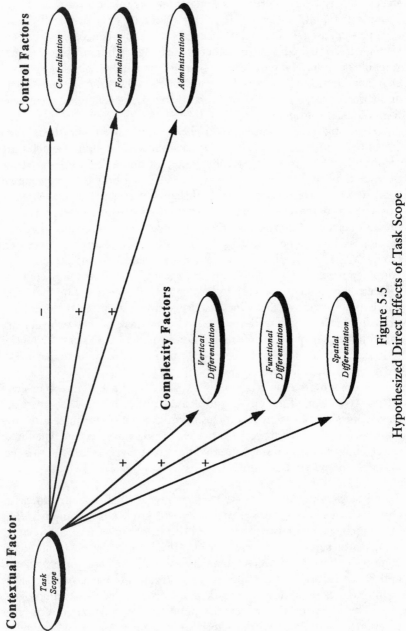

Figure 5.5
Hypothesized Direct Effects of Task Scope

> [P]olice departments are entering a new period of organizational trans-
> formation in which material technology will be reduced to the role of
> an equal player with social technologies—social technologies that are
> both underdeveloped and under-utilized in the police organizational
> context. These are the social technologies of research problem solving,
> of engineering social relationships, and of organizational techniques
> for managing human problems.

While material technologies like the automobile, communications equipment, and computers are a vital aspect of modern policing, they are not
the "core" technology of the police. The job of the police centers on
police-citizen encounters, and the core technology of the police is the
sum total of the ways that they handle or respond to these encounters.
Discretion enables the police to choose from a variety of responses, from
arguing, advising, cajoling, recommending, referring, warning, citing,
arresting, and using physical coercion, to simply listening or just doing
nothing. The notion that social technologies are a central aspect of modern policing has been suggested by a number of police theorists. Manning (1992, p. 351), for instance, shows how technology "is an apparatus, or the means by which work is accomplished, and it may be
material, logical, or social in its manifestations." Jermier (1979) suggests
that "the problems of the police are social and human and defy technological solutions." Similarly, Mastrofski and Ritti (1995) highlight the
social technology functions of the police and their implications for structure. Thus, although the police tend to seek out material "technocratic"
solutions to their problems (Reiss, 1992), most informed critics suggest
that the core technology of policing is social in nature.

The social dimensions of police work seem especially important
when we focus on the transformational processes, or technologies, that
police organizations employ to convert raw input materials into
processed outputs (Scott, 1992; Perrow, 1967). Because the raw materials of human service organizations such as the police are people, many
theorists have referred to these types of organizations as "people-processing" enterprises (Hage and Aiken, 1969; Hasenfeld, 1972, 1992b;
Mastrofski and Ritti, 1995). In 1972, Yeheskel Hasenfeld published a
groundbreaking article in the *American Sociological Review* on people-
processing organizations. Hasenfeld drew a distinction between those
organizations whose role is simply to process people, and those whose
goal is actually to change people in some direct way. I will demonstrate
in this section how Hasenfeld's framework for analyzing agencies
responsible for processing or changing people is integral for understanding how technological routineness might affect the formal structures of large police agencies.[12]

Hasenfeld (1972, p. 256) describes people-processing organizations as those whose function is "not to change the behavior of people directly but to process them and confer public statuses on them." Since processing functions are a basic element of the technologies of these organizations, their employees spend much of their time classifying and disposing of clients. Research has consistently highlighted the processing functions performed by police officers. For many years, policing has been described (and criticized) as a people-processing enterprise characterized by a variety of impersonal techniques for "slotting" clients into categories (Lipsky, 1980; Prottas, 1978; Waegel, 1981). For instance, patrol officers are known to make rapid judgments about people; judgments which tend to influence their own behavior and the services they provide to the citizen. Someone deemed to be an asshole receives very different treatment from someone deemed to be an innocent victim (Van Maanen, 1978). Police develop typified methods for responding to different kinds of calls: a loud party elicits a different response than a hot call; a chronic complainer a different response from a first-time caller. By regularly reducing individuals into a set of predefined categories for the purpose of simplifying processing routines (Prottas, 1978), police often provide canned responses to unique social problems.[13] Though the actions of police officers might occasionally prompt direct behavioral change in clients, their mandate has traditionally been to process clients, confer some kind of public status on them (e.g., arrested, referred, cited, or warned), and then either let them go, or direct them to other agencies who either process them further (e.g., juvenile and criminal courts), or who attempt to directly change the clients in some way (e.g., hospitals, counseling centers, mediation services, and prisons). In people-processing organizations, the actual client change occurs outside the boundaries of the organization.

People-changing organizations, on the other hand, attempt to change their clients directly in some way. Hospitals cure the sick and patch the injured, schools educate our children, prisons incapacitate and attempt to deter and/or rehabilitate convicted offenders, and psychologists help the mentally ill and distressed overcome their personal difficulties. People-changing organizations also perform processing functions, but unlike people-processing organizations, the client change occurs *within* the boundaries of the organization as a direct result of a technology designed to elicit change. Moreover, since staff-client encounters in people-changing organizations are designed to change the client directly, their duration is typically longer and more sustained than in people-processing organizations. Table 5.1, taken directly from Hasenfeld (1972, p. 258), summarizes the distinction between people-processing and people-changing organizations.

Table 5.1
Differences Between People-Processing and
People-Changing Organizations According to Hasenfeld (1972)

Variable	People-Processing Organizations	People-Changing Organizations
Type of Product	Altered Status	Behavioral Change
Technology	Classification-Disposition	Socialization-Resocialization
Locus of Technology	Organizational Boundary	Intra-Organizational
Relative Duration of Staff-Client Encounter	Short Term	Long Term

While people-processing functions are typically routine and predictable, people-changing functions are often nonroutine and unpredictable. The technologies used to change people's behavior are indeterminate and complex because the raw materials they act upon—people—are so complex. The less knowledge that an organization possesses about its raw materials, the less explicit, predictable, or determinate the technologies used to process those raw materials will be. Social technologies in people-changing organizations are particularly indeterminate because, as Mastrofski and Ritti (1995, p. 16) suggest, "there is little validation of what works under what conditions." In a factory, when the blade of a mechanical cutting device slams down heavily upon a thin piece of shoe leather, there is a strong chance that the operation will achieve the desired effect of cutting the leather. When a jobless mother with hungry children waits in line and fills out forms to receive Aid for Dependent Children, there is a good possibility that she will receive some form of assistance. But when a psychologist engages a depressed patient in therapy, the chances for recovery are not nearly so strong. The crucial point is that different types of technologies rank differently in terms of routineness and predictability of outcome, or in the relationship between means and ends (Mastrofski and Ritti, 1995, 2000).

All people-processing and people-changing organizations employ some type of social technology to act upon, or confer value upon their clients. Just as a factory might implement an assembly line process to produce goods, police organizations must also select an operational technology to accomplish their work. Social technologies in policing are the result of strategic decisions about how police work should be done. Some police departments focus on responding to calls-for-service, applying generic solutions to unique human problems, and generally reacting to, rather than proactively working with the community. Other police departments work actively with their communities, engaging them as coproducers of public safety, seeking out and reacting to their input, generating "custom" police responses to social problems by participating in proactive problem solving and community engagement strategies. All police departments lie somewhere on a continuum from generic to custom policing; from routine to nonroutine policing.

Patrol officers rarely know what incidents they will respond to during any given shift. They may roust a drunkard, issue a citation, arrest a vandal, and scatter some loiterers, or they may be have the misfortune to confront an armed felon. In this sense, patrol work is a nonroutine activity. Yet, most departments attempt to impose some sort of routinization on how police officers do their day-to-day work.[14] In some departments, officers are expected to, or at least are given the latitude to "solve" a local problem like loitering, whereas in others, officers are expected to make an arrest and move on. Traditional policing, in its ideal sense, is routine policing: responding to calls for service and processing encounters in the usual way. Community policing is nonroutine policing: interacting with and engaging the community to identify and solve local problems. Police work is a generally nonroutine activity, but police departments vary in the extent to which they engage in routine and nonroutine approaches to the job of policing.

In a compelling theoretical analysis, Mastrofski and Ritti (1995, 2000) suggest that as police departments move from traditional to community oriented styles of policing, they are making a fundamental shift from people-processing organizations to people-changing organizations. Mastrofski and Ritti (2000, p. 192–193) argue that community policing strategies:

> . . . will move police organizations to technologies that are relatively less explicit than those people-processing ones to which they are currently wedded. Police know quite a bit more about how to make arrests and how to get convictions than they do about how to change people and their environments in ways that reduce crime and disorder. They know a lot more about how to avoid accumulating lots of complaints against officers than they do about creating a sense of community and accumulating 'social capital' for self-policing.

The shift from traditional styles of policing to community policing type strategies introduces an element of technological indeterminacy into police organizations. Most importantly for this analysis, the shift to a less routine, less determinate, people-changing style of policing has distinct implications for formal organizational structure (Maguire, 1997;

Mastrofski and Ritti, 1995). In response to technological shifts, organizations attempt to maximize their technical rationality by adapting their formal structures to achieve a "fit" between technology and structure (Maguire, 1997). Although this adaptation process is a longitudinal event, evidence of technology-structure relationships should also be apparent in cross-sectional research that captures differences in technology and structure across a large sample of police organizations.

Police organizations that implement nonroutine technologies for accomplishing their core tasks should become less differentiated vertically and functionally as the department's structure adjusts: simplifying and becoming more flexible in order to accommodate the nonroutine nature of the department's technology. Indeterminate technologies grant greater levels of discretion and more opportunities for line level employees to develop creative and customized client treatments than more determinate people-processing technologies. Employees who employ such technologies require less supervision from a rigid hierarchy, and depend less on a structure that isolates large numbers of responsibilities into specialized units. Although community policing reformers frequently urge police departments to de-specialize, "people-changing technologies do not necessarily demand despecialization" (Mastrofski and Ritti, 1995, p. 21). However, police agencies that employ nonroutine technologies should exhibit some level of despecialization as front line employees become more well-versed in dealing with a variety of social issues. Nonroutine people-changing technologies demand front-line employees to spend more time with clients and to solve problems within the boundaries of the organization when possible, rather than referring clients to other agencies for direct change processes. To the extent that these technologies result in longer and qualitatively different police-client interactions, then agencies tending toward the people-changing end of the technology continuum should be less functionally differentiated.

In addition, police organizations using nonroutine technologies should exhibit greater levels of spatial differentiation. The organization decentralizes spatially as lower level employees expand the reach of their flexibility and influence, and try to bring the boundaries of the organization within closer proximity to their clients. Thus we see one of the important benefits of breaking structural complexity into its component parts: under nonroutine technologies, police organizations should become less complex vertically and functionally, and more complex spatially.

Nonroutine technologies should also prompt police agencies to require lower levels of structural coordination and control in all of its formats: centralization, administration, and formalization. These changes will develop in direct response to the shift in technology, as the organization adjusts to allow front-line officers more autonomy and flexibility in carrying out their nonroutine tasks. First, I have already suggested that police organizations will often decentralize their operations spatially under a nonroutine technology. This geographic shift should also be accompanied by a concomitant decentralization of authority as well. Since nonroutine peoplechanging technologies (by definition) require front-line employees to make autonomous operational decisions during employee-client contacts, centralization of authority is not amenable to a non-routine people-changing strategy. Second, as front-line employees develop generalist skills and orientations, the need for organization-wide coordination and control mechanisms lessens, thus decreasing the size of the administrative component. Finally, formal written rules, standards, policies, and procedures may be effective means of controlling police discretion in arrest and shooting situations, but since there is little evidence about what strategies are most effective for changing people, formalization is probably not appropriate strategy for achieving control in nonroutine people-changing organizations.

In summary, this section contains a number of hypotheses about the direct effects of technological routineness on organizational structure. First, police organizations employing nonroutine technologies will be less differentiated both vertically and functionally, and more differentiated spatially. Also, organizations employing nonroutine technologies will be less centralized, less formalized, and will employ smaller administrative staffs. These hypotheses are illustrated in Figure 5.6.

Technology Dimension: Recapitulation. As described earlier in this chapter, technology is a multidimensional concept. Two key dimensions of an organization's technology are task scope and task routineness. The routine nature of the technologies that an organization uses to accomplish its core tasks, together with the scope of those tasks, has important implications for how an organization is structured. These two concepts have been used extensively in prior research, with varying degrees of success, to explain the link between technology and structure (Dewar and Hage, 1978; Van de Ven and Delbecq, 1974; Scott, 1992). We now turn to another important conceptual element in the context of police agencies: organizational environments.

Organizational Environments

As described in chapter 3, the environment within which an organization is located is one of the most influential and least understood concepts in organization theory. Much of the conceptual complexity regarding organizational environments arises because unlike other elements of organizational context, environmental perspectives bridge numerous

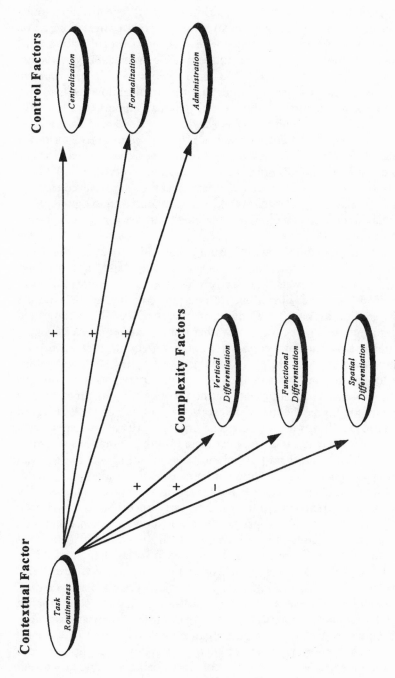

Figure 5.6
Hypothesized Direct Effects of Task Routineness

theoretical boundaries. Institutionalism, resource-dependency, population ecology and several other theoretical perspectives are all based on different propositions about what elements of an organization's environment are most important for understanding organizational structure and process (Donaldson, 1995). To some perspectives, the environment is seen as a crucial source of something the organization needs to survive, including resources, information, political support, or legitimacy (Aldrich, 1979; Galbraith, 1973; Meyer and Rowan, 1977; Pfeffer, 1978). For others the environment is a vast selection mechanism for sorting out which organizations are fit to survive and evolve, and which should fail and become extinct (Carroll and Delacroix, 1982). Perhaps even more important than its theoretical complexity, the concept of organizational environments—unlike size, age, and technology—continues today to be further explored, researched, and refined in the literature (Donaldson, 1995).

Wrestling with the vast literature on organizational environments is cumbersome, but fortunately some researchers and theorists have made the job easier by synthesizing various aspects of the research. Some have examined the operationalizations of environmental variables across studies, looking for common measures. Others have completed similar syntheses at a conceptual, rather than operational level, looking for similar environmental concepts across a variety of different theoretical frameworks (Aldrich, 1979; Dess and Beard, 1984). A few people have looked beyond individual environmental measures and concepts and have focused instead on integrating theories (Gupta, Dirsmith, and Fogarty, 1994). Like theoretical integration in criminology (e.g., Bernard and Snipes, 1996), merging different organization theories involves a number of controversial issues, including: (1) the assumptions on which different theories are based are often incongruent; (2) certain theories may explain phenomena at different levels of explanation (e.g., individual vs. structural level theories); and (3) loyalists to more traditional theories are often reluctant to accept integrated theories. As Donaldson (1995) and Bernard and Snipes (1996) argue, however, theoretical integration can overcome these obstacles with the obvious benefit of increasing the amount of explained variance in social phenomena.

Perhaps the most important work on organizational environments to bridge a variety of theoretical approaches is Aldrich's (1979) *Organizations and Environments*. Aldrich argues clearly and forcefully, that in spite of a scholar's theoretical stance, organizational environments have six generic dimensions that impact organizations in a variety of ways: (1) capacity; (2) homogeneity-heterogenity; (3) stability-instability; (4) concentration-dispersion; (5) domain consensus-dissensus; and (6) turbulence. Aldrich introduces these six dimensions in the midst of a theoretical argument that combines two theories: resource-dependence and population ecology. However, the most appealing aspect of Aldrich's environmental dimensions is their *theoretical portability*. While the choice of a theoretical framework may alter the measures of these dimensions, it will not alter the nature of the dimensions themselves. Aldrich's conceptual scheme is parsimonious and elegant in describing the relationship between these six environmental dimensions and a number of organizational properties, including formal structure. Although it is a resource-based theory, Aldrich's conceptual format for understanding organizational environments can easily be adapted to focus on the more important sociopolitical aspects of police organizational environments.

Police organizations, perhaps more than any other type of public service institution, are deeply embedded in and affected by the social and political aspects of their organizational environments. These external factors affect police at every organizational level, from front-line officer through police chief executive. The police and other street level bureaucracies, unlike production organizations, have a number of employees at different levels serving in a "boundary spanning" capacity that negotiates the organization's relationship with its environment (Lipsky, 1980). At the lowest level, the majority of police officers work in direct response to environmental imperatives, responding to citizen complaints, calls-for-service, or other encounters that are often initiated by those other than the police (Reiss and Bordua, 1967). For organizations that do not generate their own workloads, such constant reactivity is a tremendous source of uncertainty. Even higher levels of environmental uncertainty are found in police departments because not only must their workers constantly react to the environment, but they often must react to antagonistic and dangerous situations where their involvement is unwanted and possibly coercive. Managing such high levels of uncertainty in police departments often results in structural adaptations that are designed to maintain adequate levels of command, coordination, and control (Reiss and Bordua, 1967). Environmental uncertainty creeps into the organization at the upper levels as well, where police managers and administrators confront a variety of issues emerging from a complex array of external sources: managing departmental crises, negotiating with civilian superiors in local government, developing and maintaining relationships with influential third party organizations, planning strategies for how lower levels will deal with social issues, constructing and maintaining the department's image, dealing with threats to the organization's legitimacy, and attempting to ward off threats to their own personal job security (Lunden, 1958; Manning, 1977; Mastrofski, 2001;

Reiss and Bordua, 1967). The extent to which social and political issues create uncertainty within the upper levels of an organization has distinct implications for how police agencies are structured. The notion that social and political factors are a source of uncertainty in police organizations that lead to structural modifications will be explored in more detail throughout the rest of this study.[15]

Although resources are vital to police organizations, the resource-dependence examples that Aldrich employs to explain his environmental dimensions probably do not exert a global influence on the formal structure of large municipal police organizations.[16] Tolbert (1985) discovered evidence that colleges and universities depending more on external funding sources tend to have larger administrative components. Although police agencies are not nearly as dependent on diverse sources of external funding as colleges and universities, many large police organizations now maintain full-time staff members whose function is to attain and manage state and federal grants. Thus, resource acquisition activities might impact some elements of structure. For instance, Katz, Maguire, and Roncek (2001) found that police agencies that had sought federal funding to deal with a local gang problem were more likely to have implemented a specialized gang unit, even after controlling for the volume of gang-related crime. In other words, external funding had an independent effect on the formation of specialized units. However, these influences do not apply universally to a broad range of structural features, and therefore should not occupy a central role in a theory of police organizational structure. Rather, the social and political influences in the environment of a police organization are the most important in shaping its formal structure.

Adapting Aldrich's (1979) environmental dimensions for theories other than resource-dependence is quite simple. Aldrich conceives of resources broadly, including among his list of potentially important resources: power, influence, reputation, money and knowledge (62). There is a fundamental assumption common throughout the literature that environments influence organizations because they contain something the organization needs to survive, prosper, change, or grow. For resource-based theories, the vital something is *resources*. For information-dependence theorists such as Galbraith (1973), however, environments influence organizations by withholding or making available valuable *information* that the organization must process in order for decision makers to operate effectively. Similarly, for institutional theorists, the environment is a crucial source of *organizational legitimacy* (Crank and Langworthy, 1992; Meyer and Rowan, 1977). The theoretical portability of Aldrich's dimensions also permits a sociopolitical view, in which environments provide (or fail to provide) organizations with social and political support, stability, and the freedom to adjust to changing technical and environmental contingencies.

Only the first four of Aldrich's dimensions have received widespread support in the literature, and they are the only ones that will be discussed here.[17] They are environmental capacity, homogeneity-heterogeneity, stability-instability, and concentration-dispersion. The following discussion shows how these four dimensions fit within a socio-political view of organizational environments.

Environmental Capacity. The study of environmental capacity features some of the same inconsistencies in terminology that have led to confusion about many of the other organizational concepts already discussed. Aldrich (1979, p. 63) defines environmental capacity as "the relative level of resources available to an organization within its environment." Most writers, based on resource-dependency theory, define capacity in terms of the resources that an environment makes available or withholds from an organization (Aldrich, 1979; Dess and Beard, 1984). Dess and Beard (1984) have equated Aldrich's capacity dimension with "environmental munificence," or the extent to which the environment can support growth (Castrogiovanni, 1991; Starbuck, 1976). They also suggest, however, that the capacity-munificence dimension is almost identical to the environmental component that Child (1972b) calls "environmental illiberality." Child (1972b), applying a strategic-choice perspective, defines illiberality as "the degree of threat that faces organizational decision-makers in the achievement of their goals" from external entities. He then suggests that illiberality is similar to Khandwalla's notion of environmental "stress." Clearly, these similar terms—capacity, munificence, illiberality and stress—appear to be abstract and disparate because they are often used within specific theoretical frameworks that are based on fundamentally different assumptions. Nevertheless, these concepts share one basic feature: they all relate to the means by which an environment controls the ability of an organization to change in response to technical or environmental contingencies. Thus, defined generically, capacity (like its sister terms) is the degree to which an environment constrains or enables an organization to implement changes or achieve growth by providing or failing to provide some crucial element that the organization needs to thrive. Organizations located in high capacity environments are free from environmental constraints, whereas those located in low capacity environments must fight for support, resources, legitimacy, or some other product in their environments. The concept of environmental capacity is similar across theories; defining and measuring the nature of the crucial environmental element depends upon the particular theory of interest.

Since our interest in the environment is sociopolitical, environmental capacity is viewed here as the ability of a police organization to change in the face of constraints imposed by third-party organizations, such as civil service bodies, employee unions, or professional groups (as described briefly in chapter 4). The more third-party constraints that an organization faces, the more it will try to achieve internal control through increased vertical and functional differentiation, and decreased spatial differentiation. As Aldrich (1979, p. 67) notes, structural complexity in organizations is maintained by "consistent environmental pressures." Similarly, in the face of significant external threats to organizational autonomy, police agencies will attempt to tighten internal control processes through increased administration, centralization, and formalization (Child, 1972a). This discussion of environmental capacity is one area in which the theory espoused in this chapter overlaps with institutional theory. Dimaggio and Powell (1983), for instance, argue that various influences in the environment can exert significant normative, mimetic, or coercive pressures on organizations to change their structures. For instance, Marsden, Cook, and Knoke (1996) measure institutionalization using a series of survey items asking whether the organization is subject to accreditation or licensing, whether it belongs to a professional association, whether it pays attention to the practices of other organizations, and whether it is subject to governmental regulation. While their measure of institutionalization was developed for a wide variety of organizational types, it is not difficult to conceive of police organizations being subject to similar external constraints (Crank and Langworthy, 1992; Maguire and Mastrofski, 2000). Chapter 6 will contain a more detailed discussion of third-party organizations in policing and how they might affect the structures of police agencies.

To summarize, organizations that are free from sociopolitical constraints have the fundamental capacity to adjust their organizational processes and activities without interference from environmental entities. The capacity of organizations to determine their own organizational forms affects how they are structured. Those with a low capacity for change (or a high degree of external interference) will be structured tightly to achieve greater control. Specifically, they will be more vertically and functionally differentiated, and less specially differentiated. In addition, they will be more formalized and centralized, and they will employ larger administrative staffs. The direct effects of environmental capacity on organizational structure that were hypothesized in this section are illustrated in Figure 5.7.[18]

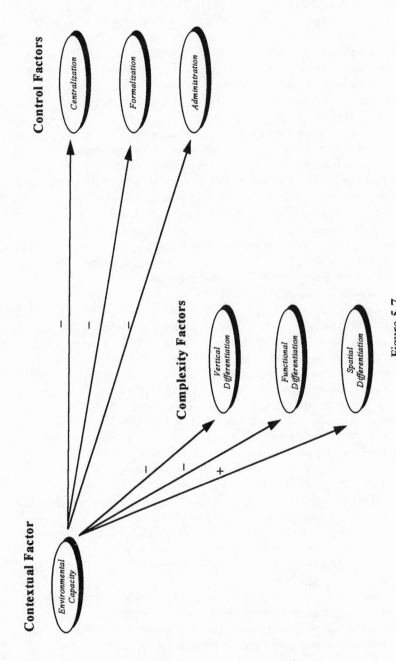

Figure 5.7
Hypothesized Direct Effects of Environmental Capacity

Environmental Complexity. Aldrich (1979, p. 66) defines environmental homogeneity-heterogeneity as "the degree of similarity or differentiation between the elements of the population dealt with. . . ." For purposes of simplicity and uniformity, this study will follow the lead of several other scholars who use the term "environmental complexity" to address this dimension (Dess and Beard, 1984). The effects of environmental complexity on structure are not entirely clear because the proposed theoretical effects lead in opposite directions.

The first view, which I call the *technology perspective*, looks at the way complex environments affect organizational technologies, which in turn impact how organizations are structured. According to Aldrich (1979), simple homogeneous environments lead organizations to adopt standardized methods and undifferentiated products or services (Thompson, 1967). And, we know from our earlier discussions that such routine technologies (like people-processing) are typically associated with complex and controlling organizational structures. Thus from a technology perspective, simple environments produce complex structures, and complex environments produce simple structures.

The second view, which I call the *organizational control perspective*, suggests that complex environments should be associated with complex structures. Complex heterogeneous environments make competing demands on organizations and therefore produce some degree of organizational uncertainty. One of the most well-established ideas in organizational sociology is that organizations faced with environmental uncertainty attempt to seal off their boundaries so that the environment doesn't penetrate the technical core (Thompson, 1967, pp. 14–24). Scholarly studies of the police have confirmed that police organizations employ such buffering strategies constantly in order to keep outsiders from meddling or getting in the way of the agency's operations. Police departments have historically buffered their organizational boundaries by employing the classic paramilitary bureaucratic form of administration. Although this structural form has been criticized for decades, police organizations have traditionally relied on complex and controlling structures in order to maintain an optimal level of control and coordination. Thus from an organizational control perspective, simple environments produce simple structures, and complex environments produce complex structures.

Two popular perspectives on the link between environmental complexity and organizational structure lead to nearly opposite conclusions. According to the technology perspective, population homogeneity simplifies organizational activities by promoting the use of routine technologies, which we know lead to more complex and controlling structures. Yet, population homogeneity (simplicity) also enables organizations to be less defensive in sealing off their boundaries from the environment, which often leads to more simplistic and flexible structures. While at first this dilemma might seem to indicate that theoretical perspectives on environmental complexity are at odds with one another, a clearer focus on the nature of the effects helps to illuminate this web of relationships. The technology perspective suggests that the effect of environmental complexity on structure is indirect, operating through technology. On the other hand, the control perspective posits that environmental complexity will directly affect organizational structure.[19] Since we would expect direct effects to be stronger and more influential than indirect effects, it is likely that the control perspective would be a stronger candidate for explaining structure than the technology perspective. Nonetheless, if these theoretical relationships are empirically valid, then the opposite effects should cancel each other out to some extent, with the control perspective emerging dominant.[20]

Environmental complexity is often troublesome for organizations, especially people-processing organizations whose technology involves transforming "a population of heterogeneous clients into highly specialized outputs" (Aldrich, 1979, p. 66; also see Hasenfeld, 1972). Police organizations in the largest urban areas of the United States are often responsible for providing services to extremely heterogeneous populations, serving people from a wide variety of racial, educational, occupational, and socioeconomic backgrounds. Police departments in these areas are often called upon to deal with diverse client-bases with competing demands. The challenge of juggling the needs of diverse populations has historically been one of the most pressing issues for police agencies to deal with, and has on many occasions erupted into full-scale crises such as riots, protests, civil disobedience, and media frenzies. These types of charged crisis situations are a classic example of what organizational researchers call an "environmental jolt" (Meyer, 1982). The persistent threat of such crises occurring as a result of dealing with complex environments is one of the most important reasons that police agencies continue to rely on command and control bureaucracies.

To summarize, according to the organizational control perspective, police organizations in complex environments will attempt to seal off their boundaries from penetration by elements of the environment, and will tend to rely on structural arrangements that enable the greatest amount of control. First, they will be more vertically and functionally differentiated than police organizations in simpler environments. Second, they will be less spatially differentiated, since spatial elaboration leads to greater uncertainty and lesser control. Third, they will be more formalized, more centralized, and they will employ larger administrative staffs.[21] The direct effects of environmental complexity on organizational structure that were hypothesized in this section are illustrated in Figure 5.8.

Environmental Stability-Instability. Aldrich (1979, p. 67) defines environmental stability as "the degree of turnover in the elements of the environment." The more stable the environment, the less the organization needs to institute buffering mechanisms that protect the organization from its environment. One of the most consistent ways that an organization protects its boundaries from penetration by unstable environments is through the use of boundary-spanning positions. Actors occupying boundary-spanning positions are responsible for interacting with, controlling, and sometimes neutralizing elements outside of the organization (Mastrofski, 2001).[22] If organizations fail to seal off their environments in turbulent unstable environments, then they become vulnerable to outside influence. As Aldrich (1979, pp. 220–222) notes, organizations that are unable to successfully close off their boundaries: "are opened to external influence and authorities seek means of closing off vulnerable segments and coping with heterogeneous and varying demands from clients, members, and others." *If unchecked, unstable environments produce unstable organizations.* There are volumes of anecdotal, case-study, and historical evidence to support this notion. The most popular case is when local politicians make arbitrary decisions about internal processes within a police agency because the police chief is afraid to intervene for fear of being fired (Greenberg, 1992; Mastrofski, 1988; Reiss and Bordua, 1967; Woods, 1993). Most important for this study is the understanding that when boundary actors fail to secure the organization from the environment, instability prompts a variety of structural accommodations.

The idea that environmental instability (also known as turbulence and dynamism) affects organizations has been explored from a number of different theoretical perspectives, each with different ideas about the nature of the relationship. For Thompson (1967), instability in the task-environment causes various forms of structural adaptation. The task environment (also called the technical, or the rational environment) is that portion of the environment that provides the organization with the substantive components it needs to function, such as: resources, clients, workers, raw materials, tools, and information. Resource-dependence theorists, for example have argued that an unstable funding environments prompt structural adaptations (Tolbert, 1985). Similarly, information-dependence theorists like Galbraith (1973) attribute the effect of

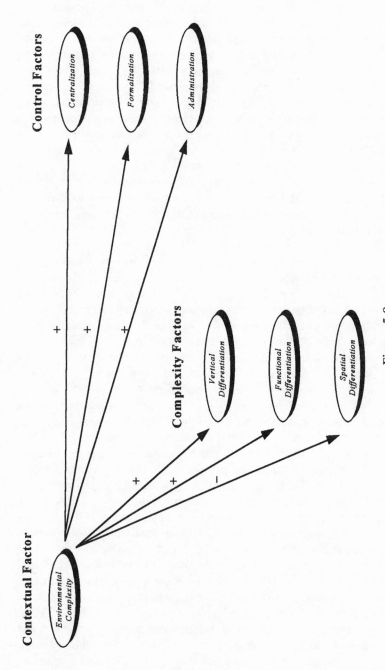

Figure 5.8
Hypothesized Direct Effects of Environmental Complexity

unstable environments on structure to the amount of information that needs to be processed. Opposite the task-environment approach to instability is the institutional approach. Institutional theorists, as discussed in prior chapters, suggest that instability in the institutional portions of the environment is responsible for shaping structural features in organizations. The institutional approach holds that structure may be the result of differing conceptions and resulting contests among environmental and organizational actors about how police agencies should be structured and what structural forms are most legitimate. Researchers continue to debate the relative influences of the task-environment and the institutional environment in shaping organizational structure.

The two primary perspectives each present very different pictures about the process of how instability affects organizations and their structures. They represent fundamental differences in organization theory, and indeed they have been used together rarely (Donaldson, 1995; Tolbert, 1985). Dess and Beard (1984) implicitly offer some sound advice for evaluating the potential effects of these two perspectives. They suggest that the key focus of instability research needs to be not just on changes in the environment, but on "change that is hard to predict and that heightens uncertainty for organizational members" (p. 56). In addition, as stated earlier, the structural effects of instability are dependent on the degree to which instability bypasses boundary actors and penetrates the organizations. Thus, whether the uncertainty arises in the institutional or the technical (task) environment, the key question for research on structure is neither whether there is instability, nor where did it come from, but on whether instability penetrates organizational boundaries. When environmental instability actually causes uncertainty within the organization, there will be structural adaptations.

Unstable environments that penetrate the organizational boundaries of a police department will prompt a number of predictable structural adaptations. These adaptations are instituted to achieve internal control in the face of external uncertainty.[23] First, police agencies will attempt to reduce uncertainty by becoming more complex functionally and vertically. Segmented workloads and rigid chains-of-command make it easier to achieve control and coordination when uncertainty threatens administrative and technical functions. Second, police organizations will centralize spatially and administratively. Decentralization heightens the effect of uncertainty and reduces the capacity for control, and thus police agencies will centralize in order to buffer themselves more effectively. Third, police departments will develop larger administrative staffs to manage the uncertainty, and they will become more formalized to achieve greater control.[24] Although all of these structural modifications imply a temporal adaptation process, evidence of these effects should be readily observable in cross-sectional research. The direct effects of instability on structure that were hypothesized in this section are illustrated in Figure 5.9.[25]

Environmental Dispersion. Aldrich (1979, p. 68) defines environmental concentration-dispersion as "the degree to which resources, including the population served and other elements, are evenly distributed over the range of the environment or concentrated in particular locations." This dimension, perhaps the most conceptually straightforward, refers to the size and density of the organization's territory. The more dispersed the population, the more difficult it is for the police organization to control its members through informal means, and the more elaborate the requirements for formal structure. In order to tap new markets, for example, many corporations are decentralizing their operations spatially, expanding into multidivisional firms with operating sites all over the world. Bayley (1985) describes a number of police organizations around the world that have extremely complex structures because they serve large regional territories or entire nations. Banal as it may appear, independent of an organization's size, the dispersion of the jurisdiction has a direct impact on structure.[26]

The most obvious relationship to emerge from this dimension is that police organizations responsible for larger, more densely populated jurisdictions will be more spatially differentiated. Quite simply, the "spread" of the jurisdiction defines the spread of the organization's structure. Similarly, organizations in more dispersed environments will be less centralized, since information processing requirements are more difficult for commanders to handle in larger, more spatially diverse, geographically dispersed jurisdictions. In addition, because the coordination requirements of larger, denser jurisdictions are greater and more complex, police organizations in these areas will be more functionally and vertically differentiated, more formalized, and will employ smaller administrative staffs. Chapter 6 will expand on the relationship between area and density in producing interactive effects on organizational structure. The direct effects of environmental dispersion on structure that were hypothesized in this section are illustrated in Figure 5.10.

Structural Complexity

Recall from the basic theoretical model discussed earlier in this chapter, and illustrated in Figure 5.1, that in addition to the effects of context on structure, the model also proposes that there is a causal relationship from structural complexity to structural control and coordination mechanisms.

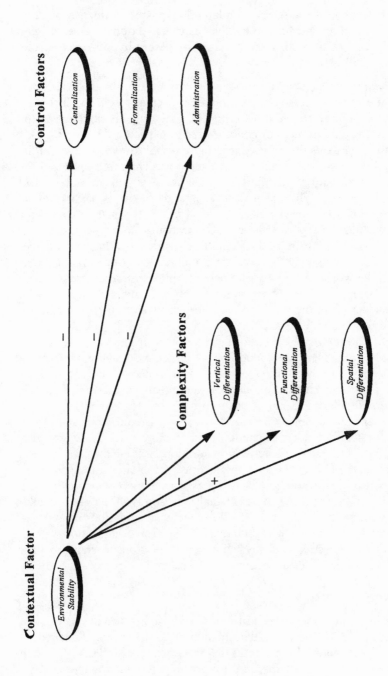

Figure 5.9
Hypothesized Direct Effects of Environmental Stability-Instability

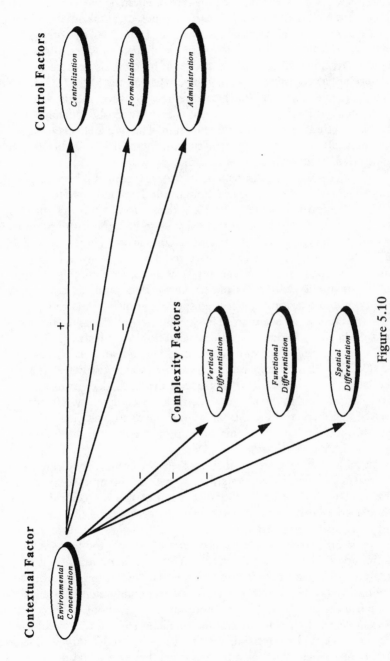

Figure 5.10
Hypothesized Direct Effects of Environmental Dispersion

Although few researchers have attempted to disentangle the web of causal effects between elements of structure, the proposed causal order is based on a simple sociological premise. As Rushing (1976, p. 676) notes: "one of the oldest ideas in sociology is the proposition that as social systems become increasingly differentiated they tend to develop structures and mechanisms that coordinate the actions of the various parts." Based on this thesis, this section will introduce a number of hypotheses about how the individual elements of structural complexity affect the individual elements of structural control and coordination. The direct effects of structural complexity on structural control that are hypothesized in this section are illustrated in Figure 5.11.

As police organizations become more structurally differentiated—dividing their labor vertically, functionally, and spatially—they experience coordination problems. Echoing a theme found throughout this study, prior research has found inconsistent results about the patterns of organizational response to increasing complexity. Hage and Aiken (1967b), for example, found a positive relationship between complexity and centralization (recall the previous discussion in this chapter about their unique definitions of structure). Pugh and his colleagues (1968) found no relationship between specialization and centralization, and Hsu, Marsh, and Mannari (1983) found no relationship between various complexity variables and centralization. And lastly, in a replication of the Aston Group study conducted by Pugh and his colleagues, Child (1972a) found that centralization was negatively related to "structuring of activities." This measure of structure, derived using factor-analysis, is similar, though not identical to complexity. Given the variety of measures and definitions used in these studies, it is difficult to rely on these studies for inspiration about the relationship between complexity and centralization.

Although the research is unclear, there are some very clear theoretical reasons for specifying a relationship between complexity and centralization. Recall from our earlier discussion of size and centralization that larger police organizations have difficulty centralizing their decision making because the overall volume of information needing to be processed in order to make decisions centrally is simply too large. A similar point applies here. Centralization is inefficient in organizations that are spatially dispersed because central commanders cannot possibly be as familiar with local conditions as local-level commanders. Similarly, functional units presumably have more knowledge about how to perform their tasks than centralized commanders, so again, it would be inefficient to centralize decision making in functionally differentiated police organizations. Vertical differentiation should also be negatively

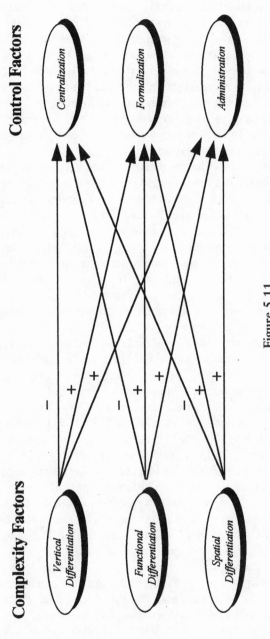

Figure 5.11

Hypothesized Direct Effects of Structural Complexity Factors

associated with centralization, because rank systems are in some sense an alternative method of achieving control and coordination. Where there is a tall hierarchy, lower-level commanders presumably filter out various decisions so that upper command levels do not need to make all decisions in the organization. Though prior research has not been very helpful for understanding the relationship between complexity and centralization, insights derived from information-based theories—most notably that organization structures are influenced by the volume of information needing to be processed—have been useful for generating some hypotheses. To summarize, every form of complexity should have a negative effect on centralization.

The same reasons that lead us to suspect a negative relationship between complexity and centralization would lead us to hypothesize a positive relationship between all forms of complexity and formalization. Complexity, in all of its forms, makes it more difficult to achieve coordination among the disparate parts of an organization. Complexity, like formalization, is an impersonal means of achieving control (Van de Ven, Delbecq, and Koenig, 1976). As the organization develops and becomes more complex—vertically, functionally, and spatially—personal control mechanisms such as personality, charisma, or friendship become less efficient and must be augmented or replaced by less personal techniques for achieving control and coordination (Van de Ven, Delbecq, and Koenig, 1976). Formalization is one of the easiest ways for an organization to achieve control, and therefore more complex organizations should be more formalized.

Similarly, as a result of increasing complexity, organizations enlarge their administrative components to manage the frequent problems of communication, coordination, and control that are common in more complex organizations. Vertical, functional and spatial differentiation all have a direct positive effect on administrative intensity (Blau, 1970,1994). Scott (1992, p. 260) eloquently describes how structural complexity "creates pressures to increase the size of the administrative component. This occurs because differentiation increases the heterogeneity of work among the various subunits and individuals, creating problems of coordination and integration. The administrative component expands to assume those responsibilities." Rushing (1967, p. 273) terms this the "complexity-administrative growth hypothesis" and credits its initial formulation to Durkheim (trans. 1949, p. 367): "the more complex an organization is, the more is the need for extensive regulation felt." Although a number of conceptual problems have plagued the literature on administrative intensity (discussed in chapter 2 and elsewhere in this chapter) studies using consistent definitions have confirmed the complexity-administrative growth hypothesis (Rushing, 1967).

To summarize, complexity in all of its forms should have a negative impact on centralization, and a positive impact on formalization and administration. We now discuss some general themes in the contextual theory outlined in this chapter, providing some insights about how the theory fits into the broader arena of organizational sociology.

Discussion

This chapter has introduced a new theory to explain the formal organizational structures of American municipal agencies. This theory is "new" in two senses: first because it explicitly outlines fifty-five separate hypotheses (summarized in Figures 5.3 through 5.11) about the relationships between the elements of context, complexity, and control in police organizations; and second because it develops a coherent, systematic framework for organizing and arranging these hypotheses. However, this new theory has its roots in a number of established areas. First, as mentioned previously, some of this theory is a direct extension of the propositions outlined in Robert Langworthy's (1986) book, *The Structure of Police Organizations*. Though Langworthy was more concerned with complexity than control, there is a great deal of overlap between the two perspectives. Second, this theory also incorporates a variety of propositions derived from a growing body of organizational scholarship in policing, especially the works discussed at length in Chapter Four, including: Bayley (1992, 1994); Bordua and Reiss (1966); Crank and Langworthy (1992); King (1999); Manning (1977, 1988a, 1992); Mastrofski (1998, 2001); Mastrofski and Ritti (1996, 2000); Mastrofski, Ritti, and Hoffmaster (1987); Reiss (1992); Reiss and Bordua (1967); Weiss (1997); Wilson (1968); and Zhao (1996). Third, the major source of information used in constructing this theory was the vast literature in structural organization theory. We now turn briefly to a discussion of where the present contextual theory of police organizational structure fits into the broader realm of structural organization theory.

Much of the literature used in constructing this theory was derived from themes that were immensely popular in the organizational literature from the 1960s through the 1980s. Researchers of that era were primarily concerned with extending, refining, and/or refuting the early ideas about bureaucracy and administration outlined by Max Weber. Thus, a disproportionate amount of research activity in organizational sociology was devoted to isolating the dimensions of organizational structure, and discovering the factors that explain variation in these dimensions (Lammers, 1974). Most of these works were rooted in various forms of structural contingency theory: a broad perspective that viewed organizational structures as dynamic systems that adapt rationally to a variety of contextual features (contingencies) in order to remain effective. Contemporary organizational theorists have moved beyond many of the "simpler" contingency theory propositions and into a number of far more specialized lines of scholarly inquiry including resource-dependency theory, organizational economics, institutional theory, population ecology theory, and several other less influential theories (Donaldson, 1995). According to some analysts, these theories represent such fundamental divisions in the study of organizations that they can be considered distinct paradigms. The proponents of each perspective, according to critics, are so blinded by their theoretical loyalties that they make it difficult for the field to progress in an orderly fashion (Aldrich, 1992; Donaldson, 1995). The answer to these "paradigm wars" according to Donaldson (1995) is not to abandon structural contingency theory, but to use it as an empirically supported foundation upon which to build more sophisticated theoretical formulations.[27] Donaldson suggests that structural contingency theory was abandoned prematurely, even though it received a great deal of empirical support for more than two decades. Subsequent theories can contribute a great deal to our contemporary understanding of organizational structure and process if they build upon, rather than reject, contingency theory propositions (Hall, 1999, pp. 106–107). In addition to Donaldson's contributions to this debate, a small handful of scholars have combined different organizational theory perspectives, including Gupta, Dirsmith, and Fogarty (1994), Mastrofski and Ritti (1996), and Tolbert (1985). The failure of organization theorists to embrace theoretical integration more rapidly is paralleled by similar problems among criminologists (Bernard and Snipes, 1996).

Although the theory of police organizational structure outlined in this chapter has largely been derived from these various organization theories, it is true to no single dominant paradigm. This is due in part to the problems highlighted by Donaldson, but also because none of these theories alone is able to explain the unique features of large municipal police organizations in the United States. Thus, bits and pieces of these theories can be found scattered throughout this chapter. For example, although the links between technology and structure are derived almost exclusively from contingency theory, the Age section contains some implicit population-ecology notions, and the Environment section contains elements of contingency theory, resource-dependency theory, and institutional theory. Although testing the integrated theory presented in this chapter would not provide adequate evidence for refuting or accepting any one of the component theories, it could possibly be used as partial evidence one way or the other. For example, as described in this chapter, the concept of environmental stability has clear ties to institutional theory. However, a valid test of institutional theory would need to account for a much larger scope of institutional propositions that fall outside the environmental stability-instability dimension.

Three other comments should be emphasized about the theory presented in this chapter. First, it is a thoroughly macro-sociological theory. Thus, although its propositions could possibly be extended to describe the behaviors of individual actors within organizations, its main focus is on organizations, not individuals. That is why the theory describes general processes that might be expected to occur within organizations based on adaptation to contextual conditions, but it does not attempt to specify exactly how those change processes are undertaken. For example, although environmental instability might prompt the closing of a substation or a precinct house (spatial differentiation), this theory is not designed to explain the specific processes and activities which lead to the expected structural changes. Those types of activities fall outside the scope of a macro-sociological theory. Second, although much of the theory is based on change or adaptation processes that are ideally tested using longitudinal data, the relationships should also be apparent in cross-sectional data with a large number of organizations. Third, every hypothesis introduced in this chapter assumes that the variables not explicitly included within the hypothesis are held constant. For example, when I suggest that technology impacts structure, I mean that the relationship is independent of size, age, and environment. This condition has significant implications for designing research methods that are capable of testing the theory with "all else held constant." With that said, we now move on to chapter 6 for an introduction to the sample, the data, and the variables used to test the theoretical model.

CHAPTER 6

Methodology and Descriptive Statistics

This chapter introduces the sample, the data, and the variables that will be used to test the theoretical model outlined in chapter 5. After specifying each of the individual measures (or measurement models in some cases) used to describe the concepts in the theoretical model, this chapter will statistically describe context, complexity and control in large municipal police agencies. Since most of what we know about police organizational structure came from data collected nearly twenty-five years ago by Elinor Ostrom and her colleagues, the descriptive data presented in this chapter represents the current state-of-the-art on how large municipal police organizations in the United States are structured (Langworthy, 1986; Ostrom, Parks, and Whitaker, 1978a, 1978b).

Sample

The focus of this study is large municipal police agencies. These are the police departments with the largest amount of variation in organizational structure, and they are the ones in which structure is most often blamed for organizational or "bureaucratic" failures. For purposes of this study, a "large" police agency is one that employs one hundred or more full-time actual (not authorized) sworn police officers;[1] a "municipal" police agency is one whose primary jurisdiction is a city or town, and not a state, a county, a territory, or a specialized district such as a school or an airport; and a "police agency" is any general-purpose law enforcement agency that responds to calls-for-service from citizens and enforces a wide-range of state criminal laws and local ordinances.[2] According to the 1992 Directory Survey of Law Enforcement Agencies, conducted jointly by the Bureau of Justice Statistics and the Census Bureau, there were 432 large municipal police agencies in the United States fitting this definition in 1992 (Reaves, 1993).[3]

Data

Only two decades ago, data on American police departments was of such poor quality that experts routinely estimated the number of police departments in the United States to be about 40,000—more than twice what we now know to be the actual number (Bayley, 1994; Maguire et al., 1997b; Reaves, 1993; Reiss, 1992). Fortunately, data collection initiatives have improved considerably, thanks to the efforts of several agencies, including the Bureau of Justice Statistics (BJS), the Bureau of the Census, the National Institute of Justice, the Police Foundation, and several others. Data from several of these sources were combined to create a new and unique database on the context and structure of large American municipal police agencies.

LEMAS DATA

In 1987, the Bureau of Justice Statistics launched the first wave of its "Law Enforcement Management and Administrative Statistics" (LEMAS) survey series. This survey data set contains more than 500 variables which assess the organizational structures, resources, and practices of over 3,000 U.S. police organizations. The survey was mailed to all local law enforcement agencies with 135 or more sworn officers, plus a random sample of smaller departments. A second wave of this survey was distributed in 1990, and expanded to include all agencies with more than 100 sworn officers, plus a random sample of smaller departments (Reaves, 1992). A third wave was collected in 1993 using the same sampling strategy as the second wave (Reaves and Smith, 1995). In this study, I will use the 1993 LEMAS data set to measure a number of contextual and structural variables. These data are ideal for this purpose, and have been used in a similar fashion in several other studies (King, 1999; Langworthy and Chamlin, 1997; Maguire, 1997; Zhao and Lovrich, 1997). Of the 432 agencies in the sample, 425 (98.4%) responded to the 1993 LEMAS survey.

POLICE FOUNDATION COMMUNITY POLICING SURVEY

In 1993, based on a grant from the National Institute of Justice, the Police Foundation surveyed over 1,600 United States police and sheriffs' departments about their experiences with community policing strategies. This study used a sampling strategy similar to that used in the LEMAS studies (Annan, 1994; Wycoff, 1994). This data set is ideal for measuring the routine-nonroutine dimension of the social technologies adopted by police agencies. Eleven of the survey items address the degree to which patrol officers are responsibile for such nonroutine duties as making door-to-door contacts in neighborhoods, conducting crime analysis, holding meetings with citizens, and working with other city agencies to solve neighborhood problems. As I will discuss in more detail later in this chapter, these responses will be formed into an index that measures task routineness. Of the 432 agencies in the sample, 382 responded to the 1993 Police Foundation Community Policing survey, and 376 (87%) provided sufficient information for this study.

CENSUS POPULATION DATA

Every ten years, the Population Division of the U.S. Bureau of the Census collects demographic information from every local jurisdiction in the country. The 1990 Census population data are used in this study to develop a measurement model of environmental (population) complexity. Several variables, including income, education, occupation, and race are combined into an overall complexity measure as described by Gibbs and Martin (1962), Langworthy (1986), and Rushing (1976). Of the 432 municipalities in the sample, 1990 census population data are available for 423 jurisdictions (98%).

SUPPLEMENTAL SURVEY DATA

Finally, in order to fill some of the gaps in LEMAS and other police survey data sets, I conducted a brief telephone/facsimile survey of the 432 largest municipal police agencies in the United States. This survey was used to collect information on a small number of variables that are important components of my contextual-structural theory, but that are not available elsewhere. For example, no existing data sets contain the information on levels of command (rank counts) that are necessary in order to develop a valid measure of vertical differentiation. Similarly, there is also no information available on the number of police headquarters and precinct houses that are used by large police agencies, and thus it is difficult to measure spatial differentiation. The supplemental telephone/facsimile survey collected information on these and several other variables, and was essential in order to capture a full range of contextual and structural variables.

Data collection for the supplemental survey took place between February and July of 1996. Respondents were asked to provide two answers for every question: one for 1993 and one for 1996 (as of January 1 of each year). The 1993 data are used in this study so that all of the data sources are contemporaneous. Of the 432 agencies in the sample, 395 (91%) responded to the supplemental survey.

The LEMAS survey, the Police Foundation Community Policing Survey, the Census Bureau population data, and the supplemental phone-fax survey are the four primary sources of data used in this study.[4] Each of these primary data sources is linked with the others by an alphanumeric agency-level code called an "ORI Code," which was created by the FBI as a unique identifier for all police agencies in the United States (Maguire et al., 1997b; National Criminal Information Center, 1989). While using multiple data sources merged at the agency-level is a good way to develop a unique and useful data-set, this method also has its shortcomings. When using multivariate statistical techniques, the overall response rate for the merged database will be at least as small as the study and/or variable with the worst response rate (and probably smaller), because agencies who failed to complete either entire surveys or a necessary survey item from one of the primary data-sets will fall out of the analysis due to missing data. Thus, due to survey and item nonresponse in one or more of the primary data-sets, the sample of police agencies used in this study is not random. In order to be selected for inclusion in this study, a department had to respond to all of the surveys comprising the merged data-set, and also have completed every applicable survey item.[5] Previous studies that have merged some of the same data sets as this study have retained 236–333 of the 432 eligible departments (54–77%) (King, 1999; Maguire, 1997). The final data set used in this study retains from 65% to 72% of the agencies, depending on the model being estimated.

Variables

Chapter 5 described the fourteen core concepts that are central to the contextual theory of police organizational structures. These fourteen concepts are the individual elements that comprise context (8 concepts), complexity (3 concepts), and control (3 concepts), as illustrated in Figure 5.2. In this section, I describe the variables that will be used to measure these fourteen concepts. In most cases a concept will be measured using a single variable or index, but for three of the concepts (environmental complexity, vertical differentiation, and spatial differentiation), I will develop a multivariate measurement model. In addition to describing each of the measures, this chapter will also list the source of the data and provide descriptive statistics for all variables.

Context

According to the theoretical model described in chapter 5, the context of a police agency consists of four dimensions: organizational size, organizational age, technology, and environment. The technology dimension includes two separate concepts: task scope and task routineness. Similarly, the environment dimension includes four separate concepts: capacity, complexity, instability, and dispersion.

Size. As reviewed in chapter 3, organizational size has been measured in many ways, but the majority of researchers have operationalized this variable as the number of employees (Kimberly, 1976). Police researchers have followed this tradition as well, measuring organization size in large police agencies as the total number of full time sworn and nonsworn personnel (King, 1999; Langworthy, 1986; Maguire, 1997). Data on organizational size are available from the LEMAS survey for 425 of the 432 police agencies in the sample, for an overall response rate of (98.4%). Organizational size in this sample ranges from 103 to 35,480 full-time personnel, with a median of 220. This variable is not normally distributed. Over 80% of the agencies have less than 500 employees, and only about 5% have more than 2,000. Summary statistics for organizational size are presented in Table 6.1.

Age. The age of an organization has been traditionally measured as the number of years that the organization has been in existence (Frisby, 1985; King, 1999). The age of a police organization, however, is particularly difficult to define and measure (Walker, 1980). In the early history of American policing, "police" organizations adopted a number of diverse organizational forms. Most historians cite the establishment of the London Metropolitan Police in 1829 by Sir Robert Peel as the first "modern" police force (Richardson, 1992). Shortly thereafter, according to police historians, the Boston Police Department was established in 1838, and the New York City Police Department in 1844 (Lane, 1992; Walker, 1980). Although these departments are generally believed to be the first modern style police forces, most municipalities in the United States relied on some form of law enforcement arrangement long before these police agencies emerged. Marshals, constables, day watches, night watches, and vigilance committees all served as early forms of law enforcement in American municipalities (Fogelson, 1977; Lane, 1992; Woods, 1993). Many police agencies were not formed at a distinct period of time, but evolved from these earlier systems. The scattered and gradual evolution of early law enforcement arrangements into modern style police forces makes it difficult to pinpoint exactly what year particular police departments were established (Walker, 1997).

For purposes of this study, a police department was "established" when it first instituted uniformed, paid, full-time 24-hour police services within a single organization that has endured until today. Many early

Table 6.1
Descriptive Statistics and Data Sources for All Variables

Concept	Variable	Min.	Max.	Mean	Median	S.D.	N	Source
Organizational Size	Total FT Employees	103	35,480	593	220	2,039	425	1993 LEMAS
Organizational Age	Organizational Age (years)	13	159	93	93	34	355	Supplemental Survey
Task Scope	Task Scope Index	9	25	17.6	17	2.07	425	1993 LEMAS
Task Routineness	Task Non-Routineness Index	0	22	11.3	11	4.67	376	1993 Police Foundation C.P. Data
Environmental Capacity	Accreditation	0	1	0.13	0	0.34	432	CALEA
	Civil Service	0	1	0.73	1	0.44	395	Supplemental Survey
	Civilian Review	0	1	0.17	0	0.38	425	1993 LEMAS
	Unionization	0	1	0.73	1	0.45	425	1993 LEMAS
Environmental Complexity	Age Differentiation	0.89	0.94	0.93	0.93	0.01	423	1990 Decennial Census Data
	Racial Differentiation	0.03	0.67	0.35	0.37	0.16	423	
	Occupational Differentiation	0.79	0.90	0.88	0.88	0.02	423	
	Education Differentiation	0.75	0.84	0.81	0.81	0.02	423	
	Income Differentiation	0.81	0.88	0.86	0.86	0.01	423	

(continued on next page)

Table 6.1 (continued)

Concept	Variable	Min.	Max.	Mean	Median	S.D.	N	Source
Environmental Stability	Police Chief Executive Turnover	1	13	4.38	4.00	1.81	389	Supplemental Survey
Environmental Concentration	Area of Jurisdiction (Sq. Miles)	1	621.5	59.6	35	81.1	388	Supplemental Survey
	Density of Jurisdiction	415	41,437	4,295.2	2,880.8	4,420.9	388	Supplemental Survey and 1990 Census
Vertical Differentiation	Command Levels	4	12	6	6	0.99	388	Supplemental Survey
	Height	0.11	3.64	1.33	1.26	0.47	425	1993 LEMAS
	Low Rank	0.35	0.91	0.76	0.785	0.079	389	Supplemental Survey
	D_{rank}	0.16	0.74	0.38	0.364	0.09	389	Supplemental Survey
Functional Differentiation	FD Index (# FT special units)	0	13	6	6	2.8	425	1993 LEMAS
Spatial Differentiation	Police Facilities	1	76	2.27	1	5.1	392	Supplemental Survey
	Beats	3	1,013	28.45	13	69.5	358	Supplemental Survey
Centralization	Centralization Index	21	77	53.4	53	8.75	393	Supplemental Survey
Formalization	Formalization Index	6	13	10.7	11	1.58	425	1993 LEMAS
Administration	% Administrative	0.02	0.62	0.24	0.24	0.081	425	1993 LEMAS

police forces emerged from separate day and night watches that were later combined. These agencies were therefore established when they combined the separate forces into a single organization. Similarly, some early departments did not initially pay their officers. Only when they began to pay their officers, and thus began to view policing as a vocation, would they be considered here as established. Others, like New York, initially instituted nonuniformed policing services, but then later uniformed their officers. Others, like Buffalo, had an early pseudo-modern police agency that was later replaced with a more modern police force. All of these conditions—uniforms, paid officers, 24-hour services, and enduring organizational form—are necessary to define the age of a police department in this study.[6] The early histories of certain municipalities, as recorded by historians, serve to illustrate how the evolution of police agencies sometimes makes it difficult to measure a police department's age.

ATLANTA, GA

In approximately 1847, the city of Atlanta was policed by a town marshal with a complement of deputies. In 1853, a night watch was established to supplement the marshals, and then in 1862, under martial law, the marshals became a military company. Then in 1874, Atlanta discarded "an essentially frontier-type enforcement agency" and replaced it with the Atlanta Municipal Police Department, "a regularly constituted and uniformed police force" (Watts, 1992b, p. 909; Maguire, 1990).

BUFFALO, NY

Although Lane (1992, p. 16) reports that Buffalo's police department was founded in 1866, an historical account by Harring and McMullin (1992) shows a more complex evolutionary process: "Up until 1834 there had not been one watchman in Buffalo. In that year the mayor was given power to appoint as many constables as he deemed necessary who were to be paid fees according to arrests." By 1858, the force consisted of a chief and eleven constables. 1866 saw the establishment of the Niagara Frontier police force with "four captains and 100 patrolmen covering the City of Buffalo. . . . In April 1871, a law was drafted creating the first Buffalo Police Department" which superceded the Niagara Frontier Police Force, which was disbanded (Harring and McMullin, 1992, pp. 325–326).

CHICAGO, IL

In 1837, Chicago's new city charter provided for a seven man constabulary consisting of a High Constable and six Constables: one for each of the six city districts. The next eighteen years saw a confusing array of police service arrangements variously named a constabulary, a city watch, and a Marshal's office. In 1855, the city council passed an ordinance providing for the establishment of an organized police department with a complement of 80 to 90 men (Haller, 1992; Flinn, 1887).

SAN FRANCISCO, CA

The Town of San Francisco began policing itself in 1847 by hiring two constables. With the madness of the 1849 gold rush, the town hired 30 additional patrolmen to assist the constables, as well as deputizing 230 volunteer policemen. San Francisco became a city in 1850, and its new charter established the city's first modern police force by creating the elective office of City Marshal and establishing a day and night watch of no greater than 75 men. After a variety of confusing political intrusions into the structure and affairs of the police department, the state legislature "upgraded the San Francisco police system in 1856 by adopting the latest New York City arrangements. This was the last fundamental change in the legal structure of the San Francisco police before the turn of the century" (Ethington, 1992, p. 123–124).

SAVANNAH, GA

In 1796, the Savannah City Council first authorized a night watch. Until 1854, policing was accomplished through a dual system: constables and marshals provided police service in the day, and a night watch policed during the night. In 1854, Savannah established a single police force for the day and the night shifts (Maguire, 1990).

SCRANTON, PA

In 1856, Scranton elected its first law enforcement official, a constable with sixteen assistants who were paid on a system of fees. In 1858, the office of Police Chief, a paid position, was created. In 1866, when Scranton became an incorporated city, they passed an ordinance creating a city police force with officers assigned to wards, but officers were still not considered professionals, and "did not look upon the job as a career." In 1873, the city council authorized the establishment of a paid, full-time, 12-man police force with citywide jurisdiction (Walker, 1992, p. 837–839).

As these examples clearly illustrate, because of the evolutionary processes that characterized early police agencies, it is often difficult to exactly pinpoint a police department's age (Walker, 1980).[7] Of the 395 agencies who responded to the supplemental survey, only 365 (92%) responded to question asking them to estimate the year they were established. Of those 365 agencies, 10 responses were dropped because respondents estimated that their departments were formed before the 1830s, which is when most historians argue that modern police departments began to emerge. This leaves 355 usable responses on the police department age, for a response rate in the sample survey (out of 395 total respondents) of 89%, and a response rate in the overall sample (out of 432 agencies) of 82%. This variable has the lowest response rate in the study.

Organizational age is a fairly normally distributed variable, with a minimum value of 13 years (as of 1993), a maximum value of 159 years, and a mean and median value of approximately 93 years. Descriptive statistics for organizational age are found in Table 6.1.

Task Scope. Task scope is an additive index consisting of responses to 28 binary questions in the 1993 LEMAS survey regarding the primary functions performed by the police department. The survey instrument includes such questions as "does your agency have primary responsibility for enforcement of traffic laws?." The only item in this list of 28 questions that is performed by every agency in the sample is patrol. Some agencies are responsible for working in jails, responding to fires, guarding courtrooms, and a variety of other tasks. No department performs all 28 of the listed tasks, though at least one agency performs each of the individual tasks. An agency's score on this index is equal to the number of tasks it performs out of the 28 tasks listed. A score of 18, for instance, means that the department is responsible for performing 18 of the 28 tasks. Agencies with higher scores on the index are responsible for performing more tasks. All of the individual tasks and the percentage of agencies performing each one are listed in Table 6.2.

Of the 432 sample agencies, 425 provided complete information on the scope of tasks that they perform (98.4%). Respondents report a minimum value of nine on the task scope index, and a maximum value of 25, with a mean and median of approximately 17. Summary statistics for task scope are provided in Table 6.1.

Task Routineness. Chapter 3 introduced the concept of task routineness, and chapter 5 described how this concept might be expected to impact police organizational structures. Only Langworthy (1986) has examined the effect of task routineness on police organizational structure. This study will improve upon Langworthy's analysis of the technology-structure relationship in several ways. Following is a brief review of Langworthy's measure of police organizational technology.

Based on Perrow's (1967) normative theory of technology, Langworthy (1986) examined the hypothesis that "agencies employing stan-

Table 6.2
Primary Tasks Performed by Large Municipal Police Organizations

(N = 425)

Functions or Tasks	% Yes	% No
Patrol and first response to incidents	100%	0%
Assault investigations	98.8%	1.2%
Enforcement of traffic laws	99.8%	0.2%
Robbery investigations	99.8%	0.2%
Accident investigations	99.5%	0.5%
Burglary investigations	99.5%	0.5%
Larceny/theft investigations	99.5%	0.5%
Motor vehicle theft investigations	99.5%	0.5%
Rape investigations	99.5%	0.5%
Homicide investigations	99.3%	0.7%
Vice enforcement	96.7%	3.3%
Receiving calls for service from citizens	95.8%	4.2%
Traffic direction and control	93.9%	6.1%
Dispatching calls for service to officers	88.7%	11.3%
Fingerprint processing	85.6%	14.4%
Arson investigations	81.2%	18.8%
Training academy operation	36.7%	63.3%
Search and rescue	34.6%	65.4%
Animal control	32.7%	67.3%
Court security	21.9%	78.1%
Jail operations	18.8%	81.2%
Laboratory testing of substances	16.2%	83.8%
Environmental crime investigations	16.0%	84.0%
Emergency medical services	14.6%	85.4%
Ballistics testing	13.2%	86.8%
Civil defense	12.0%	88.0%
Serving civil process	6.1%	93.9%
Fire services	1.2%	98.8%

dardized methods [will] be hierarchically tall, functionally and occupationally differentiated, and spatially centralized." Arguing that patrol is a nonstandardized operational technology, he measured the degree to which an agency uses a standardized technology as one minus the percentage of employees devoted to patrol. There are some problems with this measure. First, it is a structural variable, used here to predict other elements of structure.[8] Langworthy acknowledges this point but argues that standardized policing technology "is reflective of the technological structure employed in production, while the other variables to which it is being related are the core of organizational structure—that which gives the organization shape." The difference between "technological" structure and "core" structure is not clear, however. Researchers often note the difference between technical and peripheral components of organizational structures, but it is difficult to conceive of either element of structure as being more or less structural. Nonetheless, Langworthy was working with secondary data that did not contain a better measure of technology.

The second problem with this measure is that it is substantively uninformative. It explains very little about what the police in these jurisdictions do. It is not difficult to imagine two police departments with distinctive operational and strategic differences who devote the same amount of personnel to the patrol division, therefore receiving the same score on Langworthy's measure of technology. Manning's (1988a, p. 326) main criticism of the book was Langworthy's failure to adequately specify the technology variable. Manning argues that the book:

> . . . stands to policing as square dancing does to ballet . . . to define patrol as a technology is more than stretching a point. Patrol, in its diverse forms and styles, is not a means of transforming a raw material into an output. Duties, tasks, and workload vary radically in the cities sampled.[9]

Because the only attempt to assess the relationship between technology and structure in police organizations relied on a problematic measure of technology, we still have very little evidence about the relationship between these two complex variables. In order to examine the relationship between technology and organizational structure, it is necessary to select a variable (or set of variables) measuring technology which are 1) not themselves structural, and 2) more substantively reflective of the police agency's operational tasks and technologies.

In this study, the degree to which police agencies employ standardized or routinized methods will be measured using community policing data collected by the Police Foundation in 1993.[10] Like Langworthy, I must rely on secondary data to construct a measure of technology. Although the resulting measure is not ideally suited for this purpose, it is a reasonable proxy for the extent to which the agency relies on standardized or routinized methods. Agencies were asked eleven questions about "some of the things patrol officers/deputies in your agency might be expected to do or for which they might be held responsible" (Police Foundation, 1993, p. 13). The eleven tasks are all nonroutine policing duties that might be expected in a department that practices community policing, however none of the items was explicitly described in the survey instrument as a community policing task. For each task, agencies were asked to indicate whether patrol officers are *not* responsible for performing the task, whether a *special unit* is responsible for performing the task, whether *some* patrol officers are responsible for the task, or whether *most* patrol officers are responsible for the task. Table 6.3 describes each of the tasks, and provides summary data for the responses to each question.

Each of the 11 questions was recoded so that a 0 indicated no patrol officers were responsible for the task, a 1 indicated that a special unit or some patrol officers were responsible for the task, and a 2 indicated that most patrol officers were responsible for the task. The items were then summed to form an overall index of task routineness, with a lower score indicating a routine technology and a higher score indicating a nonroutine technology.[11] The eleven items appear to cluster well together, with an alpha coefficient of (0.866). This is one indication that the index is reliable (in the sense that it is internally consistent), however it is difficult to draw inferences about validity since this is really the first attempt to measure task routineness in police organizations using data of this type.

Of the 432 agencies in the sample, 376 (87%) provided sufficient information in the Police Foundation survey to construct the task routineness index. The range of possible values for the index is 0–22, and this is also the range for the actual scores. The mean and median scores for the sample agencies are approximately 11. Descriptive statistics for this variable are listed in Table 6.1.

Environmental Capacity. Recall from chapter 5 that in this study, the notion of environmental capacity refers to the ability of a police organization to act independently in the face of constraints imposed by external or "third party" organizations. The types of third-party organizations that might impact a police organization's autonomy include civil-service boards, employee unions, citizen review panels, and accreditation agencies.

No judgement is made here about the effectiveness of these types of organizations for achieving their desired ends—the only assumption is that they all impose limits (in some way) on a police organization's autonomy. As Mastrofski (1994, p. 247) notes, "Because of union contracts, civil service requirements, state and federal regulatory bodies, courts, governing charters, and special police boards (to name a few), police chiefs are quite constrained in altering fundamental aspects of their organization." Because of these organizations, there is a certain range of actions by the police agency that will prompt some type of organized external response. If the police department "improperly" fires a police officer, the union and/or civil service board will react; if the

Table 6.3
Percentage of Agencies in which Patrol Officers are Responsible for Performing Nonroutine Tasks

Tasks	No Patrol Officers Responsible for Task	Some Patrol Officers (or Special Unit) Responsible for Task	Most Patrol Officers Responsible for Task	Mean Response (0 = None, 1 = Some, 2 = Most)
Make door-to-door contacts in neighborhoods	23.3%	52.4%	24.3%	1.01
Develop familiarity with community leaders in area of assignment	11.3%	55.1%	33.6%	1.22
Work with citizens to identify and resolve area problems	6.6%	54.7%	38.7%	1.32
Assist in organizing community	19.6%	65.2%	15.2%	0.96
Teach residents how to address community problems	18.8%	64.9%	16.2%	0.97
Work regularly with detectives on cases in area of assignment	17.8%	44.1%	38.1%	1.20
Conduct crime analysis for area of assignment	42.5%	44.4%	13.1%	0.70
Meet regularly with community groups	12.6%	68.9%	18.4%	1.06
Enforce civil and code violations in area	32.5%	34.6%	33.0%	1.00
Work with other city agencies to solve neighborhood problems	11.0%	57.0%	32.0%	1.21
Conduct surveys in area of assignment	39.8%	50.8%	9.4%	0.69

police department eliminates or changes certain policies or procedures, the Commission on Accreditation for Law Enforcement Agencies may fail to renew the department's accreditation; if an officer beats a suspect and the department fails to take required steps, the citizen's review panel might take action. In each of these instances, the internal workings of the police department are watched, probed, and evaluated by an external organization. The (less/more) external constraints that a police department faces, the (greater/lesser) its capacity to act autonomously. As Marsden, Cook, and Kalleberg (1994, p. 919) note, such powerful actors in an organization's environment may have the ability "to mandate, or at least to advocate strongly, the adoption of structural forms."

Data on civil service boards, employee unions, citizen review panels, and accreditation status were collected from several sources and combined to construct a single measure of environmental capacity. For each of the four variables on third-party organizations, the responses are dummy-coded—0 if the police agency does not associate with such an organization, and 1 if it does. We now discuss each of the four indicators more thoroughly.

CIVIL SERVICE

Data on civil service were drawn from a question on the supplemental survey asking whether or not the department hires new employees under a civil service system. Of the 432 agencies in the sample, 395 provided information on the civil-service question (91.4%). Almost three-quarters of respondents (73.4%) reported that they hire new employees under a civil-service system. Descriptive statistics for this variable are listed in Table 6.1.

EMPLOYEE UNIONS

Data on employee unions and/or collective bargaining organizations were obtained from the 1993 LEMAS survey. Two questions were used to develop the binary measure of unionization: whether there is a police membership association, and whether collective bargaining is authorized. In places where collective bargaining is authorized but the police officers do not have an organized bargaining association, there is no appreciable constraint being exerted on the police organization. Likewise, there is also probably not a significant amount of constraint exerted on those police departments that have an organized employee membership association but where collective bargaining is not authorized. On the other hand, in police agencies that authorize collective bargaining and have organized employee membership associations (either local, state, federal, or unaffiliated), these associations may exert a considerable amount of influence on how the department is run. Of the 432 police agencies in the sample, 425 (98.4%) provided information on employee associations and collective bargaining. Among these respondents, nearly three-quarters (308) have organized employee associations that are authorized to conduct collective bargaining. Descriptive statistics for the unionization variable are listed in Table 6.1.

CITIZEN REVIEW BOARDS

Data on the presence or absence of citizen review boards were obtained from the 1993 LEMAS survey. Walker and Kreisel (1996) suggest that civilian review boards come in many shapes and sizes, and I acknowledge that dichotomizing this variable tramples on the complexity of civilian review. Nevertheless, since this variable is only being used as a gross indicator of external constraint, the particulars of the type of civilian review arrangement are not absolutely essential here. Of the 432 agencies in the sample, 425 provided information on this variable (98.4%). Only 74 of these respondents (17.4%) have instituted a civilian complaint review board. Descriptive statistics for this variable are listed in Table 6.1.

ACCREDITATION

Data on accreditation were obtained directly from the Commission on Accreditation for Law Enforcement Agencies (CALEA).[12] CALEA makes its list of accredited agencies available to whoever is interested (although it does not give out its list of agencies who are rejected for accreditation). All of the primary policing information in this study was collected during or for the year 1993, thus agencies are coded as accredited if the accreditation process was completed by December 31, 1993. Because the list provided by CALEA contains *all* accredited agencies, there is no missing data for this variable—any agency that is not on the list has not been accredited. Only 13.4% of the agencies in the sample have been accredited by CALEA. Descriptive statistics for this variable are listed in Table 6.1.

The responses to each of these four dummy variables were then summed to create a single environmental capacity index with a minimum possible score of 0 and a maximum possible score of 4. For example, a police agency that has not been accredited and does not have a civil service hiring system, a civilian review board, or an employee union or bargaining association, would receive a score of 0 on this measure. A low score indicates high capacity or autonomy, and a high score indicates low capacity or autonomy. This is admittedly a crude measure of environmental capacity. Nonetheless, it is quite similar to a measure used in the recent National Organizations Study. Marsden, Cook, and Knoke (1996) developed a four-item measure of institutionalization, which they defined as the extent to which "external organizations can convey institutional pressures." Like the measure used here, their measure was based on the extent to which third-party organizations might constrain or inhibit the decisions made by actors within the focal organization. Although the measure I have adopted is admittedly crude, it is not without precedent. Unfortunately, existing data sources do not permit a more refined approach.

Altogether, 390 of the 432 sample agencies (90.3%) provided sufficient information to construct the environmental capacity index. Actual scores ranged from 0 to 4, with 22 agencies scoring 0 (5.6%), 108 agencies scoring 1 (27.7%), 199 agencies scoring 2 (51%), 58 agencies scoring 3 (14.9%), and 3 agencies scoring 4 (0.8%). I did not compute an alpha reliability coefficient for these variables because their relationship with one another is not an issue for this particular index. In many (most) indices, the indicators are all presumed to be effects of some underlying latent variable. Therefore, since they are supposed to have the same cause, they should all be correlated. This is the rationale for computing an alpha reliability coefficient—to examine the pattern of the relationships between the indicators. In this index, however, the four variables are presumed to be causes, not effects, of the underlying variable (environmental capacity). Thus, the relationship between these indicators is not an issue.[13] We now turn to another important element of an organization's environment: the nature and degree of environmental complexity.

Environmental Complexity. Chapter 5 introduced the concept of environmental complexity and discussed a number of hypotheses about how this concept might affect the structures of police organizations. The concept of environmental complexity is quite simple: it is the sum total of the ways that the residents of a community differ from one another.[14] A community in which all of the residents are white Catholic blue collar workers is less complex than one that has a tremendous amount of racial, religious, and occupational differentiation. Chapter 5 suggested a number of reasons why environmental complexity might impact police organizational structure. The main thrust of this argument was that police organizations facing extremely complex social environments must adapt their structures to the varying needs of a diverse client base. Langworthy (1986) confirmed a relationship between environmental complexity and certain elements of police organizational structure.

Communities vary in their levels and patterns of environmental complexity in almost infinite ways (Langworthy, 1986). Race, ethnicity, religion, language, occupation, industry, and economy are just some of the parameters that define a community's social complexity. Taken together, these parameters are an example of what Blau (1977, p. 89) calls "multiform heterogeneity." The idea of multiform heterogeneity is that the greater the number of heterogeneity parameters, and the greater the number of groups within each parameter, the more subgroups there are. For instance, if there are 5 categories of race, 5 categories of religion, and 5 categories of occupation, then the number of subcategories (e.g., white Catholic blue collar workers) equals 125. The more subgroups that researchers can isolate, the wider the range of heterogeneity or complexity they can identify.[15]

Multiform heterogeneity is an abstract theoretical concept which is in itself unmeasurable, but may be reflected by certain measurable characteristics of a community. Environmental complexity, like the more generic concept of multiform heterogeneity, is also an abstract theoretical construct that cannot be measured directly. It is, however, a combination of several measurable features of communities (such as the distributions of race, education, and occupation within an area), and therefore one can estimate the level of environmental complexity in a community by developing a measurement model that combines these measurable features.

In Chapter 7, I will provide a detailed explanation of measurement models, but for now a more simplistic explanation will suffice. Measurement models are used to measure theoretical or abstract concepts that cannot be measured directly, but that can be estimated with a combination of variables that are measurable. Unmeasurable theoretical concepts like environmental complexity are known as "latent variables" (Loehlin, 1992). Latent variables can sometimes be estimated by combining a series of "manifest" or measurable variables. A measurement model does exactly this—it estimates the value of a latent variable by mathematically combining a set of manifest variables. In the case of environmental complexity, a measurement model could be formed based on a set of manifest variables that might include measures of racial, occupational or religious differentiation within a community. The mathematical combination of these separate manifest variables would produce a single environmental complexity score for each community in the sample.

What manifest variables are most important for constructing a measure of environmental complexity? Langworthy (1986) focused on occupational and industrial differentiation in his examination of environmental complexity. Blau (1977, p. 8) listed 13 nominal level and 9 "graduated" level parameters in his discussion of social heterogeneity. Nominal level parameters include such items as race, sex, religion, and occupation—variables with no fundamental difference in rank between the different groups. Graduated level parameters include such items as age, education, and income—variables with a fundamental rank ordering between different groups. Although the choice of parameters is wide ranging, the types of manifest variables that are available to form a measure of environmental complexity in this study are limited by available data sources.

The traditional source of data for describing the socioeconomic features of communities in the United States is the decennial census of the population collected by the U.S. Census Bureau (1990). All of the manifest variables used to measure environmental complexity in this study are formed from information available in the 1990 decennial census (U.S. Census Bureau, 1990). The census data tape that I used contained nearly a thousand socioeconomic variables for all "places" in the United States.[16] Five of the most important elements of social complexity in large U.S. communities today are age, race, occupation, education, and income. The Census Bureau has defined a number of separate categories for each of these parameters, and the data file lists the number of people in each category. The more evenly distributed the individuals within each category, the more differentiated a city is on the particular parameter. For example, if all of the residents in a city have the same race, then the city is less racially differentiated than another city that has residents representing a number of racial categories. In order to construct a measure of environmental complexity, I will measure the degree of differentiation on each of these five parameters.

The traditional way to measure differentiation in nominal variables is the *Gibbs-Martin D* formula, which was first used to measure division of labor (Gibbs and Martin, 1962). Other excellent discussions of this measure can be found in (Blau, 1977, p. 9; Langworthy, 1986, pp. 141–145; and Rushing, 1967, p. 281). The formula is:

$$D = 1 - [\Sigma x_i^2 / (\Sigma x_i)^2],$$

where D is the level of differentiation, x_i is the number of persons in group i, and the sum is taken over all of the i groups. When data for each category are expressed as the proportion of the total number of people that are represented in each group, the formula simplifies to:

$$D = 1 - \Sigma p_i^2,$$

where p_i is the proportion of people within each group. The minimum value of D is 0 when there is only one group. The maximum value of D is 1 minus the reciprocal of the number of groups, thus the maximum value approaches one as the number of groups increases toward infinity. For example, the maximum value of D with five groups is equal to one minus one-fifth, or (0.8). The larger the value of D, the more differentiated the community is on the particular parameter in question. I will now discuss the specific measurement of differentiation for each of the five parameters: age, race, occupation, education, and income.

AGE

The Census Bureau identifies 31 separate age categories. Because there are 31 categories, the maximum possible value of D_{age} is (0.968). The values of D_{age} for each community range from (0.89) to (0.94). Thus although there is a great deal of age differentiation *within* communities (because the actual values are close to the maximum possible value), the level of differentiation is fairly stable *across* communities (because the range of scores is so small). Descriptive statistics for this variable are listed in Table 6.1.

RACE

The Census Bureau identifies 5 separate racial categories: (1) white; (2) black; (3) American Indian, Eskimo, or Aleut; (4) Asian or Pacific Islander; and (5) other. According to the Census Bureau's racial classification system, Hispanics might span these racial categories, so they are not included as a separate category. Because there are five categories, the maximum possible value of D_{race} is (0.8). The values of D_{race} for each community range from (0.03) to (0.67). This large range means that the cities in this sample vary widely in their levels of racial differentiation. Descriptive statistics for this variable are listed in Table 6.1.

OCCUPATION

The Census Bureau identifies 13 occupational categories: (1) executive, administrative, and managerial occupations; (2) professional specialty occupations; (3) technicians and related support occupations; (4) sales occupations; (5) administrative support occupations, including clerical; (6) private household occupations; (7) protective service occupations; (8) service occupations except protective and household; (9) farming, forestry, and fishing occupations; (10) precision production, craft, and repair occupations; (11) machine operators, assemblers, and inspectors; (12) transportation and material moving occupations, and; (13) handlers, equipment cleaners, helpers, and laborers. Because there are 13 categories, the maximum value of $D_{occupation}$ is $1 - \frac{1}{13}$, or (0.923). The values of $D_{occupation}$ for each community range from (0.79) to (0.90). Descriptive statistics for this variable are listed in Table 6.1.

EDUCATION

Since level of education is not really a nominal level variable, the best way to measure the degree of variation in education would be to compute the standard deviation in total years of education for the population of residents within each community. The standard deviation is a common means of describing the degree of variation in an interval-level variable. Unfortunately, the data are not available in this format in the census file used in this study. Rather, education is divided into the following 7 categories, with the number of people in each category recorded: (1) less than 9th grade; (2) 9th to 12th grade, no diploma; (3) high school graduate, including equivalency; (4) some college, no degree; (5) Associate's degree; (6) Bachelor's degree; (7) Graduate or Professional Degree. Because there are seven categories, the maximum value of $D_{education}$ is $1 - 1/7$, or (0.857). The values of $D_{education}$ for each community range from (0.75) to (0.84). Descriptive statistics for this variable are listed in Table 6.1.

INCOME

Like education, income is clearly not a nominal level variable, and the best way to measure income differentiation would be to compute the standard deviation of income for the residential population within each community. Again, unfortunately, continuous level income data are not available in the census file used in this study.[17] Rather, income is divided into the following 9 categories: (1) less than $5,000; (2) $5,000 to $9,999; (3) $10,000 to $14,999; (4) $15,000 to $24,999; (5) $25,000 to $34,999; (6) $35,000 to $49,999; (7) $50,000 to $74,999; (8) $75,000 to $99,999; and (9) $100,000 or more. Because there are 9 categories, the maximum value of D_{income} is $1 - 1/9$, or $(.89)$. The values of D_{income} for each community range from (0.81) to (0.88). These values reveal an interesting fact about the nature of income inequality in American cities. *Within* large municipalities, there appears to be tremendous variation in levels of household income (which is apparent from the clustering of D-values close to the maximum possible value). Yet, the small range and standard deviation of the D-values show that *between* large cities, this degree of variation is quite stable. Thus income inequality appears to be a normal feature of the cities in this sample. Descriptive statistics for this variable are listed in Table 6.1.

Age, racial, occupational, educational, and income differentiation are not the only indicators of environmental complexity, but they are among the most salient, and they are readily available in electronic format. In chapter 7, these indicators will be formed into a measurement model that treats environmental complexity as a latent variable. We now turn to another important element in the environment of police organizations: the degree of instability.

Environmental Instability. Chapter 5 explained that environmental instability is the degree of turbulence, unpredictability, dynamism, or turnover in the in the organization's environment. Many police executives today are responsible for managing not only their internal organizations, but also for managing unstable environments. As discussed in chapter 5, police executives occupy "boundary-spanning" roles in which they act as intermediaries between the needs of their organization and the demands of their environment. The most turbulent environments produce a great deal of uncertainty for police organizations, and especially for police chief executives, who frequently have very little job security. The most turbulent or unstable municipal environments would be expected to produce frequent turnover in police chief executives. Therefore, in this study environmental instability is measured using the level of turnover in the police chief executive position. This is clearly not an ideal measure, since police chief turnover is a consequence of environmental instability, not a direct measure of the underlying concept. Some unstable environments may produce low rates of turnover either because the police chief enjoys civil service protections or because s/he is particularly skilled at weathering political storms. Either situation would produce some unknown degree of error in this measure of environmental instability. Future studies should seek to identify better measures.

Respondents in the supplemental survey were asked to report the number of chief executives holding office between 1970 and 1993.[18] Of the 432 agencies in the sample, 389 provided responses to this question (90%). According to respondents, the minimum number of police chiefs holding office during the 23-year period from 1970–1993 was 1, and the maximum was 13. The mean response was 4.4, and the median and mode was 4. Thus, the average tenure of police chiefs in this sample is slightly more than 5 years, which is longer than reported in earlier research that found the mean tenure of police chiefs to be 4.3 years (Lunden, 1958).[19] Summary statistics for this variable are reported in Table 6.1.

Environmental Dispersion. Chapter 5 suggested that the spatial size and dispersion of a jurisdiction might have certain ramifications for how police organizations are structured. Specifically, police agencies located in small geographic areas with low population densities will be less vertically, functionally, and spatially differentiated. In addition, because they will rely on more personal modes of control, they will be more centralized, less formalized, and will employ smaller administrative staffs. Similarly, police agencies located in large, densely populated geographic areas will exhibit higher levels of differentiation, formalization, and administration, and lower levels of centralization. Large areas that are not densely populated, and small areas that are densely populated should fall somewhere in the middle of these two extremes in their effects on organizational structure.

As shown in these examples, area and population are hypothesized to impact organizational structure interactively, not independently. Therefore, these variables are treated in this study as a multiplicative interaction term.[20] This interaction term alone is used to represent the environmental dispersion dimension.[21] The individual components of the interaction term (area and population) are not included in the model because they are only expected to impact organizational structure interactively, not individually.[22] Because the metrics of these two variables are so different (see Table 6.1 for descriptive statistics), they will need to be transformed in some way before they are multiplied to form the interaction term. Chapter 7 will address this issue, including some other mathematical and statistical issues that this interaction term introduces into the model.

Although area and population do not tell us much about the distribution of police service recipients across social space, they are the only available indicators of spatial dispersion. Areas with a high proportion of nonresidential or industrial property will generally appear to be more dispersed than they actually are, since this measure assumes that the population is dispersed throughout the entire area. Spatial analyses of the police are now starting to become more popular, but they are still generally limited to case study analyses of single departments (e.g., Herbert, 1997; Langworthy and LeBeau, 1992). As more geographers start to make their way into the study of the police, analyses such as this one can hopefully become more sophisticated.

Data on area and population of the police jurisdiction were obtained from 388 of the 432 sample agencies (90%). The mean size of the jurisdictions served by large municipal police agencies in the United States is approximately 60 square miles, with a median value of 35 square miles. The mean density of the jurisdictions is approximately 4,300 people per square mile, with a median value of about 2,880 people per square mile. Both of these variables are skewed to the right, and both have right side values more than six standard deviations above the mean. Descriptive statistics for area and density are listed in Table 6.1.

Structural Complexity

According to the theoretical model described in chapter 5, complexity contains three elements: vertical, functional, and spatial differentiation. Each of these will now be explored in further detail.

Vertical Differentiation. According to Langworthy (1986), vertical differentiation has three components: segmentation, height, and concentration. Segmentation is the number of levels, height is the amount of social distance or social space between the lowest and highest ranking employees, and concentration is the vertical distribution of staff throughout the command structure. I will measure vertical differentiation in this study by constructing a measurement model with multiple indicators. Although the multiple indicator approach has not been used in the past, researchers have used a number of different variables to measure vertical differentiation.

SEGMENTATION

Segmentation is the number of command levels in an organization. In police organizations, the level of segmentation is sometimes equivalent to the number of sworn ranks, though there are some important exceptions. First, many police departments designate different rank levels within a single level of command. The higher ranks offer greater salaries and more prestige, but do not signify a difference in command authority. The most prominent example is the use of different levels within the police officer category, such as the "master police officer" position used by a number of agencies, or a set of graded categories such as police officer I, II, III, and IV. These different levels are often considered by police agencies to be separate "ranks," but they are clearly not separate levels of command. Second, a number of police agencies designate a special rank for their detectives and/or investigators. The difference in rank between detectives and police officers is usually accompanied by a difference in prestige and salary, but not in command authority. Detectives in general do not have a greater level of command authority than police officers (except in investigative situations). Furthermore, treating detectives and patrol officers as different levels of command blurs the distinction between functional and vertical differentiation. Since both detectives and police officers are generally supervised by sergeants, the detective rank cannot be considered a level of command.[23] Third, many police agencies have a "corporal" rank that is difficult to classify in terms of command levels. Some use the corporal rank as a master police officer position, but the corporal does not really have any command authority over other "regular" police officers, except in certain isolated circumstances. Others use the corporal rank as the first-line supervisor over police officers and low-level civilian employees, in which case the corporal represents a distinct level of command.[24] Though different ranks may indicate differences in pay and prestige, the concept of segmentation focuses exclusively on differences in levels of command. The difference between ranks and levels of command in large police agencies mirrors the same differences in the U.S. military. Factoring in all of the noncommissioned staff and commissioned officers, there are probably dozens of actual "ranks" in the military, but of course the number of actual command levels is much smaller (Mastrofski, 1997).

Of the 432 agencies in the sample, 388 provided sufficient information in the supplemental survey to estimate the number of command levels. Because of the confusion between number of ranks and number of command levels, it was often necessary to speak with respondents directly in order to get more detailed information. Respondents reported a minimum of 4 and a maximum of 12 command levels, with a median and mode of 6. Nearly 73% of the respondents had either 5 or 6 command levels, and approximately 93% had either 5, 6, or 7 levels. Descriptive statistics for this variable are available in Table 6.1.

HEIGHT

Height is the distance from the bottom to the top of the organization, or the amount of social space between the lowest and highest ranking employees (Black, 1976; Langworthy, 1986). In general, smaller organizations tend to be flatter, and larger organizations tend to be taller, but not all of the variation in height can be accounted for by organization size.[25] Langworthy (1986, p. 40) measured the height of police departments with a standardized pay differential constructed by "subtracting the lowest paid officer's salary from the highest paid officer's salary and dividing that difference by the lowest salary." The larger the difference, the greater the height of the organization. This measure of height has been used in two recent studies of police organizational structure (King, 1999; Maguire, 1997) as well, and it is the measure used in this study.

Of the 432 agencies in the sample, 425 (98.8%) responded to the 1993 LEMAS survey salary questions that were used to construct the measure of height used in this study. The scores range from a low of (0.11) to a high of (3.64), with a mean of (1.33) and a median of (1.26). These measures have a simple substantive interpretation. The scores represent the percentage difference between the mean salary of the police officers, and the actual salary of the police chief. A score of 0.10 indicates that the police chief makes 10% more than the average officer, whereas a score of 1.0 indicates that the chief makes 100% more, or double the salary of the average officer. The greater the salary difference, the greater the social distance, or the height, of the department. Summary statistics for height are presented in Table 6.1.

CONCENTRATION

Concentration is the distribution of personnel throughout an organization's command hierarchy. The more that an organization concentrates its personnel at just one or a few levels of command, the less it is vertically differentiated. The most vertically differentiated organization is one that has a large number of command levels, each with an equal number of employees; the least differentiated would have only one level containing all employees. As Langworthy (1986, p. 63) explains: "concentrations are concerned with unequal distribution and often referred to as inequalities." Among the three components of vertical differentiation discussed in this section, concentration is the least used measure of vertical differentiation. Chapter 7 will address a number of problems with this dimension.

Both Langworthy (1986) and Crank and Wells (1991) measured concentration as the proportion of employees in the lowest level of the police hierarchy (this measure is hereafter referred to as "LowRank"). The logic implicit in this measure is simple: the greater the number of employees at the lowest level of the hierarchy, the fewer available to be distributed among the upper levels. Thus, although this measure of concentration does not take into account the distribution of personnel in the upper levels of the organization, it is a logical proxy. However, using the Gibbs-Martin D formula described in the previous section on environmental complexity, it is possible to construct a measure that does take into account the distribution of personnel throughout the upper ranks. Of the 432 agencies in the sample, 389 (91.5%) provided sufficient rank-count information in the supplemental survey to construct the measures of LowRank and D_{rank} used in this study.[26] The proportion of police officers at the lowest command level ranges from 35% to 91%, with a mean of 76%.[27] For D_{rank}, scores range from a low of (0.16) to a high of (0.74), with a mean of (0.38). Summary statistics for LowRank and D_{rank} are presented in Table 6.1. The correlation between LowRank and D_{rank} is (−0.98), indicating that the two measures are almost identical, though measured in the opposite direction. High scores for LowRank indicate low vertical differentiation, because employees are clustered in a single rank—high scores for D_{rank} indicate high differentiation, because employees are more widely distributed throughout the rank structure.

In summary, I will develop a multiple-indicator model to measure vertical differentiation. Four separate indicators of vertical differentiation have been listed here: segmentation, height, LowRank (the proportion of officers at the lowest rank), and D_{rank}. The multiple indicators approach will improve on prior studies that have treated these indicators as separate variables (Crank and Wells, 1991; Langworthy, 1986), and on those that use only single indicators of the overall dimension (King, 1999; Maguire, 1997). We now explore another element of structural complexity: functional differentiation.

Functional Differentiation. Functional differentiation is the degree to which the organization divides and assigns its tasks into functionally distinct units. An organization with a sales force, separate production staffs for each product, a planning staff and an engineering group is more functionally differentiated than an organization containing only one department. This variable is sometimes confused with occupational differentiation, which is the degree to which an organization uses different types of specially trained workers.[28] Occupational differentiation and functional differentiation are sometimes, but not always, related. Functional differentiation measures the division of tasks, while occupational differentiation measures the division of staff (Langworthy, 1986).

In this study, functional differentiation is measured with an additive index consisting of responses to fourteen separate questions in the 1993 LEMAS survey that ask whether the department has a full-time specialized unit to deal with a variety of issues. Each component item is scored zero for no special unit, and one for a full-time special unit.[29] Higher scores indicate greater functional differentiation. Of the 432 agencies in the sample, 425 (98.4%) provided sufficient information to form the functional differentiation index. Respondents reported a minimum of 0 and a maximum of 13 specialized units (out of 14 listed), with a mean and median of approximately 6. Table 6.4 lists the percentage of agencies having each of the different types of special units. Recent evidence suggests that despite pressure from community policing reformers to despecialize, large municipal police organizations have actually become *more* functionally differentiated in the late 1980s and early 1990s. Ironically, the increase in specialization may be due to the addition of specialized problem-solving and community policing units (Maguire, 1997). Perhaps even more ironic is the recent finding by Kraska and Kappeler (1997) that police agencies are implementing police paramilitary units at an increasing rate, partly in response to the idea of "proactive" policing stemming from the community policing movement. Summary statistics for the functional differentiation index are listed in Table 6.1.[30]

Table 6.4
Percentage of Agencies with Certain Specialized Units

Type of Special Unit	% Yes	% No
Victim assistance	25.2%	74.8%
Neighborhood/community crime prevention (e.g., Neighborhood Watch, Operation ID)	87.8%	12.2%
Career criminals/repeat offenders	23.5%	76.5%
Police/prosecutor relations	36.9%	63.1%
Domestic/family violence	31.5%	68.5%
Child abuse	64.2%	35.8%
Missing children	52.9%	47.1%
Juvenile delinquency	74.8%	25.2%
Gangs	53.4%	46.6%
Drug education in schools	85.2%	14.8%
Drunk drivers	32.5%	67.5%
Bias/hate crime investigation	19.1%	80.9%
Environmental crime investigation	5.2%	94.8%
Other	4.5%	95.5%

Spatial Differentiation.[31] Langworthy (1986) measured spatial differentiation using two separate variables: number of police stations and number of separate patrol beats.[32] In chapter 7, I will combine these two variables into a single measurement model that treats spatial differentiation as a latent construct. Both of these measures will now be explored in further detail.

POLICE STATIONS

All respondents in the supplemental survey were asked to report the number of "fixed 24-hour police service facilities staffed by sworn officers (headquarters, precinct houses, police stations, etc. . . . .)." Of the 432 agencies in the sample, 392 provided usable responses to this question (90.7%). The modal reply given by nearly 80% of the respondents was one police station. The largest number of police stations was 76, as reported by the New York City Police Department, the nation's largest police agency.[33] 80 agencies (20.4%) had 2 or more 24-hour police stations, and 15 (3.8%) had 10 or more. Summary statistics for this variable are provided in Table 6.1.

Social scientists, government agencies, and police departments appear to have a great deal of difficulty collecting and compiling information on the number of patrol beats that are used by large municipal police agencies. The Federal Bureau of Investigation (FBI) once collected beat information in the Police Employees component of its Uniform Crime Reports series, but has since discontinued this practice. Depending on the specific variable, only 0–3% of the 18,000+ police agencies in the 1993 Police Employees data file contain information on the number of beats (Federal Bureau of Investigation, 1993). The 1990 LEMAS survey collected beat information, but this portion of the data set was not released to the public, presumably due to problematic responses. The 1993 LEMAS survey collected beat information and released the full data set to the public. Unfortunately, there are fundamental flaws with the beat variables in this data set that render the data unusable. I now briefly discuss these flaws, together with their implications for future research on levels of police patrol coverage in large U.S. cities.

The 1993 LEMAS survey asked respondents to list the number of several different types of patrol units deployed on shifts of seven hours or longer during a 24-hour period on the most recent Wednesday and Saturday. The types of patrol units that are listed include automobile, motorcycle, foot, horse, bicycle, and other, and a distinction is made in each case between a one-person or a two-person assignment. The main problems with these data stem from the way the survey question is worded. It is apparent from manually inspecting the beat data that some agencies responded with the number of patrol units per shift, and some responded with the number of patrol units per 24-hour period, which is usually three shifts. Checking through the responses manually, it is quite easy in some cases to tell which type of response the agency provided, yet for many others it is very difficult to tell. Thus, the overall level of measurement error in these data is quite pronounced—any given response may have approximately 1/3 of the value of the correct response. For this reason, beat information in the 1993 LEMAS data is probably not useful. In 1997, the Bureau of Justice Statistics responded to concerns expressed by policing scholars and revised the wording of the question on beats so that it is easier for respondents to understand clearly how to respond appropriately.

Fortunately, the supplemental survey collected information on the average number of patrol beats used by large municipal police agencies. The types of beat data that are available in the supplemental survey are not nearly so comprehensive as those in the LEMAS data, but they are very similar to the measures used by Langworthy (1986). The survey asked all respondents to provide the average number of motorized patrol vehicles that were deployed during the day shift and the night shift in 1993. Responses to these questions were received from 368 of the 432 sample agencies, for a response rate of 85.1%. These data are not ideal. First, they do not contain information on the various types of non-motorized patrol, including foot patrol, bicycles, horses, and other patrol strategies. Second, respondents were frequently confused by the term "night shift," and often wondered whether it referred to the evening shift or the midnight shift. The question should have been asked for all three shifts in order to produce a more accurate estimate of average patrol coverage. Third, some of the responses were discarded because 49 of the initial surveys that were sent out asked for the number of motorized patrol beats, rather than the number of motorized patrol vehicles. Ten of these respondents provided incorrect responses, presumably because of these differences in the wording of the question. Once these 10 responses were eliminated, 359 usable responses remained, for a response rate of 82.9%.[34] Lastly, it appears that the very largest agencies were the ones most often unable to provide beat information, thus presenting a serious possibility of sample selection bias. This possibility will be explored further in chapter 7.

Although the beat data from the supplemental survey are not ideal, they do not present the same problems with measurement error as the beat data from the 1993 LEMAS survey. The beat data from the supplemental survey are used in this study to develop a measure of the average number of patrol beats in large American cities. For each department, the average number of patrol beats is computed by taking the mean of the responses for the number of patrol vehicles on the day shift and the night shift. The average number of motorized patrol beats ranges from a low of three in the West New York Police Department (NJ), to a high of 1,013 in New York City. The median number of beats is 13, and 344 agencies (96%) have fewer than 100 beats. Summary statistics for this variable are listed in Table 6.1.

What does the number of motorized patrol vehicles tell us about spatial differentiation? A police car is a rolling office, complete in many cases with a trained street-level bureaucrat representing the agency, blank forms designed for many different situations, multiple means of contacting the central office (the dispatch center), and in recent years, even a mobile computer. The greater the number of vehicles that police agencies use on patrol, the greater the spatial coverage of the agency. Although spatial differentiation will be highly driven by department size, the two variables will not be perfectly correlated due to differences in patrol coverage, shift patterns, and deployment. For example, consider two similarly sized agencies, with one department relying more heavily on two-officer patrols than the other. All else being equal, the department with one officer cars will tend to cover more territory than the other because it relies on more separate patrol units. Like my measure of environmental dispersion, this variable tramples on the complexity of spatial dynamics in large municipal police organizations. Nevertheless, on its face, it seems to be a valid measure of patrol coverage.

Spatial differentiation is composed of two separate measures: number of police stations, and the number of patrol beats. Because the patrol beat measure has such a low response rate and other assorted problems, chapter 7 will address a number of methodological issues regarding spatial differentiation. We now examine the various modes of structural coordination and control that are used by large municipal police organizations.

Structural Control and Coordination

According to the theoretical model described in chapter 4, there are three distinct elements of structural control and coordination: centralization, formalization, and administrative density. Each of these will now be explored in further detail.

Centralization. Centralization was measured in the supplemental survey using an index that was adapted from Robbins (1987, pp. 491–493). Respondents were asked to complete twenty questions about the levels in the organization where decisions are made. The point of the questions was to determine whether the police chief executive and his or her *immediate* subordinates make all important decisions in the organization, or whether lower level supervisors have the discretion to make some strategic and operational decisions as well. Ten of the questions covered the range of decisions made by the chief executive and his or her immediate subordinates ("senior management"), and ten covered the range of decisions made by the lowest-level supervisor, who in most police organizations is a sergeant. Response categories were coded as Likert scales, with a 0 indicating low centralization and a 4 indicating high centralization. The individual responses were then combined to form an overall centralization scale with a possible range of values from 0 (low centralization, or high decentralization) to 80 (high centralization, low decentralization). Table 6.5 lists the responses to the ten questions on decision

Table 6.5
Locus of Decision Making by Senior Management

To what extent would top management* make actual decisions (not just signing off) in the following areas?

(a = never, b = rarely, c = sometimes, d = often, e = always)

#	Type of Decision	a	b	c	d	e	Mean (a = 0, e = 4)
1	Adoption of new programs (e.g., DARE, or gun safety programs)?	0.5%	2.8%	6.4%	21.7%	68.6%	3.55
2	Adoption of new personnel policies (e.g., dress codes)?	1.0%	2.8%	9.4%	16.8%	69.9%	3.52
3	Creating a new specialized unit (e.g., a missing children's unit, or a drunk driving unit)?	0.5%	3.8%	8.2%	14%	73.5%	3.56
4	Establishing the content and methods for training employees?	0.3%	10.9%	30%	32.3%	26.5%	2.74
5	Selecting the type or brand of new equipment?	2.8%	13%	28.5%	30.5%	25.2%	2.62
6	Selecting the suppliers of materials to be used?	10.4%	29.3%	29%	18.3%	13%	1.94
7	Setting priorities about what criminal offenses the department should focus its resources on?	1%	3.1%	20.4%	40.2%	35.4%	3.06
8	Setting priorities about what geographic areas in the community the department should focus its resources on?	1.5%	3.1%	25.4%	39.7%	30.3%	2.94
9	Setting standards for measuring department performance?	2.3%	6.4%	15.3%	28.2%	47.8%	3.13
10	Controlling the release of information to the media?	1.3%	8.4%	25.5%	33.9%	30.9%	2.85

*Top management includes the chief executive position, and those that report *directly* to the chief executive.

Table 6.6
Locus of Decision Making by First-Line Supervisors

How much discretion does the typical first-line supervisor* have in the following areas?
(a = total, b = great, c = some, d = little, e = none)

#	Type of Decision	a	b	c	d	e	Mean (a = 0, e = 4)
1	Establishing his or her unit's budget?	1%	2.8%	23.7%	31.3%	41.2%	3.09
2	Determining how his or her unit's performance will be evaluated?	1%	16%	43.8%	21.9%	17.3%	2.38
3	Hiring and firing personnel?	1.5%	5.3%	15.5%	24.2%	53.4%	3.23
4	Personnel rewards (i.e., salary increases, promotions)?	1%	7.9%	19.1%	20.4%	51.7%	3.14
5	Personnel discipline (i.e., suspensions, warnings)?	1.5%	36.6%	43.8%	13.7%	4.3%	1.83
6	Purchasing of equipment and supplies?	1%	8.7%	39.7%	28.2%	22.4%	2.62
7	Establishing a new project or program?	0.8%	14.2%	53.4%	22.6%	8.9%	2.25
8	Alter shift schedules of front-line employees?	4.1%	22.4%	30.5%	23.9%	19.1%	2.32
9	Authorize overtime for front-line employees?	10.9%	45%	31.6%	6.4%	6.1%	1.52
10	Allocation of work among available workers?	20.4%	51.7%	22.1%	4.1%	1.8%	1.15

*First-line supervisors include those with direct responsibility for supervising front-line employees.

making by senior management, and Table 6.6 lists the responses to the ten questions on decision making by front-line supervisors.

Of the 432 police agencies in the sample, 393 provided sufficient information to form the centralization scale (91%). The lowest centralization score was 21, and the highest was 77, with a mean and median of approximately 53. The 20 items appear to cluster well together, with an alpha reliability coefficient of (0.798). Summary statistics for the centralization scale are reported in Table 6.1.

Formalization. Formalization is an additive index consisting of responses to 13 separate binary questions in the 1993 LEMAS survey asking whether the department has a formal written policy or directive on a number of subjects, including the use of deadly force, the handling of domestic violence cases, off-duty employment, pursuit driving, and several other areas. Table 6.7 provides a list of the questions used to form the index and a summary of the responses. An agency with a 0 on the index would have none of the formal written policies listed, while a score of 7 indicates that the department has

Table 6.7
Percentage of Agencies with Certain Formal Written Policies

Does your agency have written directives on the following?
(N = 425)

	% Yes	% No
Use of deadly force/firearm discharge policy	99.5%	0.5%
Handling mentally ill/ handicapped	82.8%	17.2%
Handling the homeless	30.1%	69.9%
Handling domestic disturbances/ spousal abuse	94.8%	5.2%
Handling juveniles	97.4%	2.6%
Pursuit driving	99.3%	0.7%
Relationship with private security firms (information exchange/processing of detainees and arrestees, etc.)	29.2%	70.8%
Off-duty employment of sworn personnel	95.8%	4.2%
Strip searches	78.8%	21.2%
Code of conduct and appearance	98.8%	1.2%
Use of confidential funds (e.g., "buy" money for drug purchases)	82.4%	17.6%
Employee counseling assistance	84.9%	15.1%
Citizen complaints	98.8%	1.2%

written policies governing 7 of the 13 specific subject areas. Of the 432 agencies in the sample, 425 (98.8%) provided sufficient information to form the formalization index used in this study. The minimum score reported was 6, the maximum score was 13, and the mean and median were approximately 11. Summary statistics for this variable are available in Table 6.1.

Administrative Intensity. Administrative intensity is the percentage of full-time actual employees whose primary function is the completion of administrative tasks. In the organizational literature, administrative personnel are generally contrasted with production personnel, whose main function is the completion of the agency's primary tasks.[35] Administrative personnel are the supportive component of the organization. They are the personnel who only contribute indirectly to the organization's production or service function.

This study relies on a measure of administrative intensity from the 1993 LEMAS survey. The LEMAS survey instrument asks respondents to list the number of full-time actual (as opposed to authorized) employees in six areas: administration, field operations, technical support, jail operations, court operations, and other. The survey instrument suggests that the administration category should include the chief executive and his or her assistants, and all other personnel who work in an administrative capacity, including finance, personnel, and internal affairs. The survey intrument also suggests that the technical support category should include dispatchers, clerks, and other personnel providing support services, including communications and training. Together, the jobs that the LEMAS survey describes as administration and technical support positions are the precise types of functions that comprise an organization's administrative component. The measure of administrative intensity used in this study is computed by summing the number of personnel in these two categories and dividing by the total number of full-time employees in the organization. The result of this computation is the proportion of employees who work in an administrative or support function.[36]

Respondents to the LEMAS survey provided sufficient data to compute a measure of administrative intensity for 425 of the 432 sample agencies (98.8%). Administrative intensity ranges from 2% to 62%, with a mean and median of 24%. The range is fairly well distributed up through about 45%, and then there are two outliers: New Brunswick, New Jersey with 50%, and Long Beach, California with 62%. Whether or not these outliers are errors is unknown. Descriptive statistics for administrative intensity are listed in Table 6.1.

Conclusion

This chapter has outlined in detail all of the data sources and the variables that are used in this study. Data are drawn from numerous sources, all contemporaneous at or about 1993, and then combined at the agency level by the use of a unique FBI code assigned to all police agencies. Combining all of these separate data sources produces a rich data set on large municipal police agencies in the United States. However, because agencies respond to some surveys and not others, many departments have missing data on one or more of the variables described in this chapter. When I test the full multivariate model, any agencies with missing data on one of the primary measures will be excluded from the analysis. This is the pitfall of combining multiple data sources, and whether there is any pattern in the types of agencies that have missing data remains to be explored. Chapter 7 will examine the issue of sample selection bias in detail, in order to determine whether the types of agencies left in or out of the sample will bias the findings.

This chapter has also provided detailed descriptive statistics about large municipal police organizations in the United States. Although much of this information is not interesting theoretically, some practitioners and researchers might find value in these figures. Detailed descriptive data on the structures of American police organizations has not been available since the early 1970s, thus this information represents the current state-of-the-art on police organizational structure. Large municipal police organizations vary in many ways: the number of police stations ranges from 1 to 76; the number of beats from 3 to over 1,000; the number of ranks from 4 to 12; the number of special units from 0 to 13. Chapter 5 outlined a theoretical model that might explain some of this variation. In chapter 7 I will test that model.

CHAPTER 7

Testing the Theory

Using structural equation models, this chapter tests the full multivariate theory of police organizational structure outlined in chapter 5 using the survey data described in chapter 6. While this chapter presents some fairly technical material, I urge readers to try wading through the statistics presented in this chapter rather than skipping around them to the final chapter. Even readers with very little knowledge of statistics will gain a new appreciation for the close relationship between theory, data, and statistics from reading this chapter. I have tried to dilute as much of the technical material as possible. Some graduate students have already found the entry-level description of both structural equation modeling specifically, and theory-testing more generally, to be very helpful. I hope new readers will have the same experience.

The chapter begins by introducing structural equation models and describing their applicability to the present theory of police organizational structure. Next, a number of structural equation models are estimated, together with a detailed discussion of how well these models fit the sample data. Next, I explore whether there is any latent sample selection bias in the sample of police agencies represented in this analysis. Finally, I integrate the results of all analyses and discuss the implications of these findings for the theory outlined in chapter 5. The analyses presented in this chapter represent a unique contribution to two literatures: the study of the police, and the study of complex organizations.

Structural Equation Modeling

Structural equation modeling (SEM) is a general term used to describe a set of statistical techniques for estimating the parameters of causal models with one or more latent, or unobserved variables. SEM can be thought of as a combination and extension of two common analytical methods used by social scientists—path analysis and factor analysis— and is most easily introduced by explaining these techniques (Carmines, 1986; Loehlin, 1992). For reasons that will become obvious, SEM is also referred to as latent variable modeling (Loehlin, 1992), analysis of covariance structures (Carmines, 1986), and to a lesser extent, analysis of moment structures (Arbuckle, 1997).[1] I begin by introducing path models and factor analysis, and then discuss how SEM is a logical extension of these common techniques. Readers familiar with these topics should skip ahead to the section entitled "A Theoretical Model of Police Organizational Structure" (p. 186).

Path Analysis

Path analysis is a technique used for graphically expressing the numerical relationships and causal order among a set of variables. Path models were first developed in the early twentieth century by American geneticist Sewell Wright (e.g., Wright, 1934), and later applied to the social sciences by sociologist Otis Dudley Duncan in the early 1960s (e.g., Duncan, 1966). Since the early work by Duncan and others, path models have become a basic element in the social scientist's statistical tool kit.

Figure 7.1 shows a hypothetical path model with three variables: two independent variables, A and B, and a single dependent variable, C. This might be the model we would specify based on a hypothetical theory that police officers with negative attitudes and low job satisfaction are the ones who will generate the highest number of complaints against them by citizens. The path from A to C represents the direct effect of attitude on the number of complaints. Similarly, the path from B to C represents the direct effect of job satisfaction on number of complaints. The curved arrow from A to B represents the unanalyzed correlation between A and B. We use the term "unanalyzed" because the relationship between A and B is due to variables that lie outside the model, and that presumably are not theoretically important. Note that the causal order in this example runs from left to right, and therefore according to the specified model, C cannot "cause" A or B.[2] We call a path model with unidirectional causation a "recursive" model. Nonrecursive models can be specified and estimated, but they are computationally complex.

When we "estimate" a path model such as the one illustrated in Figure 7.1, we typically use ordinary least squares regression to calculate the strength of all the linear relationships that are specified by the model, and then place the resulting coefficients on each path, as illustrated in Figure 7.2. The unanalyzed correlation between A and B in this hypothetical example is (0.3). The numbers placed above the two direct paths are standardized regression coefficients that summarize the independent effects of A and B on C. All three coefficients have p-values associated with them to test the hypothesis that the coefficient is significantly different from zero.

A = attitudes (negative to positive)
B = job satisfaction (low to high)
C = number of citizens' complaints

Figure 7.1
Example of a Basic Path Model

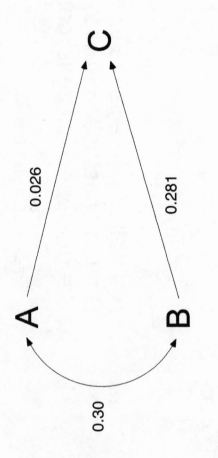

R-squared = 0.27
p = 0.02

Figure 7.2
Example of a Path Model with Coefficients

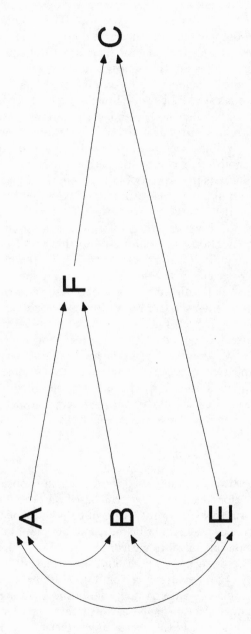

E = Courteousness
F = Number of Times Force Used

Figure 7.3
Example of Alternative Model Specification

In addition, we calculate a squared multiple correlation coefficient, or R^2, to estimate the amount of variance in C that is explained by A and B.

Another path model is shown in Figure 7.3. This alternative model was made more complex than the others to illustrate three additional concepts that are integral to understanding structural equation models: indirect effects, exogenous variables, and endogenous variables. Two variables, E and F, have been added to the model. A, B, and E are known as exogenous variables because none of them is "caused" by any other variable within the model, and these variables are all linked by curved paths representing unanalyzed correlations. F and C are called endogenous variables because they are dependent on other causal variables in the model. The compound paths from A to F to C, and B to F to C, both illustrate the notion of indirect effects. This alternative model specification indicates that attitudes (A) and job satisfaction (B) do not influence the number of complaints (C) directly, rather they affect the frequency with which officers use force against citizens (F), which in turn directly affects the number of complaints. Thus, A and B are said to have an indirect effect on C through F. The path from E to C represents the direct effect of courteousness on the number of complaints. Note that E has no direct influence on F. To estimate this path model using ordinary least squares regression, we would need to estimate separate regression models for the two endogenous variables: one in which A and B are used to predict F, and another in which E and F are used to predict C. We would calculate squared multiple correlation coefficients for the two endogenous variables to estimate the amount of variance explained in each by the variables specified in the path model. The equations used to estimate the parameters of each separate causal model are known as "structural" equations.

Factor Analysis

Factor analysis is a statistical technique used to examine how observed (measured) variables cluster together in patterns based on other unobserved (unmeasured) variables. Factor analysis is often used to measure abstract theoretical variables that cannot be measured directly, but that can be estimated based on one or more measurable variables. Analysts frequently distinguish between exploratory and confirmatory factor analysis. In exploratory factor analysis, researchers examine a set of variables to find any empirical patterns and relationships among the variables.[3] In confirmatory factor analysis, researchers specify the expected relationships up front and then confirm whether the theoretical model fits the data. Structural equation modeling uses techniques similar to confirmatory factor analysis for specifying measurement models for latent variables.

Although confirmatory factor analysis is a complex technique, its basic principles are a simple extension of path analysis. Factor analysts draw a distinction between observed variables, or indicators, and unobserved, or latent variables. Consider Figure 7.4, which illustrates how the concept of job satisfaction discussed in Figures 7.1 to 7.3 is a latent variable composed of four measured indicators, b_1 to b_4. According to this model, we cannot measure job satisfaction directly, but we can estimate its level by measuring these four indicators of job satisfaction. Observe that unlike the previous path models we have discussed, this model contains an unknown, B, which must be estimated based on the values of b_1 to b_4. Because such models are concerned with the measurement of latent variables, they are known as "measurement" models.

Combining Path and Factor Analyses

The techniques used to estimate the parameters of path (structural) models and factor (measurement) models were developed separately from one another. Thus, prior to the emergence of structural equation modeling, researchers could not estimate the structural and measurement portions of a model simultaneously (Carmines, 1986). To estimate the causal relationships among latent variables, analysts had to factor analyze a set of measured indicator variables to obtain a single composite score for each latent variable, and then introduce these composite scores as variables in a path model. Carmines (1986, p. 24) argues that:

> . . . [t]he problems with this approach, however, are severe and readily apparent. Theoretically, this procedure treats measurement and causal inferences as completely separate and distinct instead of intimately related to one another. Methodologically, the approach is essentially ad hoc and lacks an explicit statistical justification. As a result, the properties of the parameter estimates derived from this procedure are unknown.

Since path analysis does not distinguish between concepts and indicators, it is unable to account for measurement error in observed variables. Analysts using this technique have had to either: (1) use observed variables in place of latent variables within a path model, thus making the untenable assumption that all variables in the model are measured perfectly; or (2) use the two-step method described above, generating single factor composites from multiple indicators and introducing them as variables into a path model. Both of these options are problematic.

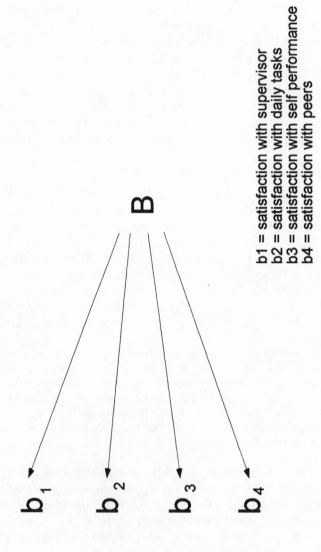

b1 = satisfaction with supervisor
b2 = satisfaction with daily tasks
b3 = satisfaction with self performance
b4 = satisfaction with peers

Figure 7.4
Example of a Factor Model

According to Alwin (1986, p. 73), errors in the measurement model introduce bias into estimates of structural parameters, and therefore they should be modeled into the system of structural equations and estimated simultaneously. Based on this approach, structural equation modeling emerged as the solution to the problem of estimating causal models with latent variables.

Structural Equation Models

SEM was first developed in the late 1960s and early 1970s by Swedish psychometrician Karl G. Jöreskog and his colleagues (Hayduk, 1987), and made available to the social science community with his popular Linear Structural Relations (LISREL) computer program for estimating SEM models (Jöreskog and Sörbom, 1989). Although much of the early work in structural equations was done using LISREL, many other programs have appeared since, including EQS (Bentler, 1989); CALIS (SAS Institute, 1990), which is affiliated with SAS; AMOS (Arbuckle, 1997), which is now a component of SPSS; and M-Plus, a newcomer from Muthén and Muthén (1998).

SEM combines the structural (causal) features of path modeling with the measurement features of factor analysis, and is therefore useful for estimating causal models with latent variables. Structural equation models estimate the structural and measurement portions of a model simultaneously, allowing the analyst to model measurement and equation error into the system of structural equations, therefore avoiding the problems described in the previous section. In addition, SEM allows the analyst to customize the model in a number of helpful ways: fixing or constraining model coefficients to equal either 0 or one another (or other theoretically meaningful constraints); investigating the possibility of correlated error terms or reciprocal causation; and performing a variety of complex computational tasks within a single analytical framework. Because they are applicable to so many different analytical problems faced by social scientists, structural equation models are now used frequently in a number of fields, including sociology, criminology, and criminal justice.[4]

Covariance Structures. The practice of estimating structural equation models is sometimes referred to as the analysis of covariance structures, or covariance structure modeling. To understand structural equation modeling, it is necessary to have a basic knowledge of covariances and correlations. A covariance, like a correlation, is used to summarize the linear relationship between two variables. The difference between a correlation and a covariance is that the former is standardized and the latter is unstandardized. To obtain a correlation (r) from a covariance (Cov), simply divide the covariance between x and y ($Cov_{x,y}$) by the product of the standard deviations of x and y ($s_x s_y$). Similarly, to obtain a covariance from a correlation, multiply the product of the standard deviations of x and y ($s_x s_y$) by the correlation between x and y ($r_{x,y}$). These formulas are presented below:

$$r_{x,y} = Cov_{x,y} / s_x s_y \quad \text{and} \quad Cov_{x,y} = r_{x,y} \times s_x s_y$$

We say that a correlation coefficient is standardized because it always ranges from -1 to +1, regardless of the units of the variables being measured. The closer the correlation between two variables comes to 0, the weaker the linear relationship between them; the closer to +1 or −1, the stronger the linear relationship. Unlike the correlation, the values of the covariance depend on the units of measurement of the variables. Two variables will have the same correlation whether they are measured in inches, centimeters, or feet, but their covariance will differ with each unit of measurement. Structural equation models rely heavily on the covariances between variables to estimate model parameters.

The relationships among a set of variables can be expressed in the form of a variance-covariance matrix (hereafter referred to as a covariance matrix). Every row and column in a covariance matrix represents a single variable. Therefore, to find the covariance between any pair of variables in a covariance matrix, one must simply locate the intersection of the row and column for each variable. The diagonal of the matrix lists the variance of each variable, since the covariance of any variable with itself is its variance. The first step in estimating a structural equation model is to develop a covariance matrix that summarizes the relationships among all variables in the model. Most SEM computer programs will automatically compute the covariance matrix summarizing the linear relationships between the variables in the model. This is known as the sample (or actual) covariance matrix, and is designated here as S.

To estimate a structural equation model, the analyst must then specify the form of the relationships among the variables in the model, as illustrated partially in Figures 7.1 through 7.4. Theory dictates how a model should be specified, and analysts employing structural equation models are implored by SEM textbook authors to rely heavily on theory when developing models (Hayduk, 1987; Schumacker and Lomax, 1996). In specifying the model, we make a number of crucial decisions based on our theory, including which indicators should be used to represent each latent variable, what unit of measurement to apply to the latent variables, what is the causal order between variables, which paths should be estimated (free), and which paths should be fixed or constrained to certain pre-set values such as 0. Once we specify a model, we are then ready to estimate its parameters using one of the widely available computer programs for estimating structural equation models.[5]

The model we specify implies a particular set of relationships among the variables, and these implied relationships can be represented in a covariance matrix. The model-implied covariance matrix is denoted as Σ (sigma). The goal of structural equation modeling is to develop a model (based on theory) that reproduces the sample covariance matrix S as closely as possible with the implied covariance matrix Σ, or to minimize Σ–S. A model that reproduces the sample covariance matrix closely is said to have a good fit. As we will discuss later, there are a number of different techniques for assessing "goodness of fit" in structural equation models. When we specify a model that fits the sample data well, we then conclude that because the model implied by our theory is capable of reproducing the actual relationships in the sample data, the theory is a valid description of the social reality that we are trying to model, or understand. If the model does not fit the data well, we must then determine whether the poor fit is due to poor model specification (problems with the theory), measurement error, sampling error, or some combination of these factors. With proper diagnosis, we can then make appropriate adjustments.

Having provided a basic introduction to structural equation modeling, I now describe the process of testing the theory outlined in chapter 5 using these techniques.

Testing a Theoretical Model of Police Organizational Structure

In this section, I test the theory of police organizational structure. I begin by reviewing a number of preliminary steps, ironing out any advanced measurement issues not covered in Chapter Six, and exploring several diagnostic issues including (1) testing for severe multicollinearity, (2) determining whether the variables in the model form a multivariate normal distribution, and (3) deciding the most appropriate estimation technique. I then estimate a separate structural equation model for each endogenous variable, assessing how well each model fits the data and whether these preliminary models explain a substantial amount of the variance in each endogenous variable. Next, I explore a number of alternative models to learn whether various modifications based on the initial findings might help to increase explained variance and/or model fit. Finally, I summarize the results obtained throughout the chapter.

Measurement Issues

Chapter 6 described the measurement of the eight exogenous and six endogenous concepts in the theoretical model. Five of the exogenous variables, including organizational age, task scope, task routineness, environmental capacity, and environmental instability, were explained sufficiently in chapter 6 and present no further measurement issues. Three of the variables, however, have more complex measurement issues that must be resolved before continuing. These variables include organizational size, which will be logged; environmental complexity, which is a latent variable with five (initial) indicators; and environmental dispersion, which is a product term. Similarly, four of the endogenous variables were explained sufficiently in chapter 6, including functional differentiation, centralization, administration, and formalization. Two of the variables require further discussion, including vertical and spatial differentiation, each of which is a latent variable with multiple indicators. The five variables requiring further explanation of measurement strategies will now be discussed in more detail.

Organizational Size. There has been some degree of controversy in the literature about whether organizational size should be expressed in raw score or logarithmic format. Criticizing the bulk of prior research, Kimberly (1976) argued that whatever choice analysts make regarding this issue, the decision should be explicitly justified on both theoretical and methodological grounds. Similarly, Klatzky (1970) argued that although a logarithmic curve fit his data well, it was not useful for explaining why the relationship between size and structure was curvilinear. Blau's (1970, p. 204) hypothesis that "increasing organizational size generates differentiation along various lines at decelerating rates" is a reasonable, though perhaps banal justification for assuming that a log transformation of organizational size is appropriate. Structure may simply be more sensitive to size differences in smaller organizations than in larger ones. In a department with 100 employees, the addition of 50 new officers may produce massive structural changes; in a department with 1,000 or 10,000 employees, an extra 50 officers may have little or no effect on structure.

In addition, there are a number of methodological reasons for log transforming organizational size. Kimberly (1976, p. 583) summarizes the three primary reasons reported in the literature for using a log transformation: "reducing the variance in the distribution of values of size across observations, testing a hypothesis of curvilinearity between size and one or more structural variables, and testing a theory in which size is hypothesized to be related with other variables in a multiplicative fashion." In addition to these reasons is a more practical consideration: a large body of research has confirmed that the relationship between size and structure resembles a logarithmic curve, not a straight line (Blau and Schoenherr, 1971; Child, 1973; Holdaway and Blowers, 1971; Hsu, Marsh, and Mannari, 1983). Finally, without the log transformation, size is highly skewed and leptokurtic, therefore contributing to a condition of multivariate non-normality, a problem which will be discussed later in the chapter. As shown in Figure 7.5, the natural log transformation does not completely cure the problems with skewness and kurtosis, but it does help to normalize the distribution somewhat. In addition, the log transformation of organizational size increases the correlation between size and structure for seven of the eight observed endogenous variables. The log transformation makes sense for a number of theoretical and methodological reasons.

Environmental Complexity. Chapter 6 described the general strategy used to measure environmental complexity, which is treated as a latent variable with multiple indicators. The five indicators measure differentiation in age, race, education, income, and occupation using the Gibbs-Martin D formula. Since these five variables are presumed to share a common latent cause, we begin by checking the zero-order correlation matrix for these variables (see Table 7.1) to see if they are all correlated with one another. Some of the correlations between variables are insignificant, and all of the insignificant correlations involve age and occupational differentiation.

Next, I estimate the initial measurement model with all five indicators. The model is overidentified with five degrees of freedom, thus there is sufficient information to solve for all unknown parameters. The results are illustrated in Figure 7.6 (Model A) with standardized regression coefficients (factor loadings) on each path, and reliabilities located above each indicator. According to the likelihood ratio statistic ($\chi^2 = 56.8$, df = 5, p < 0.000), the model fits the data poorly. It is customary practice in factor analysis to drop indicators with loadings less than

Table 7.1
Correlations Between Possible Indicators of Environmental Complexity

	D_{educ}	D_{income}	D_{race}	$D_{occupat}$
D_{income}	0.390 (p = 0.000)			
D_{race}	0.346 (p = 0.000)	0.386 (p = 0.000)		
$D_{occupat}$	0.065 (p = 0.184)	0.074 (p = 0.131)	0.206 (p = 0.000)	
D_{age}	−0.059 (p = 0.225)	0.091 (p = 0.063)	−0.178 (p = 0.000)	0.170 (p = 0.000)

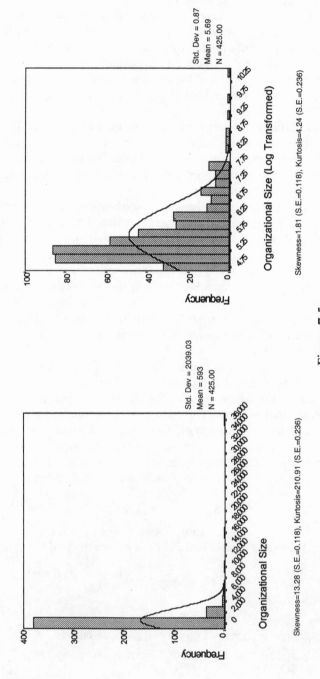

Figure 7.5

Histograms of Organizational Size Before and After Log Transformation

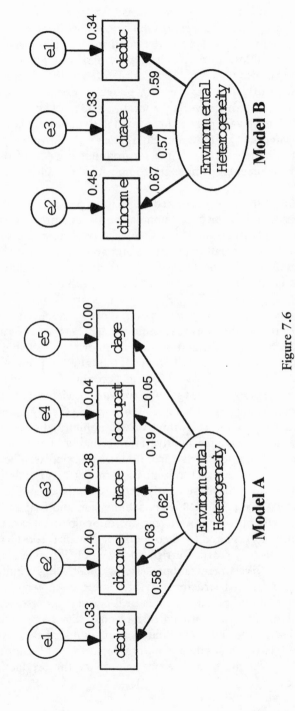

Figure 7.6
Alternative Measurement Models of Environmental Complexity

(.3) since they will contribute mostly measurement error to the model. Loadings for occupation and age are well below this threshold, so I first dropped age from the model, and after confirming that the loading for occupation was still low, I dropped it as well.[6] The resulting model with three indicators is also illustrated in Figure 7.6 (Model B). This model is just identified (0 df), so it fits the data perfectly. Environmental complexity explains 45% of the variance in D_{income}, 33% of the variance in D_{race}, and 34% of the variance in D_{educ}.[7] The reliability of the latent variable, as estimated using Heise and Bohrnstedt's (1970) omega coefficient, is approximately (0.64).[8] Thus, approximately 64% of the variance in the environmental complexity composite is reliable.

Environmental Dispersion. As stated in chapter 6, I selected a multiplicative interaction term between population (P) and area (A) to measure environmental dispersion. While the majority of communities in the sample have relatively small populations and areas, a handful are quite large. As a result, both P and A are skewed to the right and leptokurtic, and the product of their raw scores (PA) is even more severely skewed and leptokurtic (see Figure 7.7). Product terms are typically not normally distributed, and this tendency is even more pronounced when the components of the product term are nonnormal. There are several good reasons to transform this variable so that it is normally distributed: (1) to reduce the variance in the distributions of the values of P and A across observations (Kimberly, 1976); (2) to account for curvilinearity observed in scatterplots between PA and the various elements of organizational structure; and (3) allowing PA to remain severely nonnormal will contribute to a condition of multivariate nonnormality. As will be discussed later in this chapter, multivariate normality of the exogenous variables is an assumption of the maximum likelihood technique frequently used to estimate structural equation models, and violations of this assumption sometimes result in biased test statistics and standard errors (Arbuckle, 1997; Bollen, 1989b; Schumacker and Lomax, 1996).

Although complex product terms are difficult to interpret, their use is sometimes necessitated by theory and/or practical considerations of model estimation (Jaccard, Turrisi, and Wan, 1990). Theoretically, the effect of PA (like organizational size) probably has diminishing effects on organizational structure; beyond some unknown threshold level, the effects of additional increases in PA begin to decrease. On a more practical level, the nonnormal distribution of the raw product term contributes to a severe condition of multivariate nonnormality. To overcome both problems, I first take the natural logarithm of P and A separately, and then add the logged terms to produce the product term.[9]

Although the distributions of A, P, and PA are all severely nonnormal, the distribution of the transformed product term [ln (P × A)] is approximately normally distributed (see Figure 7.7). In addition, the log transformation of PA increases the correlation between environmental dispersion and structure for seven of the eight observed endogenous variables (for the one remaining endogenous variable, the correlation with ln[PA] is lower by only [0.003]). The log transformation of environmental dispersion makes sense for a number of theoretical and methodological reasons.

Vertical Differentiation. As described in several earlier chapters, there are three dimensions of vertical differentiation (Langworthy, 1986). First is height (*H*), which is the social distance from the top to the bottom of the organization. Second is segmentation or stratification (*S*), which is the number of separate command levels. Third is concentration (*C*), which focuses on the vertical distribution of workers throughout the command structure. Chapter 6 introduced the measures of these variables and suggested that they would be evaluated as potential indicators in a multiple indicator measurement model of vertical differentiation. Here we explore a number of theoretical, conceptual, and measurement issues related to vertical differentiation that make it difficult to select the best overall measure of the concept.

In the past, researchers have measured vertical differentiation (VertDiff) in many ways, but none to my knowledge has ever relied on a multiple indicator approach. The most popular measure of vertical differentiation is segmentation. A number of analysts have used *S* alone to measure VertDiff, including Beyer and Trice (1979); Blau and Schoenherr (1971); Dewar and Hage, 1978; and Hall, Haas, and Johnson (1967). The standardized pay differential, *H*, is less popular, but has been used alone to measure VertDiff by Evers, Bohlen, and Warren (1976); King (1999); and Maguire (1997). Langworthy (1986) used several variables *separately* to measure VertDiff, including *S*, *H*, and *C*. Similarly, Crank and Wells (1991) used *S* and *C* as independent measures.[10] Because nobody has explored these separate measures as indicators of a single latent concept, we have little knowledge about how they relate to one another. Before settling on an appropriate measurement model, it is crucial to explore whether the separate indicators appear to be related to a single latent variable.

The first step is to determine how well these variables relate to one another, since as indicators of a latent variable, they are presumed to share a common cause. The correlations between segmentation, height, and concentration (using both LowRank and D_{rank}) are shown in Table 7.2.

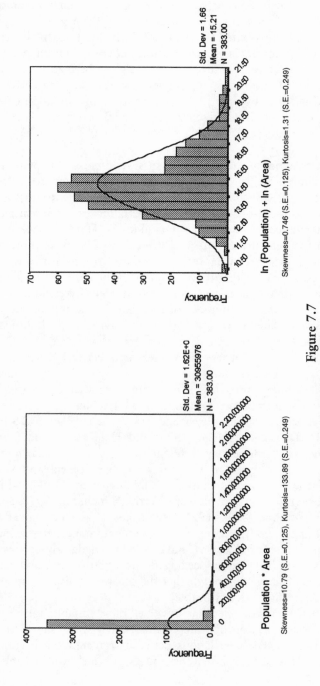

Figure 7.7
Histograms of Environmental Dispersion Before and After Log Transformation

Table 7.2
Correlations Between Possible Indicators of Vertical Differentiation

	Segmentation	Height	LowRank
Height	0.310 (p = 0.004)		
LowRank	–0.159 (p = 0.002)	–0.009 (p = 0.856)	
D_{rank}	0.145 (p = 0.004)	–0.000 (p = 0.999)	–0.962 (p = 0.000)

LowRank and D_{rank}, the alternative indicators of concentration, have a zero order correlation of (–0.96). These alternative measures also have very similar correlations with segmentation and height, suggesting that they are essentially interchangeable measures of concentration. Although LowRank is a far more intuitive measure, D_{rank} takes advantage of more information (the distribution of personnel throughout the rank structure rather than at a single level), and will be used in all subsequent discussions. The largest correlation between the remaining three indicators is between height and segmentation, the two most popular measures of vertical differentiation (r = 0.31). The correlation between D_{rank} and height is approximately 0, yet the correlation between D_{rank} and segmentation is (0.145). In general, we would expect variables sharing a common cause to have high intercorrelations, yet D_{rank} is uncorrelated with height. The small correlation between D_{rank} and segmentation is probably due, in part, to the fact that segmentation is used in the calculation of the D_{rank} score.[11] From examining the intercorrelations, it appears that concentration does not share a common cause with segmentation and height.[12]

Before deciding which measures should be used as indicators, I will attempt to estimate two alternative measurement models, as shown in Figure 7.8. Model A contains segmentation, height, and D_{rank}; model B contains only segmentation and height. Model A is just-identified, with 0 degrees of freedom. Estimating model A using maximum likelihood produces an inadmissible solution. One of the error variances is negative, and some of the standardized regression coefficients and squared multiple correlation coefficients are out-of-range. Estimating the measurement model in the context of a larger structural model (to increase degrees of freedom) produces similar results. Model B is under-identified (-1 df), with too little information in the model to estimate a unique solution. However, the measurement model can be estimated in the context of a larger structural model, since the additional information contributed by the structural portion of the model increases the degrees of freedom and allows the estimation of the unknown parameters. As I will

Model A

Model B

Figure 7.8
Alternative Measurement Models of Vertical Differentiation

demonstrate shortly when I estimate the structural equation models, Model B is clearly superior to model A. Concentration, either measured as LowRank or D_{rank}, does not appear to share a common cause with segmentation and height.

Although concentration has been used by past researchers to measure vertical differentiation, the present analysis casts some doubt on its relationship with both the latent concept of vertical differentiation, and with segmentation and height, the primary indicators used to measure this concept. Intuitively, concentration does seem to be an element of an organization's vertical dimension. However, just as the length of a person's legs might contribute to their height, we would not use leg length to measure a person's overall height. Concentration is related to vertical differentiation, but it cannot be used as a measure of the overall dimension. The two most popular measures of vertical differentiation, segmentation and height, are the ones that should be used as indicators in a measurement model. The multiple indicator approach will allow me to estimate the reliability of these measures for the first time. Since the model alone is under-identified, however, I will discuss the reliability of the concept and the indicators once I begin to estimate the structural models.

Spatial Differentiation. As described in chapter 6, spatial differentiation is a latent variable with two indicators, number of patrol beats and number of full-time general purpose police stations (Langworthy, 1986). As with the revised measurement model of vertical differentiation, the model is under-identified (-1 df), which means it cannot be estimated alone because it does not contain enough information to calculate all unknown parameter estimates. Once the measurement model is placed within the context of a larger structural equation model, the extra information provided by the structural model will increase the degrees of freedom and allow the estimation of unknown parameters. The two indicators of spatial differentiation are severely skewed to the right and leptokurtic, and therefore must be normalized to decrease multivariate nonnormality. The skewness and kurtosis scores for the indicators are listed below:

- Police Stations: (Skewness = 9.44, S.E. = 0.123; Kurtosis = 119.02, S.E. = 0.246).
- Beats: (Skewness = 9.50, S.E. = 0.129; Kurtosis = 118.19, S.E. = 0.257).

To reduce the nonnormality of the distributions, I took the natural logarithm of each variable, resulting in the following skewness and kurtosis scores:

- Police Stations: (Skewness = 2.45, S.E. = 0.123; Kurtosis = 5.81, S.E. = 0.246).
- Beats: (Skewness = 1.71, S.E. = 0.129; Kurtosis = 4.08, S.E. = 0.257).

While the resulting distributions are clearly not normal, the log transformation did help to normalize the distributions somewhat. Because the model is under-identified, I will reserve further discussion of the measurement of spatial differentiation until I estimate the structural equation models.

Diagnostic Issues

Collinearity. One of the assumptions shared by ordinary regression models and structural equation models is that there is no perfect multicollinearity or linear dependency between the exogenous variables. In both types of models, strong multicollinearity results in unstable coefficients with large standard errors. In structural equation models, multicollinearity among the predictors often leads to an inadmissible or improper solution.[13] To diagnose multicollinearity, researchers frequently take two steps: examine the correlations between exogenous variables, and determine how much of the variance in each exogenous variable can be explained by the others. Diagnosing multicollinearity in the context of structural equations is slightly different than for ordinary regression models when one or more of the exogenous variables is unobserved. First, traditional Pearson correlation coefficients cannot be used to measure the linear relationship between two variables when one or both of the variables is unobserved. Second, since OLS is unable to estimate models with latent variables, it cannot be used to estimate the proportion of variance explained in each exogenous variable by the others. Since one of the exogenous variables in my model is unobserved (environmental complexity), both of these steps must be taken within a structural equation framework.

Table Fourteen shows the correlations between the eight exogenous variables. In diagnosing problems with collinearity, we should look closely at correlations greater than 0.8 or 0.9 (Berry and Feldman, 1985, p. 43; Hayduk, 1987, p. 176). In addition, at the bottom of Table 7.3 I list two values that are helpful for diagnosing collinearity: R^2 and the variance inflation factor (VIF). R^2 is the proportion of variance in each exogenous variable explained by the others, and VIF is calculated with the formula: $1/(1-R^2)$. Variance inflation factors above three generally warrant some level of caution, and VIFs of four or five usually indicate a problem with collinearity (Fisher and Mason, 1981). Two variables in

Table 7.3
Collinearity Diagnostics

	Organizational Size	Organizational Age	Task Scope	Task Non-Routineness	Environmental Capacity	Environmental Dispersion	Environmental Instability	Environmental Complexity
Organizational Size	1.00							
Organizational Age	0.410*	1.00						
Task Scope	0.197*	0.125*	1.00					
Task Non-Routineness	0.178*	0.052	0.033	1.00				
Environmental Capacity	0.166*	0.171*	0.032	−0.013	1.00			
Environmental Dispersion	0.819*	0.262*	0.101	0.139*	−0.002	1.00		
Environmental Instability	0.295*	0.198*	−0.050	−0.044	0.147*	0.188*	1.00	
Environmental Complexity	0.526*	0.568*	0.043	0.209*	−0.003	0.319*	0.217*	1.00
R^2	0.794	0.376	0.084	0.071	0.149	0.718	0.132	0.500
VIF	4.85	1.60	1.09	1.08	1.18	3.55	1.15	2.00

*$p < 0.05$

the model have a high variance inflation factor: organizational size (4.58), and environmental dispersion (3.55). The highest correlation is also between organizational size and environmental dispersion (r = 0.819). The reason for this high correlation is clear: cities with large territories and high populations have bigger police departments. Approximately 67% of the variance in each variable overlaps with the other (0.819² = 0.67). This level of shared variance is very high, and will require further attention throughout the remainder of the analysis. For now, I will proceed on the assumption that it is probably not large enough to require respecification of the model. The remaining pattern of large correlations between organization age, organization size, environmental dispersion, and population complexity suggests that larger cities also tend to have larger, older police departments (most likely because the cities themselves are older, though such data are unavailable) and more diverse populations. The low VIFs for these variables suggest that they will not present a collinearity problem. Given the strong relationship between organizational size and environmental dispersion, I will continue to discuss collinearity throughout the remainder of the chapter.

The Assumption of Multivariate Normality. Maximum Likelihood (ML) is the most widely used method for estimating structural equation models, though a handful of other estimators are available as well. One of the assumptions of ML is that the variables in the model form a multivariate normal distribution. Univariate normality of the individual variables in the model is a necessary condition for multinormality, but not a sufficient condition. Because multivariate normality takes into account the covariances between variables, a model in which all variables are univariate normal might still be multivariate nonnormal, though this would probably not happen very often in practice. Although ML is fairly robust to some level of nonnormality, excessive violations of the multinormality assumption result in biased test statistics and standard errors, thus influencing significance tests for overall model fit and individual parameter estimates (Benson and Fleischman, 1994; Bollen and Stine, 1993; Hayduk, 1987, p. 230; Schumacker and Lomax, 1996, p. 104). Research has demonstrated that such problems generally arise as result of multivariate kurtosis rather than skewness, though the two are generally correlated (Bentler, 1997; Bollen, 1989b; Browne, 1984). Therefore, Mardia's (1970) coefficient of multivariate kurtosis is most often used to test the normality assumption (Arbuckle, 1997; Schumacker and Lomax, 1996).

There are a number of techniques for dealing with multivariate nonnormality in structural equation models. These include deleting outliers from the analysis, using an alternative estimation technique (other than ML), transforming the units of the variables, or correcting biased test-statistics and standard errors for nonnormality. Because there is such diversity in the size and structure of police agencies in the United States, there are a number of agencies that appear as outliers in the distributions of several variables in the model. Very large police agencies such as New York, Chicago, Los Angeles, and Detroit appear repeatedly as outliers. I am reluctant to trim these outliers from the analysis because they represent the very kind of variation that I am seeking to explain in this study.

The second option is to use an estimator other than ML. Asymptotically Distribution Free (ADF) estimators have no distributional assumptions, so they can be used to estimate models with nonnormal data. Monte Carlo (simulation) research has shown that while ML and ADF produce similar parameter estimates, ML chi-squares and standard errors are more biased than ADF estimates. On the other hand, ADF requires a large sample size (Schumacker and Lomax, 1996, p. 104), and simulation research has consistently shown that it produces incorrect estimates with small samples (Chan, Yung, and Bentler, 1995; Chou, Bentler, and Satorra, 1991; Curran, West, and Finch, 1996; Henly, 1993; Kaplan, 1991; Muthen and Kaplan, 1992). In addition, the ADF fit function is computationally intensive and often fails to produce estimates for complex models (Curran, West, and Finch, 1996; Muthen and Kaplan, 1992). Efforts to modify the fit function have not produced improvements in the performance of ADF estimates (Chan, Yung, and Bentler, 1995). Because of these shortcomings, ADF does not appear to be a viable option for estimating the models in this study.

The third option is to transform the units of measurement for variables that are not univariate normal. Log transformations are frequently helpful for reducing the variance of variables with large outlier values, thereby "normalizing" otherwise nonnormal distributions. Although log transformations make it difficult to interpret parameter estimates, the researcher can always estimate the model with a log term and later convert the data into their original form (Hagle, 1995). Despite the appeal of log transformations, critics have warned that they imply a particular functional form that should make sense theoretically (Kimberly, 1976). As described earlier in this chapter, I transformed some of the variables in the model using the natural logarithm.

The last way of dealing with violations of the multinormality assumption is to estimate the model using maximum likelihood, but then to correct biased test statistics and standard errors for nonnormality. One method of correcting for nonnormality is bootstrapping, which is defined by Schumacker and Lomax (1996, p. 193) as follows:

The bootstrapping approach treats a random sample of data as a substitute for the population and resamples from it a specified number of times to generate sample bootstrap estimates and standard errors. These sample bootstrap estimates and standard errors are averaged and used to obtain a confidence interval around the average of the bootstrap estimates. This average is termed a bootstrap estimator. The bootstrap estimator and associated confidence interval are used to determine how stable or good the sample statistic is as an estimate of the population parameter . . .

Bollen and Stine (1993) describe a bootstrap resampling technique for correcting biased chi-square values that has now been implemented in the AMOS program (Arbuckle, 1997). They argue that "naive" bootstrapping of the original sample will produce incorrect estimates of bias and that the data must be transformed before bootstrapping. Their recommended technique is now referred to in the literature as the Bollen-Stine correction procedure. In addition, most of the major SEM programs now contain bootstrap resampling techniques that can be used to correct the standard errors of parameter estimates for nonnormality. Because these bootstrap correction procedures re-estimate the standard errors of parameter estimates, they enable the researcher to use significance tests in the face of multivariate nonnormality.

The EQS program (pronounced "X") for estimating structural equation models contains another technique used to correct ML estimates for nonnormality: an optional "robust" maximum likelihood estimator. For nonnormal data with a small N, the program uses the Satorra-Bentler technique to correct biased chi-square test statistics, and a robust estimator to correct standard errors (Bentler, 1997; Chou, Bentler, and Satorra, 1991). Because bootstrapping generally requires a large sample, the Satorra-Bentler χ^2 is probably a better alternative for nonnormal data with a small sample. Simulation research has shown that with nonnormal data, the $SB\chi^2$ provides better estimates than ML or ADF (Chou, Bentler, and Satorra, 1991; Curran, West, and Finch, 1996). In addition, "the $SB\chi^2$ had the desirable property of simplifying to the $ML\chi^2$ under multivariate normality" (Curran, West, and Finch, 1996, p. 27). At the time the models in this book were estimated, the $SB\chi^2$ was only available in the EQS program. Since then, both LISREL and M-Plus have implemented new methods for dealing with nonnormality.

Because large municipal police agencies vary so widely in context, complexity, and control, many of the models that are estimated in the following section do violate the multinormality assumption. Four techniques were described for dealing with this problem, and many of these will be explored in further detail in the coming pages. I now estimate a number of initial structural equation models. We will return to the multi-normality issue many times throughout the remainder of the chapter.

Initial Model Estimation

In this section I estimate initial structural equation models for each of the six endogenous variables. The software package that I use to estimate the models is called AMOS (version 3.61), which stands for Analysis of Moment Structures (Arbuckle, 1996). AMOS allows the analyst to specify a structural equation model using traditional path notation, and offers all of the major benefits of other popular SEM packages (like EQS and LISREL), including every major goodness of fit index, modification indices, normality checks, and various other options.

The results for all six models are shown in Table 7.4. For every model, parameters and standard errors are estimated using normal-theory maximum likelihood (ML) which assumes that the data in the population follow a multivariate normal distribution (Curran, West, and Finch, 1996). As I will demonstrate, the sample data are *not* multinormal, and therefore it is important to explore the robustness of the ML estimates. Research has shown that under non-normality (especially non-zero kurtosis), ML parameter estimates are generally correct but the ML test-statistics and standard errors are biased (Benson and Fleischman, 1994; Curran, West, and Finch, 1996). I use bootstrapping to correct the biased test statistics and standard errors. The bootstrap estimates were derived by resampling (with replacement) from the sample data 250 times. The p-value for the χ^2 test of model fit has been recomputed using the Bollen-Stine correction procedure (Bollen and Stine, 1993). The differences between the ML and bootstrap estimates can be used to gauge the extent of bias introduced into the model by violating the multinormality assumption. To demonstrate the instability of ADF estimates with small samples, I also provide them for the first model (vertical differentiation) only.

Following the parameter estimates, at the bottom of Table 7.4 I provide a great deal of additional information useful for evaluating each model. First is the squared multiple correlation coefficient (R^2), which indicates the percentage of variance in the dependent variable that is explained jointly by the independent variables. Second is the likelihood ratio chi-square statistic, which summarizes how well the model fits the data. Large significant chi-squares indicate a poor fit, whereas small insignificant chi-squares indicate that the model fits the data well. Third is the chi-square divided by the degrees of freedom, which is often used

Table 7.4
Initial Structural Equation Models for all Endogenous Variables

NOTE: Metric coefficients are on the first line of each row, standard errors are on the second line in parentheses, and critical ratios are on the third line. ML = maximum likelihood and ADF = asymptotic distribution free estimator. Bootstrap corrections for standard errors and χ² are based on 250 samples. The Bollen-Stine (1993) correction procedure is used to adjust the significance level of the chi-square for nonnormality.

	Vertical Differentiation (N = 302)			Spatial Differentiation (N = 280)		Functional Differentiation (N = 306)		Centralization (N = 275)		Formalization (N = 276)		Administration (N = 276)	
	ML	ADF	Bootstrap	ML	Bootstrap	ML	Bootstrap	ML	Bootstrap	ML	Bootstrap	ML	Bootstrap
LogSize	0.657	0.554		0.616		1.21		-13.38		1.87		0.354	
	(0.106)	(0.141)	(0.151)	(0.047)	(0.057)	(0.344)	(0.408)	(22.64)		(3.08)		(0.438)	
	6.17	3.92		13.07		3.5		-0.591		0.606		0.806	
Age	0.004	0.002		0.001		-0.007		0.009		0.003		0.000	
	(0.002)	(0.001)	(0.002)	(0.001)	(0.001)	(0.005)	(0.006)	(0.058)		(0.008)		(0.001)	
	2.27	1.45		2.03		-1.28		0.151		0.375		0.277	
Task Scope	0.007	-0.008		0.001		0.054		-0.171		0.035		-0.002	
	(0.020)	(0.018)	(0.018)	(0.008)	(0.009)	(0.068)	(0.078)	(0.308)		(0.049)		(0.005)	
	0.33	-0.448		0.091		0.796		-0.556		0.726		-0.505	
Task Non-Routineness	-0.017	-0.016		0.005		0.110		-0.222		0.023		0.003	
	(0.009)	(0.008)	(0.009)	(0.003)	(0.003)	(0.029)	(0.032)	(0.252)		(0.034)		(0.004)	
	-1.96	-2.17		1.32		3.81		-0.884		0.680		0.837	
Environmental Capacity	-0.066	-0.039		-0.004		0.344		-0.001		0.128		-0.012	
	(0.054)	(0.051)	(0.055)	(0.021)	(0.020)	(0.181)	(0.182)	(0.900)		(0.137)		(0.013)	
	-1.21	-0.768		-0.21		1.91		-0.001		0.930		-0.945	

(continued on the next page)

Table 7.4 (continued)

	Vertical Differentiation (N = 302)			Spatial Differentiation (N = 280)		Functional Differentiation (N = 306)		Centralization (N = 275)		Formalization (N = 276)		Administration (N = 276)	
	ML	ADF	Bootstrap	ML	Bootstrap	ML	Bootstrap	ML	Bootstrap	ML	Bootstrap	ML	Bootstrap
Environmental Dispersion	-0.053	-0.017		0.035		0.191		-2.38		0.024		0.023	
	(0.045)	(0.053)	(0.060)	(0.017)	(0.017)	(0.15)	(0.176)	(1.41)		(0.197)		(0.026)	
	-1.18	-0.315		2.01		1.28		-1.68		0.123		0.893	
Environmental Instability	0.006	-0.020		0.025		-0.094		-0.707		0.075		0.013	
	(0.023)	(0.023)	(0.029)	(0.009)	(0.010)	(0.076)	(0.083)	(0.918)		(0.125)		(0.017)	
	0.27	-0.869		2.85		-1.24		-0.771		0.602		0.755	
Environmental Heterogeneity	0.635	0.796		-0.258		0.304		-6.65		-1.63		-0.161	
	(0.759)	(0.547)	(0.929)	(0.305)	(0.333)	(2.54)	(2.93)	(15.93)		(2.35)		(0.263)	
	0.837	1.46		-0.848		0.12		-0.418		-0.693		-0.613	
Vertical Differentiation								3.55		-0.343		-0.003	
								(3.51)		(0.546)		(0.027)	
								1.01		-0.629		-0.13	
Spatial Differentiation								23.06		-2.25		-0.546	
								(36.25)		(4.89)		(0.705)	
								0.636		-0.461		-0.774	
Functional Differentiation								-0.318		0.054		-0.000	
								(0.217)		(0.039)		(0.002)	
								-1.46		1.41		-0.008	

(continued on next page)

Table 7.4 (continued)

	Vertical Differentiation (N = 302)			Spatial Differentiation (N = 280)		Functional Differentiation (N = 306)		Centralization (N = 275)		Formalization (N = 276)		Administration (N = 276)	
	ML	ADF	Bootstrap	ML	Bootstrap	ML	Bootstrap	ML	Bootstrap	ML	Bootstrap	ML	Bootstrap
R^2	0.83	0.77	0.87	0.98		0.31	0.33	0.16		0.07		0.40	
χ^2	94.37 p=0.000	84.25 p=0.000	p=0.004	58.81 p=0.000	p=0.004	62.2 p=0.000	p=0.004	133.84 p=0.000		136.44 p=0.000		139.6 p=0.000	
χ^2/df	94.37 / 25 = 3.78			58.81 / 25 = 2.35		62.2 / 16 = 3.89		133.84 / 50 = 2.68		136.44 / 50 = 2.73		139.6 / 50 = 2.79	
GFI	0.952			0.967		0.966		0.945		0.944		0.943	
AGFI	0.851			0.898		0.861		0.85		0.847		0.845	
IFI	0.934			0.976		0.951		0.952		0.951		0.950	
CFI	0.932			0.975		0.948		0.951		0.949		0.947	
Kurtosis	15.83 (C.R.=7.5)			14.26 (C.R.=6.5)		11.11 (C.R.=5.7)		21.13 (C.R.=7.3)		18.79 (C.R.=6.5)		25.65 (C.R.=8.9)	

together with the chi-square to assess model fit.[14] Finally, I include a number of alternative goodness-of-fit indices.

Initially, researchers used only the significance level associated with the likelihood ratio chi-square to evaluate model fit. Unfortunately, "nearly all models they tested with reasonable sample sizes failed to fit the data according to the p-value of the χ^2 statistic" (Gerbing and Andersen, 1993, p. 41). Many new goodness-of-fit indices have been developed over the past two decades, and most SEM software programs enable the user to choose from a number of alternatives. AMOS, for instance, has approximately 20 such measures. I include 4 of these measures in Table 7.4: the goodness of fit index (GFI), the adjusted goodness of fit index (AGFI), the incremental fit index (IFI), and the comparative fit index (CFI). All of these measures range from 0 to 1 (except AGFI, which has no 0 lower bound), with scores closer to one indicating a good fit. The GFI and AGFI indices are included because they are among the more well-known measures of fit. The AGFI adjusts the GFI for the degrees of freedom available in the model, thus penalizing very complex models. The IFI and CFI indices are included because they were recommended in a review of fit indices by Gerbing and Andersen (1993). The derivations of these indices are beyond the scope of this study, but for a thorough review, see Gerbing and Andersen (1993) or Arbuckle (1997, p. 551–572). Using a number of different indices gives the analyst a much better impression of how well the model fits the data than using any single measure.

The last line of Table 7.4 contains Mardia's (1970) coefficient of multivariate kurtosis. The normal distribution has 0 kurtosis, so the further this coefficient is from 0, the greater the non-normality. There is very little indication in the literature how high kurtosis needs to be before it becomes problematic. Further study is clearly needed to determine the robustness of ML estimates under various levels of kurtosis, different sample sizes, and other varying conditions. This issue appears frequently in SEM research, and practical guidelines need to be developed that address the conditions under which multivariate kurtosis is problematic and when it might safely be ignored (Bollen, 1997). I now explore the results from estimating each model.

Vertical Differentiation. Recall from our prior discussion that the measurement model for vertical differentiation was underidentified because it contained only two indicators. In the context of the larger structural model (illustrated later in Figure 7.9), the parameters of the measurement model can now be estimated due to the increased degrees of freedom. The loading for height is (0.47) and the loading for segmentation is (0.69). Squaring these loadings reveals that 22% of the variance in height and 47% of the variance in segmentation is reliable, or accounted for by the latent variable. The reliability of the latent variable, as estimated using Heise and Bohrnstedt's (1970) Ω coefficient, is approximately (0.50). This is a very low level of reliability, and is one indication that the variables used to measure the vertical differentiation construct (both in this study and in the past) are not accounting for the full range of variance. With 50% of the variance in vertical differentiation unmeasured, it seems important for researchers to develop new indicators to reflect this latent concept.

Turning our attention to the structural model, we find only 3 of the 8 independent variables have a significant effect on vertical differentiation at the (p = 0.05) level: organizational size, organizational age, and nonroutineness of tasks.[15] Larger and older police organizations are more vertically differentiated than smaller and younger ones. Although the effect is borderline significant, police organizations that rely on less routine technologies are less vertically differentiated. While all of these effects are in the expected direction, neither task scope, nor any of the 4 environmental variables exert a strong effect on vertical differentiation. The bootstrap standard errors are larger than the ML standard errors for 5 of the 8 variables, and equal in another 2. This is one indication that the standard errors estimated using non-normal data are negatively biased, therefore increasing the critical ratios and statistical significance levels for predictor variables. While the ADF standard error estimates are similar to the ML and bootstrap standard errors, the ADF parameter estimates vary greatly, sometimes taking the opposite sign. The resulting critical ratios from the ADF estimates appear unstable as well. ADF has repeatedly been shown to generate incorrect estimates for small samples, and as suggested earlier, does not appear to be a good method to correct for nonnormality in this study.

The R^2 value indicates that the 8 predictor variables jointly explain 83% of the variance in vertical differentiation. According to the likelihood ratio χ^2 statistic and the χ^2/df, the model does not fit the data well, though the bootstrap corrected p-value demonstrates that the ML χ^2 was inflated due to nonnormality. The unadjusted alternative fit indices range from 0.932 to 0.952, suggesting that although the model might be a reasonable approximation, there is still room for improvement.

Spatial Differentiation. Recall from our prior discussion that like vertical differentiation, the measurement model for spatial differentiation was underidentified because it contained only 2 indicators. In the context of the larger model (illustrated later in Figure 7.10), the parameters of the measurement model can now be estimated due to the increased degrees of freedom. The loading for number of police stations is 0.81 and the loading for number of beats is 0.89, thus 66% percent of the variance in number of police stations and 80% of the variance in number of beats is reliable, or can be explained by the latent variable. In addition to the reliability of the indicators, we can also calculate the reliability of the latent variable. According to Heise and Bohrnstedt's (1970) omega coefficient, the spatial differentiation construct is reasonably reliable ($\Omega = 0.80$).

Focusing now on the full structural model, we find that 4 of the 8 predictors are statistically significant at the ($p = 0.05$) level: organizational size, organizational age, environmental dispersion, and environmental instability. Larger police organizations, older police organizations, those serving more dispersed environments, and those serving politically unstable environments tend to be more spatially differentiated. Bootstrapped standard errors are larger than ML standard errors for 4 of the 8 variables, and equal for another 3. Substituting the larger bootstrapped standard errors does not result in critical ratios lower than 2 for any of the 4 significant variables.

The R^2 value indicates that the 8 predictor variables jointly explain 98% of the variance in spatial differentiation. Again, the majority of this explanatory power can be attributed to organizational size. According to the likelihood ratio χ^2 statistic and the χ^2/df ratio, the model does not fit the data well, though the bootstrap corrected p-value demonstrates that the ML χ^2 was inflated due to nonnormality. The unadjusted alternative fit indices range from 0.967 to 0.976, the highest values among these 6 initial models. These indices suggest that the model reasonably approximates the data, although there is still some room to improve the fit of the model.

Functional Differentiation. Only 2 of the 8 predictors have a statistically significant effect on functional differentiation at the ($p = 0.05$) level: organizational size and task nonroutineness. Larger police organizations and those that perform nonroutine tasks are more functionally differentiated. While the effect of organizational size is in the expected direction, the effect of task nonroutineness is in the opposite direction suggested in earlier chapters. I predicted that as police organizations begin to embrace nonroutine community policing strategies, they would become less functionally specialized. This hypothesis is backed by a large body of normative literature on community policing that seeks to transform police agencies into squads of "uniformed generalists." However, this unexpected effect is not entirely suprising. In a recent study of structural change in large municipal police organizations, I found that despite normative rhetoric to the contrary, police agencies have become more specialized during the community policing era (Maguire, 1997). Further research is necessary to determine why police organizations are becoming more functionally differentiated if they are in fact adopting nonroutine technologies.

The R^2 value indicates that the eight predictors jointly explain 31% of the variance in functional differentiation. The χ^2 suggests that the model fits the data poorly, though the bootstrap corrected p-value for the χ^2 demonstrates that the uncorrected MLχ^2 was inflated due to nonnormality. The χ^2 adjusted for df is fairly low and indicates a reasonable fit. The unadjusted goodness of fit indices range from 0.948 to 0.976, implying that the model fits the data reasonably well but can be improved.

Centralization. None of the 8 predictors in the structural equation model for centralization is statistically significant. Bootstrapped standard errors are unavailable because AMOS was unable to generate 250 bootstrap samples. Bootstrapping generally requires large samples, and the sample size here is smaller and the model more complex than the previous 3 models. Bootstrapped standard errors would probably not have made much of a difference in calculating the critical ratios for the parameters in this model. For the 24 bootstrapped standard errors that have been estimated so far, 17 have been larger than the ML standard error, 5 have been equal, and only 2 have been slightly smaller. Thus, the available evidence suggests that even if bootstrap standard errors were available for this model, they would decrease the statistical significance of the predictors (by increasing the S.E. in the denominator of the critical ratio).

The R^2 value indicates that the predictors jointly account for 16% of the variance in centralization. The χ^2 suggests that the model fits the data poorly, though the χ^2/df ratio implies a more reasonable fit. Bollen-Stine corrections for the ML χ^2 are unavailable because the requisite bootstrap samples could not be generated. The unadjusted goodness of fit criteria range from 0.945 to 0.952, implying a somewhat reasonable fit that can be improved substantially.

Formalization. None of the 8 predictors in the structural equation model for formalization is statistically significant. As with the centralization model, bootstrapped standard errors are unavailable because AMOS was unable to generate 250 bootstrap samples. Again, if bootstrap standard errors were available for this model, they would probably have the effect of decreasing the statistical significance of the predictors.

The R^2 value indicates that the predictors jointly account for only 7% of the variance in formalization. The χ^2 suggests that the model fits the data poorly, though the χ^2/df ratio implies a more reasonable fit. Bollen-Stine corrections for the ML χ^2 are unavailable because the requisite bootstrap samples could not be generated. The unadjusted goodness of fit criteria range from 0.944 to 0.951, implying a somewhat reasonable fit with substantial room for improvement.

Administration. None of the 8 predictors in the structural equation model for administrative intensity is statistically significant. As with the models for centralization and formalization, bootstrapped standard errors are unavailable because AMOS was unable to generate 250 bootstrap samples. Again, if bootstrap standard errors were available for this model, they would probably have the effect of decreasing, rather than increasing the statistical significance of the predictors.

The R^2 value indicates that the predictors jointly account for 40% of the variance in administrative intensity. It is difficult to say why there is such a high R^2 value when none of the predictors are statistically significant. One possibility may be that the model is too complex for the sample size, resulting in unstable parameter estimates. I will explore this possibility in more depth later in the chapter. The χ^2 suggests that the model fits the data poorly, though the χ^2/df ratio suggests a more reasonable fit. Bollen-Stine corrections for the ML χ^2 are unavailable because the requisite bootstrap samples could not be generated. The unadjusted fit indices range from 0.943 to 0.950, implying a somewhat reasonable fit that can be significantly improved.

Recap of Initial Model Estimation. The 6 models that have been estimated so far presented a number of interesting issues. First, bootstrapping confirms for three of the models that in the presence of multivariate kurtosis, ML standard errors and χ^2 estimates were biased. ML standard errors were smaller than bootstrap standard errors in the majority of instances, therefore critical ratios computed with uncorrected ML estimates tended to be larger. In the presence of kurtotic data, one might find statistically significant effects that would not be so if the standard errors were corrected appropriately. Similarly, the Bollen-Stine corrected p-values for the ML χ^2 test statistic confirmed that the ML χ^2 is positively biased with nonnormal data. Curran, West, and Finch (1996) report that inflated ML chi-squares might lead to an inflated Type One error rate in which researchers end up rejecting models that fit the data well. Although bootstrap samples could not be computed for all of the models, the limited results confirm the types of bias found in other studies.

Another clear pattern emerging from the initial analyses is that the various types of structural complexity appear to be fairly predictable, whereas structural coordination and control mechanisms seem to be unrelated to all of the predictors used in this study. There is a possibility that the latter three models are unstable because they contain too many free parameters (those to be estimated), and not enough cases. A quick look at the last three models confirms that they are far more complex than the first three models. In addition, the sample sizes are slightly smaller. Although there is no strict rule, researchers generally suggest a ratio of 5 to 10 cases per free parameter.[16] For the first three models, the ratios are 5.7 for vertical differentiation, 5.3 for spatial differentiation, and 6.1 for functional differentiation. For the last three models, the ratios are approximately 3.2 for centralization, formalization, and administration. Clearly the last three models have far fewer free parameters per case and should be investigated further to determine whether the estimates are somewhat unstable. I explore this possibility in the next section.

Finally, none of the initial models estimated in this section fit the data very well. All of the p-values for the likelihood ratio χ^2 statistics, including those that were bias-corrected, were statistically significant, indicating a poor fit. Some of the alternative fit indices suggested a decent fit, but even these implied that there was substantial room for improvement. In the next section, I consider a number of modifications to these models that might improve their fit.

Modifying the Initial Models

Structural equation modelers frequently proceed as I have thus far: specifying and estimating an initial model, evaluating the fit of the model, and then attempting to improve the fit by making a variety of modifications to the initial model. The difficulty is determining how to improve the fit of the model in ways that make sense theoretically. Schumacker and Lomax (1996, p. 106) call this process a specification search: "The purpose of a specification search is to alter the original model in the search for a model that is "best fitting" in some sense and yields parameters having practical significance and substantive meaning." While a specification search might result in a better fitting model, Loehlin (1992, p. 191) cautions that "changing a structural model is changing one's theory" and clearly this step should not be taken lightly.

There are a number of techniques for respecifying models to achieve a better fit. Some analysts prefer a "theory trimming" approach that consists of deleting all nonsignificant paths and re-estimating the model (e.g., Gupta, Fogarty, and Dirsmith, 1994). Others might consider such an approach to be either atheoretical or statistically unjustified because it capitalizes on chance. Modification indices, available in most structural equation estimation programs, show how much the chi-square test statistic would decrease by freeing (allowing a path to be estimated for) each fixed (or constrained) parameter. It is up to the analyst to decide which of the changes suggested by the modification indices make theoretical sense (Arbuckle, 1997, pp. 232–233). The Lagrange multiplier functions as a multivariate analogue to the modification index by showing the effect of freeing a set of fixed parameters (Schumacker and Lomax, 1996, p. 108). The Wald statistic works in the opposite direction of the modification index and Lagrange multiplier by indicating which parameters should be dropped from the model (Bentler and Chou, 1987, p. 95; Schumacker and Lomax, p. 108). Unfortunately the Lagrange and Wald methods are not widely available in all structural equation modeling programs, though with the rapid improvements taking place in this line of software, these features may be added soon. Another method for respecifying models is to compare nested models (in which one model is a more restricted version of the other) using the hierarchical chi-square approach, as described by Bentler and Chou (1987, p. 106; also see Loehlin, 1992): "In this approach, both the restricted and less-restricted models are estimated, and the significance of the model-differentiating parameters is investigated by a chi-square difference test. The χ^2 and degrees of freedom are obtained by calculating the difference between the two goodness-of-fit χ^2 tests, as well as their degrees of freedom." All of these techniques permit the analyst to respecify a poorly fitting model and gauge the subsequent improvement in model fit.

Despite earlier hypotheses to the contrary, three of the exogenous variables listed in Table 7.4 did not have a significant effect on *any* of the endogenous variables: task scope, environmental capacity, and environmental complexity. I am reluctant to simply drop all of these variables from the model simultaneously, so I first explore the possibility of dropping one of them and then re-estimating the models. To decide which of them to drop, I used a hierarchical chi-square test. The results are listed in Table 7.5. As indicated clearly by the significant differences in the chi-square test statistics, dropping environmental complexity produces much better fitting models than dropping either of the other two variables.[17] I now reestimate all of the models without environmental complexity, then reevaluate their fit, and explore other possible modifications. The model respecification process for each model will now be discussed in detail. The revised models are illustrated in Figures 7.9

through 7.14 using conventional structural equation modeling diagram notation. Squares or rectangles identify observed variables, ellipses identify unobserved or latent variables, and small circles identify measurement error and equation prediction error terms (Arbuckle, 1997; Schumacker and Lomax, 1996). Coefficients are not included on the paths in these illustrations because the models are too complex.

Vertical Differentiation. Figure 7.9 illustrates the revised structural equation model for vertical differentiation. Dropping environmental complexity produces a significant improvement in the fit of the vertical differentiation model. In addition, because environmental complexity was highly correlated with other predictors, dropping it from the model provides the added benefit of reducing the overall level of collinearity. The variance inflation factor for organizational size dropped from (4.85) to (4.00), and the VIF for environmental dispersion dropped from (3.55) to (3.30). This reduction in collinearity holds for *all* of the remaining models. Dropping capacity and/or task scope from the model does not produce any further improvement in the fit. Modification indices provide a number of suggestions for improving the fit of the model, but none make any substantive sense. It is possible to specify a model that fits the data more perfectly by eliminating all nonsignificant variables, but such an approach capitalizes on chance and is not justified statistically. Therefore, no further modifications will be made to the model.

The various estimates for the revised model are shown in Table 7.6. Two cases were deleted from the initial analysis because they had incomplete data on environmental complexity, so once this variable was dropped from the model, the sample size increased by two. The R^2 for the revised model indicates that together, the predictors account for 82% of the variance in vertical differentiation. The χ^2 test statistic reflects a better fit than the initial model, but still indicates room for improvement. The unadjusted alternative fit indices range from 0.982 to 0.987, suggesting a very good fit.

The effect of task nonroutineness, barely significant in the initial model, is nonsignificant in the revised model. The two variables that appear to impact vertical differentiation most strongly are organizational size and organizational age. As I concluded from the initial model, larger and older police organizations are more vertically differentiated than smaller and younger ones.

Spatial Differentiation. Figure 7.10 illustrates the revised structural equation model for spatial differentiation. Dropping environmental complexity produces a significant improvement in the fit of the spatial

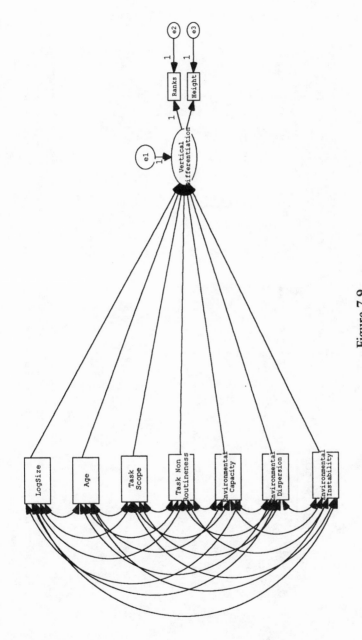

Figure 7.9

Revised Structural Equation Model for Vertical Differentiation

Table 7.5
Respecifying the Initial Models

Model	Initial Models		Dropping Task Scope		Dropping Environmental Capacity		Dropping Environmental Complexity	
	N	χ^2	χ^2	Difference	χ^2	Difference	χ^2	Difference
Vertical Differentiation	302	94.4 (25)	89.0 (22)	5.4 (3)	87.2 (22)	7.2 (3)	18.2 (6)	76.2*** (19)
Spatial Differentiation	280	58.8 (25)	54.4 (22)	4.4 (3)	51.7 (22)	7.1 (3)	7.6 (6)	51.2*** (19)
Functional Differentiation	306	62.2 (16)	58.6 (14)	3.6 (2)	52.8 (14)	3.4 (2)	(A)	(A)
Centralization	275	133.8 (50)	127.5 (46)	6.3 (4)	127.0 (46)	6.8 (4)	52.3 (22)	81.5*** (28)
Formalization	276	136.4 (50)	129.9 (46)	6.5 (4)	129.0 (46)	7.4 (4)	55.4 (22)	81.0*** (28)
Administration	276	139.6 (50)	133.7 (46)	5.9 (4)	133.2 (46)	6.4 (4)	51.5 (22)	88.1*** (28)

Note: The top figure in each row is the value of the chi-square test statistic, and the bottom figure (in parentheses) is the degrees of freedom for each model. Models containing an (A) are just-identified with zero degrees of freedom, therefore $\chi^2=0$, and the p-value for χ^2 cannot be computed. Models containing a *** have a p-value that is less than (0.001).

differentiation model. Dropping capacity and/or task scope from the model does not produce any further improvement in the fit. Modification indices provide a number of suggestions for improving the fit of the model, but none make any substantive sense. Therefore, no further modifications will be made to the model.

The various estimates for the revised model are shown in Table 7.6. Two cases were deleted from the initial analysis because they had incomplete data on environmental complexity, so once this variable was dropped from the model, the sample size increased by two. The R^2 for the revised model indicates that together, the predictors account for 98% of the variance in spatial differentiation. The χ^2 test statistic reflects a far better fit than the initial model and suggests that there are no significant differences between the observed and implied covariance matrices. The unadjusted alternative fit indices range from 0.994 to 0.999, suggesting an almost perfect fit.

In the initial model, organizational age had a barely significant positive effect on spatial differentiation. In the revised model, its effect is nonsignificant. Further research is needed to clarify the robustness of the relationship between organizational age and spatial differentiation. The one variable that impacts spatial differentiation the most strongly is organizational size. Larger police organizations, as we might expect, are more spatially differentiated. In addition, police organizations situated in unstable and/or dispersed environments are more spatially differentiated than those in stable and/or concentrated environments. Thus, three variables—organizational size, environmental dispersion, and environmental instability—explain almost all of the variance in spatial differentiation.

Functional Differentiation. Figure 7.11 illustrates the revised structural equation model for functional differentiation. Dropping environmental complexity results in a just-identified model of functional differentiation. Unlike the previous two models, I cannot assess the efficacy of dropping capacity and/or task scope from this model because doing so would result in an underidentified model. Modification indices provide a number of suggestions for improving the fit of the model, but none make any substantive sense. Therefore, no further modifications will be made to the model.

The various estimates for the revised model are shown in Table 7.6. Two cases were deleted from the initial analysis because they had incomplete data on environmental complexity, so once this variable was dropped from the model, the sample size increased by two. The R^2 for the revised model indicates that together, the predictors account for 31% of the variance in functional differentiation. The χ^2 and degrees of

Table 7.6
Revised Structural Equation Models for All Endogenous Variables

	Vertical Differentiation (N = 304)		Spatial Differentiation (N = 282)		Functional Differentiation (N = 308)		Centralization (N = 281)		Formalization (N = 282)		Administration (N = 282)	
	ML	Bootstrap	ML	Bootstrap	ML	Bootstrap	ML	Bootstrap	ML	Bootstrap	ML	Bootstrap
LogSize	0.708 (0.091) 7.77	(0.120)	0.596 (0.041) 14.55	(0.061)	1.27 (0.294) 4.32	(0.311)	-11.50 (18.57) -0.619		1.28 (2.44) 0.522		0.283 (0.304) 0.930	
Age	0.004 (0.001) 3.44	(0.001)	0.001 (0.001) 1.91	(0.001)	-0.006 (0.004) -1.43	(0.004)	0.016 (0.037) 0.443		-0.001 (0.005) -0.103		0.000 (0.001) -0.125	
Task Scope	0.002 (0.020) 0.115	(0.018)	0.002 (0.008) 0.246	(0.009)	0.043 (0.067) 0.652	(0.076)	-0.045 (0.295) -0.154		0.054 (0.046) 1.17		-0.003 (0.004) -0.702	
Task Non-Routineness	-0.015 (0.008) -1.80	(0.008)	0.004 (0.003) 1.14	(0.003)	0.111 (0.028) 3.96	(0.026)	-0.292 (0.189) -1.54		0.017 (0.025) 0.677		0.003 (0.003) 1.08	
Environmental Capacity	-0.082 (0.051) -1.60	(0.052)	0.001 (0.020) 0.043	(0.020)	0.321 (0.171) 1.88	(0.183)	-0.048 (0.767) -0.063		0.209 (0.120) 1.74		-0.011 (0.010) -1.07	
Environmental Dispersion	-0.067 (0.042) -1.57	(0.057)	0.040 (0.016) 2.46	(0.017)	0.165 (0.141) 1.17	(0.155)	-2.40 (1.41) -1.70		0.092 (0.190) 0.484		0.022 (0.022) 0.998	

(continued on next page)

Table 7.6 (continued)

	Vertical Differentiation (N = 304)		Spatial Differentiation (N = 282)		Functional Differentiation (N = 308)		Centralization (N = 281)		Formalization (N = 282)		Administration (N = 282)	
	ML	Bootstrap	ML	Bootstrap	ML	Bootstrap	ML	Bootstrap	ML	Bootstrap	ML	Bootstrap
Environmental Instability	0.010 (0.023) 0.434	(0.026)	0.025 (0.009) 2.82	(0.009)	-0.086 (0.076) -1.13	(0.084)	-0.709 (0.855) -0.829		0.070 (0.114) 0.615		0.011 (0.013) 0.844	
Vertical Differentiation							Dropped from model		Dropped from model		Dropped from model	
Spatial Differentiation							23.20 (31.23) 0.743		-2.02 (4.07) -0.495		-0.449 (0.510) -0.881	
Functional Differentiation							-0.385 (0.212) -1.87		0.065 (0.038) 1.74		0.000 (0.002) -0.230	

(continued on next page)

Table 7.6 (continued)

	Vertical Differentiation (N = 304)		Spatial Differentiation (N = 282)		Functional Differentiation (N = 308)		Centralization (N = 281)		Formalization (N = 282)		Administration (N = 282)	
	ML	Bootstrap	ML	Bootstrap	ML	Bootstrap	ML	Bootstrap	ML	Bootstrap	ML	Bootstrap
R^2	0.82	0.86	0.98	0.98	0.31	0.33	0.14		0.06		0.33	
χ^2	18.49 p=0.005	p=0.02	7.53 p=0.275	p=0.307	(A)	(A)	10.99		12.39 (p=0.192)		9.21 p=0.418	
χ^2/df	18.49 / 6 = 3.08		7.53 / 6 = 1.26		(A)		10.99 / 9 = 1.22		12.39 / 9 = 1.38		9.21 / 9 = 1.02	
GFI	0.987		0.994		1.0		0.993		0.992		0.994	
AGFI	0.903		0.956		1.0		0.949		0.943		0.957	
IFI	0.983		0.999		1.0		0.998		0.997		1.0	
CFI	0.982		0.999		1.0		0.998		0.997		1.0	
Kurtosis	16.08 (C.R.=10.0)		16.13 (C.R.=9.6)		9.66 (C.R.=6.7)		16.54 (C.R.=8.2)		15.31 (C.R.=7.6)		20.39 (C.R.=10.1)	

(A) Model is just-identified with zero degrees of freedom, therefore $\chi^2 = 0$, and the p-value for χ^2 cannot be computed.

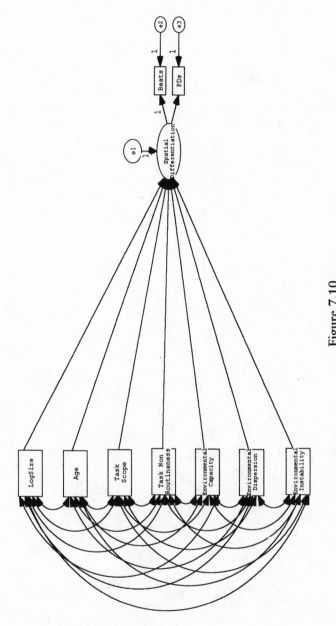

Figure 7.10

Revised Structural Equation Model for Spatial Differentiation

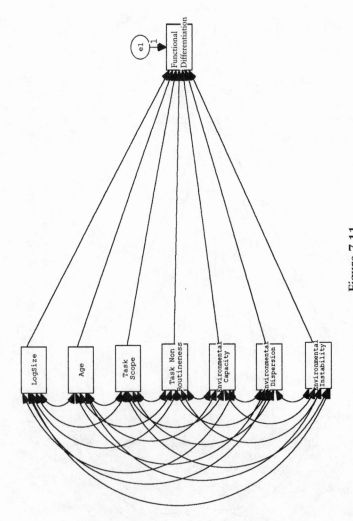

Figure 7.11
Revised Structural Equation Model for Functional Differentiation

freedom equal 0 because the model is just-identified, thus we cannot compute a p-value for the test statistic. The unadjusted alternative fit indices automatically equal 1 in a just-identified model.

The significant effects in the revised model are about the same as they were in the initial model. Larger police organizations are more functionally differentiated, as we might expect. Moreover, police agencies that engage in nonroutine tasks tend to be more specialized, which is opposite my hypothesis in chapter 5. I will discuss the significance of this unexpected finding further in chapter 8.

Centralization. Figure 7.12 illustrates the revised structural equation model for centralization. Recall from our earlier discussion that the models for centralization, formalization and administration were too complex. The ratio of free parameters to cases in these models was approximately 3.2, when as a general rule the ratio should be at least 5. Such low ratios provide cause for concern that the parameter estimates might be unstable. Thus it is important to consider alternative specifications that will simplify the model and increase the ratio of free parameters to cases.

One of the reasons that the initial centralization model is so complex is that it specifies indirect effects for all of the endogenous variables through the three structural complexity variables. Thus, the first step in respecifying the model is to test the need for each of these indirect effects individually. Using a hierarchical chi-square test for nested models, I examine the impact of dropping spatial, functional, and vertical differentiation from the model.

The initial model containing all three structural complexity variables has a χ^2 of 52.09 with 22 degrees of freedom. Dropping spatial differentiation from the model results in a χ^2 of 31.76 with 9 degrees of freedom. The difference is nonsignificant ($p > 0.05$) with a χ^2 of 20.33 with 13 degrees of freedom, thus dropping spatial differentiation from the model will not improve the fit. Dropping functional differentiation from the model results in a χ^2 of 42.79 and 18 degrees of freedom. The difference is significant ($0.01 < p < 0.02$), with a χ^2 of 11.3 and 4 degrees of freedom, thus dropping functional differentiation from the model will improve the fit. Finally, dropping vertical differentiation from the model results in a χ^2 of 11.72 with 9 degrees of freedom. The difference is highly significant ($p < 0.001$), and the resulting model fits the data extremely well. Thus, deleting vertical differentiation from the model produces an appreciable improvement in fit.

The next step in respecifying this model is to reexamine the possibility of deleting the remaining two indirect effects. Dropping each of

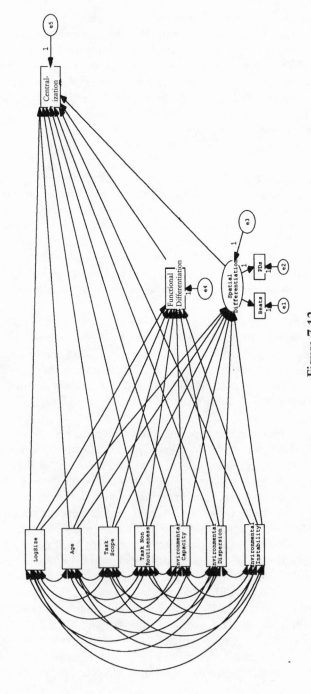

Figure 7.12
Revised Structural Equation Model for Centralization

these from the model does not produce a significant improvement in model fit. Next, as I have done with all of the models so far, I reexamine the possibility of dropping task scope and environmental capacity. Again, neither change significantly improves the fit of the model. The changes recommended by the modification indices make no substantive sense, so I will make no further modifications to this model. Dropping environmental complexity added two cases to the model, and dropping vertical differentiation added another four cases, so I reestimated the model with the increased sample size. The results of the final model are listed in Table 7.6.

The R^2 for the revised model indicates that together, the predictors account for 14% of the variance in centralization. The χ^2 test statistic reflects a far better fit than the initial model and suggests that there are no significant differences between the observed and implied covariance matrices. The unadjusted alternative fit indices range from 0.993 to 0.998, suggesting an almost perfect fit.

Due to the decrease in model complexity and the increase in sample size that resulted from dropping two latent variables, the ratio of free parameters to cases increased from 3.2 in the initial model to 4.93 in the revised model. This ratio is still below the recommended 5–10 range, and therefore there is some possibility that the parameter estimates may be somewhat unstable. Bootstrap estimates of the standard errors (and chi-square) are not available because the requisite number of bootstrap subsamples could not be obtained. As with the initial model, none of the predictors has a significant effect on centralization.

Formalization. Figure 7.13 illustrates the revised structural equation model for formalization. As with centralization, one of the reasons that the initial formalization model is so complex is that it specifies indirect effects for all of the endogenous variables through the three structural complexity variables. Thus, the first step in respecifying the model is to test the need for each of these indirect effects individually. Using a hierarchical chi-square test for nested models, I examine the impact of dropping spatial, functional, and vertical differentiation from the model.

The initial model containing all three structural complexity variables has a χ^2 of 55.45 with 22 degrees of freedom. Dropping spatial differentiation from the model results in a χ^2 of 32.21 and 9 degrees of freedom. The difference is nonsignificant ($p > 0.05$) with a χ^2 of 23.24 with 13 degrees of freedom, thus dropping spatial differentiation from the model will not improve the fit. Dropping functional differentiation from the model results in a χ^2 of 46.45 and 18 degrees of freedom. The difference is nonsignificant ($p > 0.05$), with a χ^2 of 9.0 and 4 degrees of

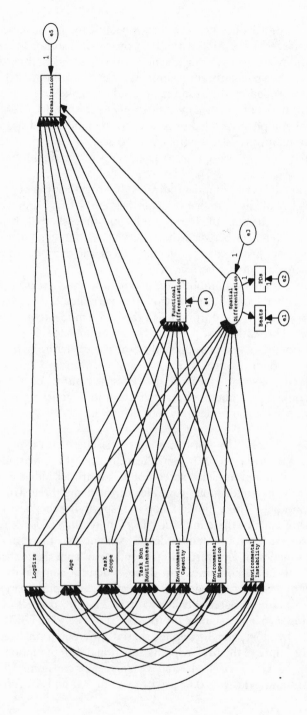

Figure 7.13
Revised Structural Equation Model for Formalization

freedom, thus dropping functional differentiation from the model will not improve the fit. Finally, dropping vertical differentiation from the model results in a χ^2 of 13.29 with 9 degrees of freedom. The difference is highly significant (p < 0.001), with a chi-square of 42.16 and 13 degrees of freedom. The resulting model fits the data extremely well, thus deleting vertical differentiation from the model produces an appreciable improvement in fit.

The next step in respecifying this model is to reexamine the possibility of deleting the remaining two indirect effects. Dropping each of these from the model does not produce a significant improvement in model fit. Next, as I have done with all of the models so far, I reexamine the possibility of dropping task scope and environmental capacity. Again, neither change significantly improves the fit of the model. The changes recommended by the modification indices make no substantive sense, so I will make no further modifications to this model. Dropping environmental complexity added two cases to the model, and dropping vertical differentiation added another four cases, so I reestimated the model with the increased sample size. The results of the final model are listed in Table 7.6.

The R^2 for the revised model indicates that together, the predictors account for only 6% of the variance in formalization. The χ^2 test statistic reflects a far better fit than the initial model and suggests that there are no significant differences between the observed and implied covariance matrices. The unadjusted alternative fit indices range from 0.992 to 0.997, suggesting an almost perfect fit. As with the initial model, none of the predictors has a significant effect on formalization.

Administration. Figure 7.14 illustrates the revised structural equation model for administrative intensity. As with centralization and formalization, one of the reasons that the initial administrative intensity model is so complex is that it specifies indirect effects for all of the endogenous variables through the three structural complexity variables. Thus, the first step in respecifying the model is to test the need for each of these indirect effects individually. Using a hierarchical chi-square test for nested models, I examine the impact of dropping spatial, functional, and vertical differentiation from the model. The initial model containing all three structural complexity variables has a χ^2 of 51.31 with 22 degrees of freedom. Dropping spatial differentiation from the model results in a χ^2 of 32.04 with 9 degrees of freedom. The difference is nonsignificant (p > 0.05) with a χ^2 of 19.27 and 13 degrees of freedom, thus dropping spatial differentiation from the model will not improve the fit. Dropping functional differentiation from the model results in a χ^2 of 41.99 and 18

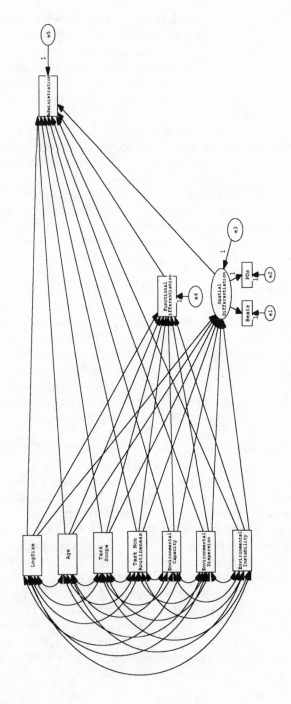

Figure 7.14

Revised Structural Equation Model for Administrative Intensity

degrees of freedom. The difference is nonsignificant (p > .05), with a χ^2 of 9.32 and 4 degrees of freedom, thus dropping functional differentiation from the model will not improve the fit. Finally, dropping vertical differentiation from the model results in a χ^2 of 10.06 with 9 degrees of freedom. The difference is highly significant (p < 0.001), with a chi-square of 41.25 and 13 degrees of freedom. The resulting model fits the data extremely well, thus deleting vertical differentiation from the model produces an appreciable improvement in fit.

The next step in respecifying this model is to reexamine the possibility of deleting the remaining two indirect effects. Dropping each of these from the model does not produce a significant improvement in model fit. Next, as I have done with all of the models so far, I reexamine the possibility of dropping task scope and environmental capacity. Again, neither change significantly improves the fit of the model. The changes recommended by the modification indices make no substantive sense, so I will make no further modifications to this model. Dropping environmental complexity added two cases to the model, and dropping vertical differentiation added another four cases, so I reestimated the model with the increased sample size. The results of the revised model are listed in Table 7.6.

The R^2 for the revised model indicates that together, the predictors account for 33% of the variance in administrative intensity. The χ^2 test statistic reflects a far better fit than the initial model and suggests that there are no significant differences between the observed and implied covariance matrices. The unadjusted alternative fit indices range from 0.994 to 1.0, suggesting a nearly perfect fit. As with the initial model, none of the predictors has a significant effect on administrative intensity. An R^2 value of 0.33 with no significant predictors may be a sign that this model is being affected by multicollinearity. In the following section, I examine this possibility.

A Final Look at Multicollinearity. Throughout the model estimation process, I have made a number of references to potential problems with multicollinearity. In the initial models, organizational size had a variance inflation factor of (4.85) and environmental dispersion had a VIF of (3.55). The two variables also had a high correlation (r = 0.819). In the revised models, we dropped one or more variables and picked up a few extra cases. This resulted in lower VIFs for organizational size (4.00) and environmental dispersion (3.30), and a slightly lower correlation between these variables (r = 0.817). In addition to reducing overall multicollinearity in the revised models, it is possible that the simpler models and larger sample sizes may have also contributed to more stable estimates. Nevertheless, there are still some signs that collinearity may be influencing one or more of the models. For example, one of the classic signs of multicollinearity is a model in which the R^2 suggests that the predictors are influential, but none are significant. This is the case with the revised model of administrative intensity, which has an R^2 of 33%, but none of the predictors are significant. I will now explore each of the revised models to see if multicollinearity might be influencing the estimates.

Organizational size, as we have seen in the initial analyses, is the primary contextual variable that shapes the structures of large municipal police organizations. Since any potential problems with multicollinearity are the result of a high correlation between organizational size and environmental dispersion, it is important to see how the estimates behave with one of these variables dropped from the model. After dropping environmental dispersion, the highest correlation among the predictors is approximately (0.20), and the variance inflation factor for organizational size is (1.38). For the first three models, the effects were similar. Dropping environmental dispersion resulted in higher parameter estimates and lower standard errors for organizational size. This makes sense, since organizational size and environmental dispersion share a large portion of their variances. The results on the remaining variables in the model were negligible. Thus, although collinearity in the first three models produces some variance inflation, this should not affect any of the substantive interpretations from these models.

For the remaining three models, dropping environmental dispersion did not produce any substantive differences—all parameter estimates remained nonsignificant. In the formalization and administration models, there were no discernible differences in the parameter estimates or standard errors. Recall that the administration model has an R^2 of 0.33 but no significant predictors. Although we would normally suspect collinearity in such a circumstance, estimating the model in the absence of collinearity produced only negligible changes in the parameter estimates. For centralization, however, collinearity may be a problem. Dropping environmental dispersion from the model resulted in a variety of bizarre changes. Some of the parameter estimates changed signs, and many of the standard errors are much smaller or larger. There are obvious problems with the stability of the estimates in the centralization model.

While multicollinearity is a problem in this study, it only appears to have a severe effect on one of the six models: centralization. However, multicollinearity only affects our ability to interpret the effects of individual predictors, not the joint effects of a set of predictors. The centralization model has an R^2 of only 0.14, thus the predictors examined in this study do not appear to have a strong impact on centralization regardless of collinearity. It may be that one or more of the variables in the model does have some effect on centralization that is being masked by the collinearity, but it is difficult to tell based on the data from this sample. Further research is needed to explore the causes and correlates of centralization in large municipal police organizations.

Checking for Sample Selection Bias

The last step of the analysis is to determine whether the results obtained so far may have been influenced by any form of sample selection or non-response bias. The sample of police agencies used in this study was not randomly selected. The study seeks to generalize only to large municipal police agencies employing 100 or more full-time sworn officers. Since there are only about 432 such agencies in the United States according to the 1992 Directory Survey of Law Enforcement Agencies (Reaves, 1993), it would be advantageous to select the entire population for this analysis. This, unfortunately, was not possible because some agencies either failed to fill out one or more of the surveys used in constructing the data set in this study, or failed to fill out requisite items on one or more of the surveys. Although all 432 agencies were surveyed, many were excluded from one or more of the models because they had incomplete data. Thus, due to survey and item nonresponse, the data set used for this analysis is based on a nonrandom sample of large municipal police agencies.

Although it is impossible to rule out sample selection bias in the presence of missing data, there are some simple methods that can be used to compare respondents and nonrespondents.[18] To test for possible nonresponse bias, I compared respondents and nonrespondents for every variable in each of the six revised models. For example, in the revised model of vertical differentiation summarized in Table 7.6, there were 304 agencies represented. There were 128 agencies that were missing data for one or more variables in this model, and were therefore excluded from the analysis. However, many of these 128 agencies did provide information for some of the variables in the model, and therefore may be useful for assessing nonresponse bias. Of the 128 agencies that did not make into the vertical differentiation model, for example, 121 provided information on organizational size, 51 on organizational age, and 85 on environmental instability. Thus sufficient information is available to compare respondents and nonrespondents on the variables used in this study.

To see if those in the models are similar to those excluded from the models, I simply compared the means of the two groups using independent sample t-tests. I did this for every variable in every model. For the models containing unobserved variables, I was only able to examine the observed indicators. Of all the variables in all six models, there was only one significant difference between respondents and nonrespondents. In the functional differentiation model, respondents exhibited significantly higher scores on environmental instability than nonrespondents (t = 2.45, p = 0.015). Recall that instability was operationalized as the number of police chief executives that held office from 1970–1993. For respondents in the functional differentiation model, the average number of police chiefs was approximately 4.49, compared with an average of approximately 3.99 for nonrespondents.

Is this difference important? Remember, I explored the differences between respondents and nonrespondents for every observed variable in each of the six revised models. There are 9 observed variables in the vertical differentiation model, 9 in the spatial differentiation model, 8 in the functional differentiation model, and 11 in each of the models for centralization, formalization, and administration. Therefore, I ran 59 separate t-tests to explore possible differences between respondents and nonrespondents. Because there were no significant differences on environmental instability in any of the other five models, and because only 1 in 59 t-tests detected a significant difference between respondents and nonrespondents, it is safe to assume that sample selection bias is not a problem in this study. Thus, although the sample is nonrandom, it is probably not significantly different from a random sample.[19]

Summary

In this chapter I used structural equation modeling techniques to test the theory outlined in chapter 5. Only a few of the hypotheses are supported in the sample of police agencies used in this study. In chapter 8 we will discuss why police organizational structures might not be responsive to the same contextual influences that impact other types of organizations. Many of the findings in this chapter have important implications for research, theory and policy on the police.

I will now summarize the results obtained in this chapter. I begin by discussing each of the six models, highlighting any differences between the initial and revised models. I then discuss each of the independent variables, assessing the evidence about their impact on organizational structure. Chapter 8 will then discuss the potential impact of these findings on police research, theory, and policy.

In the initial vertical differentiation model, I found that organizational size and organizational age both had a significant positive effect. Older and/or larger police agencies are more vertically differentiated than younger and/or smaller police agencies. This finding was replicated (and strengthened) in the revised vertical differentiation model. In addition, the initial model showed that police organizations engaging in nonroutine tasks tended to be less vertically differentiated, though the effect was only borderline significant (t = −1.96). Task nonroutineness was no longer significant in the revised model (t = −1.80). Further research is needed to examine the stability of this relationship. The effect of environmental complexity was nonsignificant in the initial model, and removing it from the revised model produced a significant improvement in fit. The complexity of the population clearly does not have an impact on the level of vertical differentiation in large municipal police organizations.

In the initial spatial differentiation model, I found that organizational size, environmental dispersion, and environmental instability all had significant positive effects. Larger police organizations, and those serving more dispersed and/or unstable environments are more spatially differentiated. These findings were all replicated in the revised spatial differentiation model. In addition, the initial model showed that organizational age had a significant positive effect on spatial differentiation (t = 2.03). Age was no longer significant in the revised model (t = 1.91). Further research should examine the stability of this relationship. The effect of environmental complexity was nonsignificant in the initial model, and removing it from the revised model produced a significant improvement in fit. The complexity of the population clearly does not have an impact on the level of spatial differentiation in large municipal police organizations.

In the initial functional differentiation model, I found that organizational size and task nonroutineness both had significant positive effects. Larger police organizations and those performing nonroutine functions are more functionally differentiated. These findings were both replicated and strengthened in the revised model. The effect of task nonroutineness, as mentioned earlier in the chapter, is in the opposite direction of that predicted by theory. This will be discussed further in chapter 8. The effect of environmental complexity was nonsignificant in the initial model, and removing it from the revised model produced a significant improvement in fit. The complexity of the population clearly does not have an impact on the level of functional differentiation in large municipal police organizations.

In the initial models of centralization, formalization, and administration, I found that none of the variables in the models had a significant effect. This finding was clearly unexpected, since there is a large body of theory and research to support the hypothesis that these structural elements should be shaped in some way by organizational context. Chapter 8 will discuss the significance of this finding at length. All of these initial models fit the data poorly, and a variety of steps were taken to improve their fit to the data. The result of my specification search for all three models was the same: dropping environmental complexity and dropping the indirect effects of the contextual variables through vertical differentiation both produced significant improvements in model fit. The level of vertical differentiation and the complexity of the population clearly do not have an impact on the level of centralization, formalization, and or administrative intensity in large municipal police organizations.

Lastly, this study highlighted some of the contextual variables that impact the way police organizations are structured. Organizational size, organizational age, task non-routineness, environmental dispersion, and environmental instability all had significant effects on one or more elements of structure. Despite earlier hypotheses, three variables demonstrated insignificant effects on structure in every model: they are task scope, environmental capacity, and environmental complexity. The absence of a significant effect for task scope suggests that the type and volume of different tasks that police agencies perform are unrelated to differences in structure. Environmental capacity, as I suggested earlier, was measured crudely, and therefore it is difficult to tell if the results for this variable are due to poor conceptualization or poor measurement. Finally, removing environmental complexity improved the fit of every model substantially. Since the reliability of the environmental complexity construct is within reasonable bounds ($\Omega = 0.64$), the improvement in fit probably cannot be attributed to a poorly fitting measurement model. Clearly, the complexity of the population that a police agency serves is unrelated to its organizational structure.

In summary, most of the hypothesized relationships were not observed among this sample of large municipal police agencies. Structural complexity is largely driven by organizational size, with a handful of other factors impacting different types of complexity individually. Knowing a little about the context of a police organization would enable us to predict the overall level of its structural complexity with some accuracy. Structural coordination and control mechanisms, on the other hand, are largely unaffected by the elements of context examined in this study. The reasons for this are not entirely clear. Certainly one strong possibility may be that hypotheses about these variables have been formulated, tested, and refined on other types of organizations than the police. In the following chapter, I will explore this notion further.

CHAPTER 8

Summary and Conclusions

After a brief summary of the findings, I will discuss the implications of this study for three areas: theory, research, and policy. The theory section shows how the findings force us to rethink many of the ideas discussed in chapter 5, and more generally to reconsider theoretical explanations for police organizational structure. One area in particular that deserves more attention is how police organizations are different from other types of organizations in which research has confirmed some of the hypothesized structural-contextual relationships that were not supported in this study. The research section will focus on the strengths and limitations of the data and methods used in this study, including a discussion of the use of nonnormal data, small samples, and multiple indicator and structural equation models in police research. This section will also highlight the importance of the findings for future research on police organizations, especially in two areas: studies seeking to explain police organizational structure, and studies using structural elements to explain other phenomena. Finally, I discuss the policy implications of this study, especially as they relate to the structural reform agendas of community policing advocates.

Summary

In this study, I used structural equation modeling techniques to test a theoretical model of police organizational structure. Six structural variables were considered: three of these—vertical, spatial, and functional differentiation—are elements of an organization's overall level of structural complexity; the remaining three—centralization, formalization, and administrative intensity—are structural tools that organizations use to maintain coordination and control. Six separate models were tested initially, and then they were modified, resulting in six revised models. All of the revised models fit the data well, and all reveal something about the correlates of formal organizational structure in large municipal police agencies. All of the findings that I discuss come from these revised models. Very few variables evidenced a significant effect on organizational structure, and thus very few of the hypotheses were supported. After summarizing the findings of each specific model, I will then discuss how these findings relate to theory, research, and policy.

VERTICAL DIFFERENTIATION

Most of the variance in vertical differentiation (82%) is explained by the contextual variables in this study. Although vertical differentiation is largely driven by organizational size, organizational age accounts for a portion of its variance as well. Controlling for other contextual variables, older organizations are more vertically differentiated. Every police organization has its own history of scandals, crises, and reform efforts, and it appears that as police organizations grow older, they add layers of command for one reason or another. Because the effects of age on structure depend in part on the unique histories of local police departments, it is difficult to draw much more out of the relationship than this. Case study or historical research methods are ideally suited to explore this trend in more detail.

SPATIAL DIFFERENTIATION

Nearly all of the variance in spatial differentiation (98%) can be explained by the contextual variables, although like other complexity variables, it is largely driven by organizational size. The other contextual features influencing spatial differentiation are environmental dispersion and environmental instability. It is common sense that police agencies with larger, more dispersed jurisdictions would be more spatially differentiated, and this study confirms such an effect. The finding that police agencies serving more unstable environments are more spatially differentiated is puzzling. It is difficult to tell whether this is a valid relationship between concepts or an artifact resulting from imperfect measurement. In chapter 6 I acknowledged the possibility that my measure of instability (police chief turnover) might be flawed. Despite my intention to explore a theoretical relationship between environmental instability and spatial differentiation, this unexpected finding could be telling us something different: that there is an inverse relationship between the average tenure of police chiefs and the level of spatial differentiation in large municipal police agencies. Police chiefs in organizations that are more spatially complex may simply have a shorter average period in office than chiefs in more spatially centralized agencies. In other words, this relationship could be telling us more about the measure of environmental instability than the concept it is intended to reflect. Clearly, if we wish to explore the impact of environmental instability on police organizations, we need to develop more precise measures of this abstract concept. This is one area in which police scholars might look to research on local or urban politics for further guidance.

FUNCTIONAL DIFFERENTIATION

Contextual variables do not explain as much of the variance in functional differentiation as they do in the other complexity factors. Organizational size has a significant effect on functional differentiation, but the influence is not as strong as it is with the other complexity factors. In addition, as tasks become more nonroutine, functional differentiation increases. Because this finding is in the opposite direction implied by the hypotheses in chapter 5, we will discuss it in more detail in the theory section. In addition, this finding has important implications for police policy, and it will be discussed in that context as well.

CENTRALIZATION

The independent variables account for only 14% of the variance in centralization. The centralization model suffered from two statistical problems: model complexity and collinearity. The complexity problem occurred because the model had too many free parameters and not enough cases, thus raising concern that the estimates may be unstable. In addition, of the six revised models, centralization was the only one evidencing strong problems with multicollinearity due to the strong relationship between two predictors: organizational size and environmental dispersion. Although these problems might make it difficult to interpret the effects of individual parameters, they do not impair our ability to evaluate the predictive capacity of the model as a whole. Thus, although this study found that none of the contextual variables in the model has a significant effect on centralization, studies using more robust models (e.g., larger sample size, simpler model, lower collinearity) might find that one or more of these contextual variables is significant. Nevertheless, these variables do not account for a substantial degree of variation in centralization.

FORMALIZATION

The independent variables in the revised model account for only 6% of the variation in formalization, and none of the predictors had a significant effect. Like the centralization model, there are not enough cases per free parameter to produce stable estimates. Unlike the centralization model, multicollinearity does not appear to be influencing this model very strongly. Despite any statistical problems, it is clear that formalization in large municipal organizations is unrelated to any of the independent variables examined in this study.

ADMINISTRATIVE INTENSITY

The independent variables in the revised model account for 33% of the variance in administrative intensity, though none of the predictors has a significant effect. Normally in the presence of such a high R^2 value we would suspect a problem with multicollinearity. However, the limited diagnostic checks that I described at the end of chapter 7 suggest that this is not a problem. Like the centralization and formalization models, this model has too many free parameters and not enough cases, and thus there is a possibility that the parameter estimates may be unstable. Further research with more robust models is needed to explore the relationship between organizational context and administrative intensity.

Theory

This study probably raises more questions than it answers about why large municipal police organizations are structured the way they are. Many of these questions are somewhat banal, since they imply the lack of a relationship between context and structure. Most of the hypotheses that I formulated in chapter 5 were not supported, and one general conclusion that can be drawn from this finding is that only a handful of contextual variables impact organizational structure. Furthermore, these effects do not apply universally to all elements of structure. Such a finding is somewhat surprising, given the massive literature confirming these relationships in other types of agencies. Therefore, it appears that although studying police agencies as organizations may be a productive form of inquiry for generating hypotheses about how they function, it is nevertheless important to keep one eye firmly focused on what makes the police a unique institution. In this section I focus on this and other theoretical questions about police organizations and how they are structured.

I have already summarized the results of this study, and therefore we know how each of the structural variables are impacted by the contextual variables. We now focus on the contextual features themselves—size, age, technology, and environment—and how the results obtained in this study might be useful in future theories of police organizational structure.

Organizational Size. The first finding which emerges strongly and clearly from this study is no surprise: organization size matters. Much of the variance in structural complexity is due to organizational size. Larger police organizations require more complex structures for a number of reasons. This is no theoretical mystery, and future theories of police organizational structure can build upon this established finding. However, size has no effect on structural coordination and control mechanisms. Later in this section I will explore some reasons for this unexpected finding.

Organizational Age. The age of a police organization has a significant positive effect on vertical differentiation, controlling for organizational size and other contextual variables. Age also had a significant positive effect on spatial differentiation in the initial model, though this variable was borderline insignificant in the revised model. This is the second study to uncover age effects on structure. King (1999), in his examination of the age-structure relationship, found that older police organizations were more vertically differentiated and that they employed fewer civilians. An earlier version of King's study was aptly named: "Do Older Police Departments Have More Wrinkles?" (King, 1994).

Theories of police organizational structure have rarely accounted for historical effects, but it seems apparent from this study that police organizations are affected by the aging process. Since our ability to draw general conclusions about the effects of historical processes on police organizations from survey research is severely limited, theories on the age-structure relationship will need to be tested using longitudinal data, historical research, and/or case-study approaches. Of particular importance is determining how often age effects are the product of local circumstances that are unique to each department, and how often they are the product of global trends such as large-scale reform movements. Finally, the finding that age affects organizational structure begs a larger and perhaps more important question—does age constrain other organizational phenomena such as performance, culture, innovation, or management?[1] Because theoretical explanations for these phenomena rarely include age effects, analysts may learn much by studying the aging trajectories of large municipal police agencies.

Task/Technology. The idea that structure is dependent on technology is intuitively appealing because it suggests a very rational process of structural adaptation: as organizations change their technologies, their structures shift to accommodate their new methods of operation. Although theoretically appealing, the findings from this study do not support a strong technology-structure relationship. The scope of tasks that a police agency performs is unrelated to every element of structure. The routine-nonroutine dimension of an agency's tasks is related only to functional differentiation, and the effect is opposite the hypothesized direction. Police agencies engaging in less routine patrol functions have higher levels of functional differentiation than agencies engaging in routine patrol functions. Prior research has established that routine technologies are associated with higher levels of functional differentiation, since routine tasks can be broken down into distinct subtasks and handled by specialists or specialized units. Because nonroutine tasks are less predictable, agencies engaging in them should be less functionally differentiated, depending primarily on the work of generalists. At least one of the implications of this finding is that police agencies may be different from other types of agencies that exhibit the expected relationship between technology and structure. For example, police agencies may not have the same incentives to seek a good fit between technology and structure that other agencies have, especially those in the private sector. I will return to this thesis later as we begin to explore the differences between police and other types of organizations.

Environment. The environment of a police organization is virtually infinite in scope, and therefore it is not useful to make generalizations about whether "environment matters" (Langworthy, 1986). This study looked at four elements of the police environment: capacity, dispersion, instability, and complexity. Two of these, environmental capacity and environmental complexity, did not have a significant effect on any element of organizational structure. Capacity is similar in principle to autonomy, and refers to the degree of external constraint that the environment places on the organization. Because this variable was measured crudely, it is difficult to draw much from this finding. Whether the lack of a relationship between capacity and structure reflects a true null relationship or poor measurement is unknown. Although the measure of environmental complexity was good (and reliable), this variable did not have a significant effect on any structural element. The demographic makeup of the population has no effect on police organizational structure. This finding was clear and strong, however, it conflicts somewhat with research undertaken on social threat theory. For instance, Katz, Maguire, and Roncek (2001) found that the proportion of Hispanics in the population has a strong effect on the likelihood that a police organization will have a specialized gang unit, even after controlling for gang-related crime. Much remains to be learned about the relationship between the demographic complexity of the community and the social structure of police organizations.

Two environmental variables—dispersion and instability—affected some elements of structure but not others. Environmental dispersion refers to the size and spread of the task environment. Dispersion had a significant effect only on spatial differentiation. This finding is nothing more than common sense: agencies serving more spatially dispersed environments are more spatially differentiated. One interesting point worth noting is that the size of the organization has a much stronger effect on spatial differentiation than the size and spread of the environment (or jurisdiction). Theories of police organizational structure need to develop explanations for why spatial differentiation is driven more by internal features of the department than external features of the environment. In addition, theoretical explanations need to be developed to account for why environmental dispersion does not impact other structural features, especially centralization. Environmental instability, as discussed earlier in the chapter, had only one significant effect. Unstable environments were associated with higher levels of spatial differentiation, a finding opposite the hypothesized direction. I have already mentioned the possibility that this relationship may be due to a flawed measure. Theories focusing on environmental instability cannot be tested adequately without better measures.

In sum, two environmental variables have no effect on organizational structure, and two have fairly isolated effects. Thus, no generalities can really be made about environment-structure relationships other than that such effects are not universal.

The Effect of Structural Complexity on Structural Control and Coordination Mechanisms. The last set of relationships that I explore are the direct effects from the complexity factors to the coordination and control factors. In short, despite a long line of elegant theoretical propositions starting with Durkheim, structural complexity has no effect on structural coordination and control mechanisms. While these three models were somewhat unstable, the findings suggest that structural coordination and control are independent of every antecedent variable in the models. All three models experienced a significant improvement in fit when I dropped vertical differentiation from the model, thus it appears that this variable is clearly not related to levels of centralization, formalization, and administrative intensity. Again, although the relationship between complexity and control has been established in other studies, police organizations do not seem to conform to these expected relationships.

This leads us directly to the next subject, that structural coordination and control mechanisms in large municipal police agencies appear to be somewhat random. Theories of police organizational structure are not currently equipped to explain why some elements of structure are systematic and predictable and others are random and unpredictable. If further research continues to confirm that some elements of structure are indeed random, then this randomness needs to be explored and built in as an element of future theories. The literature in organizational sociology contains a number of potential explanations. None of these is sufficiently developed to favor one explanation over the other, but all deserve some consideration in future theories of police organizational structure. I now explore three potential avenues that might explain some of the results obtained in this study, and that might be fruitful areas for further theoretical development in the study of police organizational structure.

Loose Coupling and Institutional Theory. I have discussed institutional theory a number of times in previous chapters, so I will not explain the theory in detail in this chapter. Of particular interest here is the idea, often echoed by institutional theorists, that organizations and their contexts contain a number of loose or weak linkages that appear to be irrational—structural features are unrelated to other structural features, technical components are unrelated to structural components, and contextual variables are unaligned with structural and/or technical variables. The phrase frequently used to describe this state of affairs is called "loose coupling." This concept has utility in a number of contexts outside institutional theory, but institutional theorists have probably spent the greatest amount of time trying to explain the process of loose coupling, therefore the two are often associated (Meyer and Rowan, 1977; Weick, 1976). Suffice it to say that institutional theory is not the only explanation for loose coupling, merely the most popular.

As applied to this study, the concept of loose coupling is useful because it suggests that some organizations are loosely coupled—in structure, technology, and environment—for rational, functional reasons. For example, loose-coupling theorists might argue that the reason there are weak relationships between context and structure in police organizations is to allow for localized adaptation. As Weick (1976, p. 6) argues: "If all of the elements in a large system are loosely coupled to one another, then any one element can adjust to and modify a local unique contingency without affecting the whole system. These local adaptations can be swift, relatively economical, and substantial." The approach of loose coupling theorists is abstract, somewhat philosophical, and difficult to summarize in a few brief paragraphs. In general however, the focus is on understanding and explaining why some parts of the organization appear to be random or wholly disconnected from other components. In the jargon of social science, those who study loose coupling seek to explore the unexplained variance (the "noise") in organizational phenomena rather than the explained (or explainable) variance. Loose coupling theorists recognize that trying to explain otherwise unpredictable features of complex organizations will require unique methodological approaches not regularly used in the social sciences (Weick, 1976). Because the focus of loose coupling is on those organizational linkages that appear to be unpredictable or random, this concept may be useful for understanding the lack of structural-contextual relationships found in this study.

Individuals, Culture, Politics, and Strategic Choice. Another view that may be helpful in understanding police organizational structure is the idea that we cannot ignore the dynamics of culture, power, politics and behavior that occur within organizations. Nearly three decades ago, Child (1972b) suggested that much of the research into organizational structure ignored the behavior of influential people within organizations: the power struggles, the formation of coalitions, and most importantly, the strategic choices made by individual leaders. This view implies that organizations are shaped less by external or contextual features than by the individuals or groups working within them. These internal factors may take several forms. In a chapter entitled "The Micropolitics of Organizations," Pfeffer (1978, p. 29) suggests that contingency approaches to organizational structure tend to ignore "the conflict in preferences among organizational participants and the resulting contest for control over the organization." Rosengren (1967), on a slightly different note, draws a distinction between organizational control that is achieved through structure, and control that is achieved through the personality features of the leader. Centralization and formalization are two of the primary structural control mechanisms used by complex organizations. Perhaps one reason why I was only able to explain a small proportion of the variance in these variables is that I did not account for the leadership behaviors and supervisory styles of those working within police organizations.

Extending this argument from individual level behaviors to institutional patterns of behavior, it is possible that organizational culture may shape structure as well. Traditionally we think of structure as antecedent to culture, but the opposite may hold as well. For instance, Hall (1999:93) argues that like size and technology, organizational culture "is part of the configuration of internal organizational factors that have been formed in interaction to yield structure and that compose the context in which future structural arrangements are developed." Cultures of control may produce control-oriented structures, and informal cultures may produce informal structures. This line of research and theory suggests that ignoring the individuals, cultures, politics, and strategic choices within organizations will produce an incomplete understanding of organizational structure. If organizations are as predictable as puppets, then context may not hold all of the strings. The challenging part of these alternative theoretical explanations, however, is determining the causal order between organizational structure and culture, politics, leadership, and strategic choice. Doing so will require research designs very different than the one employed in this study.

The Missing Link: Organizational Type and the Failure of Contingency Theory. Contingency theory, as discussed in previous chapters, is a broad-ranging theoretical framework for understanding how organizations adapt to their contexts. As forces in an organization's environment shift, or as new technologies emerge, organizational structure must adapt to the changing conditions in order to achieve maximum efficiency and effectiveness. The majority of comparative research in organizational structure is based implicitly on propositions derived from contingency theory. The problem with applying contingency theory to the police is that like all human-service agencies, judging effectiveness in police organizations requires normative judgments about agency goals (Langworthy, 1986). Measuring, maintaining, and focusing on what constitutes "success" in a police organization is very difficult (Langworthy 1986; Mastrofski, 1998; Mastrofski and Ritti, 2000; Ostrom 1973). If police agencies (and reformers) don't know what is effective, they will be hard-pressed to conform organizational structures in ways that are effective.[2] Consequently, in the absence of clear effectiveness criteria, contingency theory propositions may simply not hold.[3]

Thus, the absence of some structural-contextual linkages in police organizations may be attributable to the fact that they are public organizations. Among organizations in the private sector, there may be real consequences for not adopting a particular organizational form. Population ecologists, for example, study the birth and death rates of particular organizations, and they often find that organizational deaths can be attributed to a failure to adapt to changing contextual circumstances. However, police organizations for the most part do not die off.[4] Thus there are few consequences to be suffered for poorly structured police agencies. Perhaps this is one reason why Crank and Langworthy (1992) and others have likened police agencies to what Meyer and Zucker (1991) call "permanently failing organizations." With few incentives for police to adopt a particular structural form, and no clear roadmap that instructs police managers how to structure a police organization, it is little wonder that some elements of structure appear to be random or unexplainable.

One set of questions this study cannot answer with any certainty is the proper scope of a theory of police organizational structure. Should a theory that explains the structure of police organizations be generalizable only to the police? Or can more general theories be modified to account for those aspects of policing that are unique? More generally, what principles from the corporate world can be applied to policing and expected to produce the same results as in private industry? Former New York City Police Commissioner William Bratton instituted a number of changes using ". . . private-sector business practices and principles for the management of the NYPD, even using the business term "re-engineered" rather than the public policy term "reinventing" government" (Bratton with Knobler, 1998, p. 224). Yet very little is known about the applicability of private sector practices in the public sector more generally, and in policing specifically. Wallace Sayre once quipped that "public and private management are fundamentally alike in all unimportant respects" (Allison, 1992, p. 457). Taken literally, this aphorism suggests that theories of public and private management should be developed separately. This study has shown that relationships found in other organizational types, both public and private, may not apply to the police. Further inquiry into the similarities and differences between police and other types of organizations could generate important knowledge for both theory and policy.

Summary. In this section, I have discussed the implications of this study for theories of police organizational structure. Most of the hypotheses outlined in chapter 5 were not supported, thus many of the ideas imported from the study of other types of organizations did not apply to this sample of police agencies. Some elements of structure are highly predictable, whereas others are almost completely unrelated to the variables examined in this study. Current theories of police organizational structure are not developed sufficiently to explain this finding. I have highlighted three directions that future theoretical explanations of police organizational structure might take. All make sense and all are anchored in what we know about the realities of police organizations. Nevertheless, other possibilities certainly exist, but without further theory development and research, it will be difficult to know which of these possibilities reflects the truth about police organizations.

Research

This project has raised a number of issues about how to study police organizational structures. Langworthy (1986) initiated this line of research by using the comparative method, collecting data from a large number of police agencies, and based on theory, probing for empirical regularities. Because it was an exploratory study, he used mostly bivariate statistics and did not test a comprehensive multivariate model. In this study, I sought to build on Langworthy's foundation by testing a series of theoretically derived multivariate causal models of police organizational structure. I begin this section by discussing the benefits and hazards of using causal models to study police organizations. Second, the structural equation modeling (SEM) techniques that I used in this study are some of the most powerful tools available for testing causal models, and I highlight some of the benefits of this methodology for studying police organizations. However, using SEM, I encountered a number of statistical problems that I believe will also plague other researchers using these methods to study large samples of police organizations. I describe some of these issues and make a number of suggestions about how future researchers might best deal with them. Third, I discuss a number of data quality issues that face researchers in this area and I develop a rough blueprint for developing more meaningful and useful data sets in the future. Finally, I discuss the use of structural variables in future research on the police. This study may be a useful resource for researchers seeking to devise structural measures that are more theoretically meaningful than those used in the past.

Causal Modeling and the Idea of Causal Order. In 1972, *Administrative Science Quarterly* published a series of articles debating the use of causal modeling techniques in the study of organizational structure. The series began with an article by Aldrich (1972a), who used path analysis to re-analyze earlier data from the Aston Group. Aldrich formulated a theory about how technology impacts structure, which in turn impacts organizational size. His secondary analysis then found evidence in support of his theory. In response, Hilton (1972) argued that causal inference analysis is a "seductive" process because it is rarely capable of distinguishing between competing models. Hilton found support for three very different models: Aldrich's model, in which technology was antecedent to structure, both of which were antecedent to size; another model in which size and technology were exogenous to structure; and a third model in which technology was antecedent to structure, and structure was involved in a simultaneous causal relationsip with organizational size. After a rebuttal by Aldrich (1972b), David Heise (1972:60) concluded the debate by suggesting that causal models are valuable because they force the analyst to think through his or her hypotheses carefully, but that there are also dangers associated with these techniques:

> The results of causal analysis are valid if the input theory is valid, but garbage in, garbage out. . . . Different analysts can produce many different models from the same data, even though only one of the obtainable models is correct. What is worse, there is no way to reject wrong models (even nonsense models) by checking them against the same or different cross-sectional data. With some rare and mostly uninteresting exceptions . . . causal analysis of cross-sectional data cannot be used to reject one general theory in favor of another.

Although these cautions apply equally to the structural equation modeling techniques used in this study, there is not a lot of debate about the causal order of the variables in my theoretical model. Most researchers agree that context is antecedent to structure.[5]

Structural Equation Modeling Techniques. The first few pages of Chapter Seven provided a basic introduction to structural equation modeling. Structural equation models force a researcher to think through every possible effect that each variable in a model may have on another. When the analyst does not specify a path between two variables, for example, s/he is asserting a theoretical proposition: that there is a zero relationship between the variables. For instance, if the analyst has explicit ideas about how variables in the model are related to one another, s/he can test these hypotheses by fixing or constraining model parameters to certain theoretically informed values. Doing analyses like this is quite different from the more exploratory techniques used by most social scientists. A number of researchers have commented on the degree of thought that precedes the actual analyses in structural equation modeling. Hage (1980), for example, notes that these types of models are a "powerful technique for organizing not only one's data, but also one's ideas" (p. 6). Heise, speaking of more primitive path analysis techniques, argues that such models force researchers to think about their theories in a far more indepth manner than more traditional statistical techniques. Finally, Joreskog and Wold (1982, cited in Hayduk, 1987, p. xv) note that structural equation models are most useful for scientists who are "willing and able to spend a portion of each day in quiet,analytical thought, thinking through and anticipating possible challenges to their models as currently defined. . . ." In short, the effectiveness of structural equation models depends on the theories that go into them.

Assuming that SEM techniques are based on theories that have been developed carefully, what are their benefits over simpler techniques? Most importantly for this study, they allow us to estimate the measurement and causal elements of a model simultaneously. Measurement is treated as an integral part of the structural modeling process.

When we have multiple indicators of an abstract concept, we can estimate the reliabilities of the latent and manifest variables. For example, a number of researchers have used height and/or segmentation (defined in chapter 6) to measure vertical differentiation. Based on the multiple indicators approach used in this study, we now know that neither of these indicators is very reliable, and that when used together, only about half of the variance in the composite is reliable. In other words, the use of multiple indicators has pointed to a clear deficiency in more than a decade of research on police organizational structures. Unfortunately, I did not have multiple indicators for the majority of variables in the study, thus we still cannot be sure that they are all measured reliably.

Estimates derived from structural equation models using maximum likelihood are based on an assumption that the data are from a multivariate normal distribution. On most measures, large municipal police organizations are not normally distributed. In my sample, which is truncated at the lower end by departments with 100 or more full-time sworn officers, there are many smaller agencies (100–200 officers), and only a handful of larger agencies. Thus, the very enterprise of studying data from large municipal police organizations tends to violate a primary assumption in structural equation modeling.

Does this mean that SEM should be abandoned in research on police organizations? For the most part, as I demonstrated in chapter 7, it just means that researchers need to be cautious in building and interpreting models and in selecting appropriate statistical techniques. Simple methods such as logarithmic and other transformations may help, but their use has theoretical implications as well, and therefore they shouldn't be used lightly. My findings showed that distribution free estimators do not work well with small samples, and should not be used with limited samples of agencies. I used the bootstrapping techniques available in the AMOS program to adjust standard errors and chi-square test-statistics for nonnormality, but this practice is relatively new and the only simulation evidence on the efficacy of these techniques is still unpublished as this book goes to press. As I showed in chapter 7, violation of the multinormality assumption consistently produced deflated standard errors and inflated test statistics. Failing to account for nonnormality could produce a number of incorrect findings. Because different software programs implement unique procedures for correcting these problems, researchers contemplating the use of SEM techniques on nonnormal data should be careful to select the program appropriate for their data.

Finally, one of the major problems I faced in estimating some of the more complex models was that the sample was too small for the

number of parameters needing to be estimated. Such a condition produces unstable parameter estimates, and in this study it limited my ability to draw definitive conclusions from some of the models. There are
two ways to remedy this problem: first, testing simpler models means
estimating fewer parameters, therefore allowing the analyst to use
smaller sample sizes; second, using data sets with less missing data
allows the analyst to estimate more complex models. In the following
section, I explore the second possibility; how better data might produce
a fuller understanding of police organizational structure.

Data Issues. This study combined data from five separate sources to
produce a unique database on the structure and context of large municipal police agencies. While this approach made it possible to test
hypotheses that could not be tested in previous research, combining separate data sources is not an ideal method. Although most of the component surveys used in this analysis had response rates well in excess of
85%, when I put all of the data together the overall rate was much
lower. If a police agency failed to respond to any one of the surveys, or
a necessary item on any one of the surveys, it was excluded from the
analysis. Ideally, what is really needed is a single survey of police agencies that contains items for all the necessary variables. With an 85%
response rate, surveying the 432 large municipal police agencies that
constituted the population in this study would produce a sample size of
367 agencies, well above the sample sizes of all the models reported in
chapter 7.

In addition to the need for more cases, we also need to start focusing on collecting higher quality data. So far, researchers have had to rely
on measures developed by government agencies or other researchers
with a different intellectual agenda. One important step is to develop
multiple indicators for many of the constructs. The use of multiple indicators in this study generated a great deal of useful information on the
reliability of organizational measures.

Another important step is to learn from previous studies. For
instance, chapter 7 pointed out a number of flaws in the LEMAS questions regarding special units and beats. Also, chapter 7 discussed a number of additional problems that I encountered in the supplemental survey with the number of beats and the number of command levels. This
is all valuable information that can be used in future surveys so that we
don't continue to make the same mistakes.[6]

Organizational Variables in Future Research. Chapter 4 highlighted a
number of problems with the use of structural variables in police
research. These variables are used or discussed in two primary ways: as

independent or intermediate variables in models predicting non-structural phenomena (such as arrest rates), and as dependent variables in studies such as this one. In addition, it is likely that with the advent and popularity of hierarchical linear modeling techniques, structural-level features will probably start to be used as contextual variables in multilevel studies of police attitudes and behavior. While this study cannot speak to the effects of structural features as independent variables, it may be useful in conceptualizing and measuring these variables. As I argued in chapter 4, with the exception of a small group of researchers, nearly every usage of structural variables in the literature has been problematic. The notion of a "bureaucratic" police department tramples on theoretical complexity and is no longer useful in studies of police attitudes and behavior. Researchers are encouraged to make conceptually informed decisions about the use of structural variables in future research. For example, while the number of ranks may sometimes be a convenient and available measure, in many instances it is not useful. As I demonstrated in chapter 6, there is a clear difference between the number of ranks and the number of command levels. This study may be helpful in guiding those decisions in future research.

Summary. In this section, I highlighted the implications of this study for future research on police organizations. I discussed some of benefits and problems associated with the use of causal modeling and structural equation modeling techniques in studies of police organizations, and made a number of suggestions for researchers using these tools in the future. In addition, I made a number of recommendations for those who plan to collect data on police organizational structures. Hopefully future data collection efforts can learn from the mistakes of prior studies, thus producing a more cumulative knowledge in this area. Finally, I highlight the importance of conceptualization in future studies of any type that use structural variables. Most of the structural variables used in prior studies of police behavior, for instance, have been more convenient than conceptual. I now discuss the implications of this study for police policy.

Policy

To frame our discussion of the implications of this study for police policy, I return to Langworthy's notion that certain elements of an organization's context might exert constraints on its structure. I refer to this as the "constraint hypothesis." According to Langworthy's (1986:126) explanation of the constraint hypothesis: ". . . variables that constrain or determine structures, limit organizational options, and . . . these constraints will appear as strong correlates. Implicit in this rationale is the notion that weak correlations would not appear to impose insurmountable restrictions on the range of organizational options. That is, if the relation is weak, exceptions are frequent enough to discount the association as a determining factor." Thus, contextual variables not demonstrating significant effects on police organizational structure should not, in practice, constrain the structural options available to police administrators.

Langworthy's analysis of the effects of size, technology, and environment on structure found few constraints. Only spatial differentiation was significantly constrained by organizational size. Technology constrained functional differentiation, though as I discussed in earlier chapters, there were some conceptual problems with the technology measure. Environment exerted an effect only through population size, which was so highly correlated with organization size that it was difficult to separate the two effects. Later research on the constraint hypothesis by Crank and Wells (1991) found that although organizational size had a significant effect on segmentation (which they referred to as "height") and supervisory ratio, these effects were too small to constrain structural options in small police organizations. Thus, to date, the evidence for the constraint hypothesis is fairly weak.

This study generated a number of important findings useful for reevaluating the constraint hypothesis. The most important finding is that contextual variables account for a large portion of the variance in structural complexity factors, and very little of the variance in structural control and coordination factors. The revised models in Table 7.6 explain 82% of the variance in vertical differentiation, 98% of the variance in spatial differentiation, and 31% of the variance in functional differentiation. Thus, knowing something about an organization's context tells us a lot about how that organization is probably structured. On the other hand, contextual variables account for only 14% of the variance in centralization, 6% of the variance in formalization, and 33% of the variance in administrative intensity. Although these three models may have been somewhat unstable, context does not appear to exert significant constraints on structural coordination and control mechanisms.

The policy implications that flow from this conclusion are clear. When reformers suggest that police organizations should become more vertically or spatially differentiated, they may be asking the police to change something beyond their control. After all, nearly all of the variance in these structural features is accounted for by various elements of the organization's context. When reformers ask police organizations to change their levels of functional differentiation or administrative intensity, the police may face some constraints, but certainly not as many as with spatial or vertical differentiation. In other words, these structural features are related to organizational context, but not to such a degree as to substantially limit structural options. But, when reformers ask police organizations to change their levels of centralization or formalization, from a contextual perspective, they are asking things that are achievable. According to the results obtained in this study, reform movements that focus on changing centralization and formalization in police organizations are not bound to fail due to contextual constraints.[7]

The most influential contemporary reform movement in police organizations today is community policing. Community policing advocates have been pressuring police agencies to experiment with a number of innovations, some having to do with organizational structure. According to reformers, police organizations should reduce their levels of vertical differentiation, functional differentiation, centralization, formalization, and administrative intensity. In addition, they should increase their level of spatial differentiation.[8] These changes are supposed to produce leaner and more responsive police organizations that work more closely with the communities they serve, provide more efficient and effective services, and employ officers who are more satisfied with their work.

Yet the research findings from this study may not bode well for the structural reform agendas of community policing advocates. We know that changes in vertical and spatial differentiation may have more to do with organizational context than with the needs and wants of community policing reformers. Whether these significant associations serve in practice as constraints to the decisions made by police managers remains to be seen. Functional differentiation is not so constrained by contextual influences, but my research in this and an earlier study suggest that community policing may result in (or be accompanied by) increasing, rather than decreasing levels of functional differentiation (Maguire, 1997). Reformers may have some success in thinning out the administrative components of police organizations, since context does not exert a strong effect in this area. Lastly, deformalizing and decentralizing appear to be two structural strategies that are not subject to excessive external constraint. This study has found no reasons why police organizations should not continue to explore these strategies as part of their overall shift to a community policing strategy.[9] Of course, these are only one small part of community policing and these changes may not be meaningful if they are not accompanied by commensurate changes in the attitudes and behaviors of police officers on the street.

Conclusion

The structures of large municipal police organizations have been described for the last two decades as rigid, bureaucratic, centralized, militaristic, and often dysfunctional. This study examined police organizational structures empirically, finding that there is tremendous variation in how large municipal police agencies are structured. As I argued in chapter 4, organizational structure is a multivariate concept, and police agencies vary on a number of important structural dimensions. Because they vary on multiple dimensions, it is not appropriate to describe them using classifications like "bureaucratic" or "democratic." Furthermore, some elements of organizational structure are fairly predictable, and others appear to be thoroughly random. For theorists, this finding implies a number of unanswered questions about why police organizations are structured as they are. For researchers, the challenge is to devise increasingly sophisticated measures and a large enough sample of police agencies to test complex theories of police organizational structure. For reformers and policymakers, the findings in this study suggest that some of the structural reforms integral to the community policing movement might be more or less achievable than others. This study generated more questions than answers about the organizational structures of large municipal police agencies in the United States. If policing scholars are to provide any guidance to policy makers about structural reform in these agencies, much work remains to be done.

Notes

Chapter 1. Introduction

1. When the research for this book was being conducted, the 1992 Directory Survey contained the most comprehensive available listing of American police agencies.

Chapter 2. What is Organizational Structure?

1. The one noteworthy exception to this trend is the nomenclature used in the numerous writings of Jerald Hage and Michael Aiken, who use the terms complexity and differentiation to describe different structural elements (e.g., Hage and Aiken, 1967b, 1970; Dewar and Hage, 1978).

2. Langworthy (1986) includes a fourth element of structural complexity that I do not use in this study. Occupational differentiation is the degree to which an organization uses specially trained workers. Functional and occupational differentiation are often, but not always, related. Functional differentiation measures the division of tasks, while occupational differentiation measures the division of staff (Langworthy, 1986). Langworthy operationalizes this variable as the percentage of civilians employed by the agency. While this is a reasonable proxy, it is important to note that it has some shortcomings. Civilians in police organizations perform a variety of functions that are not necessarily specialized. Lutz and Morgan (1974), for instance, suggest that civilians engage in a broad spectrum of clerical, technical and professional duties, some specialized and some not. In many agencies, civilians take over duties formerly handled by police officers—according to this measure of occupational differentiation, the same duties would be considered non-specialized when handled by a police officer, and specialized when handled by a civilian.

3. Managerial decentralization might sometimes be considered a form of "diagonal" differentiation. For example, if a mid-manager in a centralized agency is placed in charge of a new non-centralized operating site, and given considerable responsibility over local operations, decision-making responsibility has been shifted both downward (vertical) and outward (horizontal).

Chapter 3. Explaining Organizational Structure

1. These two sources of complexity are aptly summarized by Scott (1992, p. 264): "one of the great watersheds in the design of organizations is the decision concerning whether tasks are divided and hierarchically coordinated or left in larger clusters and delegated to more highly skilled workers." Law offices and medical group practices, for example, tend to exhibit simple organizational forms because the main work of the organization is performed by autonomous professionals requiring little coordination and control.

2. Because the two concepts may be seen as structural alternatives for achieving control, the literature also reports a consistent negative correlation between formalization and centralization that persists when controlling for size (Mansfield, 1973).

3. Social technologies are also referred to in the literature as service technologies, knowledge technologies, and human technologies.

4. The concept of enactment—that organizations may impact and shape their environments in important ways—suggests that the relationship between organizations and environments may be nonrecursive.

5. While both subjectivists and institutionalists focus on the meaning of the environment, institutionalists, unlike subjectivists, do not assume that only individuals within an organization are capable of reading the meaning. Environments may have meanings for particular components of an organization, entire organizations, organization sets, organizational populations, functional organization fields, or areal organization fields.

6. Marsh and Mannari use a number of terms confusingly in this study, and they do not report all of their regression coefficients in tabular form, thus it is difficult to interpret their findings on the age-structure relationship. They discuss two separate forms of functional differentiation—number of departments and number of subunits—but do not report regression results for, define, or distinguish between the two. Finally, they multiply the number of subsections by the number of levels to form an overall complexity score, thus implicitly forming a multiplicative interaction term. This operational definition of complexity is unlike the mainstream use in the literature, and inconsistent with their own description of complexity earlier in the paper.

7. However, the other structural variables used in this analysis were clearly not among the elements of structure commonly found in the literature. These include the number of full-time paid positions, the proportion of paid to unpaid staff, the number of volunteers and students, the size of budgets, the size of budget deficits, and the total number of workers.

8. However, this model may be unstable as evidenced by (1) their use of OLS and path analytic techniques on sample data containing only 30 cases, and (2) the large difference between the age-structure correlations and the age-structure path coefficients.

Chapter 4. Police Organizational Structure

1. Sherman (1980) reviewed 62 studies of police behavior appearing since 1959, and Riksheim and Chermak (1993) reviewed 70 studies of police behavior published between 1980 and 1989. Researchers have continued to publish such studies since 1989, so the number of studies has surely grown from 132 in 1989 to at least 150 today.

2. These works typically suggest that police departments should adopt particular organizational forms in order to improve performance in one or more areas. Langworthy (1986) terms them "normative theories" because the choice of effectiveness criteria requires a normative judgment about what constitutes effectiveness.

3. There are many normative theories in policing, some of which we have already discussed. These will not be covered here because this work is more concerned with what "is" than with what "ought to be."

4. The professional autonomy model is based on the notion that removing police from party politics was part of a larger movement, implemented in the public interest, toward replacing machine governments with reform governments. An alternative perspective is that these changes were not motivated based on the public interest but on the desires of economic elites hoping to centralize their control over city politics (see Swanstrom, 1985). I am grateful to David Duffee for this observation.

5. Institutional theory has its roots in the institutional school of organizations. Though not exclusively derived from the work of Philip Selznick, the institutional school is well represented in Selznick's writings (Perrow, 1986; Scott, 1992). Selznick described institutionalization as the process by which organizations develop an "organic character" (Perrow, 1986) and become "infused with value beyond the technical requirements of the task at hand" (Selznick, 1957, p. 17). Selznick's early fascination was the paradox that organizations are created for rational action, but that they never quite succeed in conquering non-rational elements of organizational behavior because they are "inescapably embedded in an institutional matrix" (Selznick, 1948, p. 25). Many "modern" discussions of institutional theory, including most of the works that have applied institutionalism to policing, have taken the 1977 article by Meyer and Rowan as a point of departure. While Meyer and Rowan have contributed substantially to the literature, their famous 1977 article was neither the first, nor necessarily the best discussion of institutional theory. Perrow (1986, p. 265), while lauding other work on institutional theory by Meyer and Rowan as "brilliant," argues that the 1977 article is misleading because all organizational activity "is seen as myth creating; it is an unfortunate example of overextension of an important insight."

6. In their essay on police chiefs, Hunt and Mageneau (1993) conceive of institutional theory as an "external perspective on organizations" that helps us to understand organizations "as adaptations to the social contexts in which they are embedded" (pp. 7–8). Institutional analysis to Hunt and Mageneau, "is less

theoretical than it is postural." Other than noting that institutionalism focuses on the normative aspects of organizations, the authors do not separate institutional theory from the many other perspectives on organizational and environmental linkages. Therefore, their discussion is not reported here.

7. A third set of studies, using both cross-sectional and longitudinal designs, also suggests the importance of organizational variables in studying the police. Cross-sectional studies have uncovered jurisdictional differences between police departments on a variety of output measures (e.g., use of force, arrest), but have been unable to specify organizational effects for two reasons: because (a) they did not control for community-level effects (see Sherman, 1980), and/or (b) they did not include organizational-level independent variables in their models (Friedrich, 1980; also see Sherman, 1980). McDowall and Loftin (1986) encountered the same problem in their time-series analysis of police expenditures in Detroit. They use a partial adjustment process that essentially "model[s] the activities within the organization as a black box. The specification provides a way of representing the effects of organizational processes on budgetary outcomes, but it does not explain how the organizational processes work. Our purpose has been to describe the effects of the black box, rather than to examine its contents" (p. 170). Thus this set of studies does not help us to understand what elements of organizations are important, but they underscore the need for including organizational level variables in models explaining police organizational behavior.

8. This definition of centralization is much different than those found in the organizational theory literature. Centralization is typically defined as the degree of autonomy granted to lower level employees or local-level site managers (such as precinct commanders). Smith and Klein's construct works better as a measure of supervisory intensity, which can still be conceived of as a structural measure.

9. While Monkkonen uses this ratio as a measure of structure, Langworthy (1986) uses it as an independent variable (an indicator of technology) to predict structure.

10. In brief, Weber's ideal type bureaucracy contained the following characteristics: fixed distribution of personnel, hierarchical division of authority, intentional system of rules governing decisions and actions, authority based on "rank-in-office" as opposed to "rank-in-man" (see Guyot, 1979), position selection based on technical qualifications rather than election, and an assumption of employment as a career rather than a short-term commitment (Weber, 1947; Scott, 1992). While Weber is widely considered the father of modern organization theory, his conception of bureaucracy has met with considerable criticism (e.g., Gouldner, 1954; Blau and Scott, 1962; Wilson, 1989).

11. Though he uses three structural variables, Crank does not cover a wide range of structural diversity. His variables only tap different dimensions of vertical differentiation. Segmentation is the number of ranks, concentration is the ratio of administrators to sworn officers, and supervisory ratio is the proportion of police officers to sergeants.

12. Other works have examined organizational structure at a different level of analysis. Bayley (1985, 1992) and Virtanen (1979) employ an implicit population ecology approach to the emergence of police organizations cross-nationally, showing how different forms of policing emerge at the national level. Population ecologists focus on populations of organizations as their unit of analysis, rather than single organizations (e.g., Young, 1988). These works are not discussed here in detail because this study focuses on the comparison of police organizations at the "organization set" level. For a review of levels of analysis in organizational studies, see chapter 3.

Chapter 5. A Primitive Theory of Police Organizational Structure

1. I borrow the notion of a "primitive" theory from Peter Blau (1977).

2. Blau (1994) argues that theorists must commit to a theory that posits causal order. While it may be appealing to claim that everything affects everything else in a web of reciprocal relationships, the job of theorists is to untangle that web. As Blau (1994, p. 35) states: "no meaningful analysis of social structures is possible if the investigator always vacillates, attributes any concomitant variation of conditions to reciprocal influences, and refuses to commit himself to a predominant causal direction. Every major social theory makes such a commitment."

3. The increasing availability of complex statistical modeling techniques and readily available computer programs for testing social science theories will be discussed at length in chapter 7.

4. One could conceivably add together standardized measurements of each variable to obtain an overall score of complexity or control. However, this would produce no knowledge about the nature of complexity or control, only the overall magnitude. Furthermore, some of the factors thought to influence organizational structures may increase some forms of complexity and decrease others.

5. Throughout the remainder of this study, I use the following terms interchangeably: administration, administrative intensity, administrative component, administrative density, and administrative overhead.

6. Most of these works are based, either implicitly or explicitly, on propositions derived from structural contingency theory, a broad-ranging theoretical framework which links the internal features of organizations, including structure, to the environments in which they are located, the nature of their clients, the type of work they perform, and the technologies they use to accomplish their work (Donaldson, 1995). Other popular theoretical perspectives, as discussed in chapter 3, include propositions about the relationship between structure and organizational size (Blau, 1970), and organizational age (Stinchcombe, 1965; Downs, 1967).

7. There are fine shades of meaning separating such terms as goals, tasks, technologies, and technical systems. Goals are considered the stated purposes of an organization, tasks the general day-to-day work of the organization, technologies the means of accomplishing tasks, and technical systems the specific duties encompassing the technologies (Scott, 1992). For instance, in a shoe factory, the goal is to make a profit, the task is making shoes, the technologies consist of assorted machinery and a set of assembly lines, and the technical system is comprised of cutting, tanning, sewing, assembling, checking and packaging.

8. Whether these structural mechanisms are effective tools for achieving coordination and control is another question.

9. The effects of age on organizational structure might be attenuated by a number of broad general forces and unique local influences. Broad forces might include shifting professional opinions about how organizations should be structured and a variety of other organizational innovations. Local events (crises, scandals, and other organizational or political issues) may also prompt a variety of structural changes. Thus, age is a proxy for a number of social forces, and interpreting significant age effects might be difficult.

10. Normative literature on decentralization often confuses these two concepts. Under a community policing model, police organizations are urged to decentralize, both spatially (geographically) and administratively. Both forms of decentralization have roots in the early history of precinct-based police organizations.

11. The community policing reform movement, as mentioned earlier, has attempted to reverse the ongoing trend toward increasing structural elaboration. However, recent research shows that reformers have been fairly unsuccessful in implementing their structural reform agendas in large municipal police agencies (Maguire, 1997).

12. The importance of Hasenfeld's (1972) work for understanding how police organizations are structured was first suggested in a conference presentation by Mastrofski and Ritti (1995).

13. The tendency to slot clients into categories is not restricted to the police—it is a common processing function in other criminal justice agencies (McCoy, 1993; Sudnow, 1965) and in many other types of human service bureaucracies as well (Glisson, 1992; Hasenfeld, 1972,1992a,1992b; Lipsky, 1980; Prottas, 1978).

14. For example, Hall (1991, p. 64) notes that although much of the work that street-level bureaucrats like police officers and prison guards perform "cannot be programmed or formalized in advance, much of it is also routinized."

15. The uncertainty that penetrates the lowest levels of the organization frequently emerges from technical portions of the environment. The uncertainty that penetrates the upper levels of the organization generally emerges from both technical and institutional elements of the environment. Thus, structural responses to environmental uncertainty might be the result of technical and/or institutional forces.

16. This is not to say that resource issues are not important for other aspects of police organizations. Municipal police organizations must often compete for resources with other local agencies, and the resource-acquisition process prompts a number of organizational responses within police agencies and other institutions within the larger municipal arena. Resource acquisition strategies affect organizations in a number of areas, including the formation of informal coalitions, the emergence of internal and external power struggles, and the nature of certain politically volatile strategic decisions.

17. First, Dess and Beard (1984) exclude Aldrich's dimension of domain consensus-dissensus because they don't find it applicable to the profit-making institutions they examine. According to Aldrich (1979, p. 68), domain consensus-dissensus refers to "the degree to which an organization's claim to a specific domain is disputed or recognized by other organizations, including governmental agencies." Although police organizations are now beginning to face challenges to their public-safety domain from the growing private-security industry, this challenge is not expected to produce significant alterations in the formal structures of large police agencies in the near future. Second, Dess and Beard (1984) combine stability and turbulence into a single dimension called environmental dynamism. As Hall (1991, p. 211) notes about turbulence, "this is the most difficult of Aldrich's dimensions to understand, since the idea of turbulence seems a great deal like instability." Domain consensus and turbulence are not used in this study.

18. I acknowledge here that my application of the term environmental capacity is different than the way it has been used most often in research and theory on organizations. Nonetheless, its conceptual meaning is quite similar. For those who have difficulty with my use of the term environmental capacity, another term that closely matches it is autonomy.

19. Institutional theorists might see this distinction as very important. Complexity in the task environment may produce indirect effects on structure through technology, whereas complexity in the institutional environment may affect structure directly. The problem with this theoretical approach is that the line between task and institutional environments is nearly always muddied in practice.

20. This is not the first time that a theoretical relationship in organizational sociology has led to such conflicting expectations. The best known example is Blau's (1970, 1994) contention that organizational size produces opposite effects on administrative overhead (using a different definition of overhead than is used in this study). Larger organizations employ a smaller proportion of their personnel in administrative components due to an economy of scale in supervision, but at the same time they increase the relative size of the administrative component indirectly by increasing structural differentiation.

21. Freeman (1973, p. 754) summarizes the hypothesized relationship between environmental complexity and administrative intensity best: "Many administrative functions arise from the relations between organization and envi-

ronment. The more diverse or changeable that environment is, the greater the number of factors requiring administrative action."

22. Interestingly, human service bureaucracies have boundary-spanning positions at both the lowest and highest level positions of the organization. The boundary-spanners at the bottom of the hierarchy are responsible for carrying out the direct work of people-processing or people-changing. They interact with the environment in a technical capacity. Boundary spanners at the other end of the hierarchy are of more concern in this particular discussion, because they interact with the environment in a technical and an institutional capacity. In other words, their role is to represent the organization to powerful and influential entities outside of the organization (Mastrofski, 2001).

23. Wilson (1968, pp. 183–184), for example, suggests that a reform chief in a politically volatile environment must make a number of structural adaptations: "[t]o break through the governing pattern of personal relations, loyalties, and feuds to which he, as an outsider, is alien, he seeks to centralize control, formalize authority, and require written accounts of everything that transpires." Wilson cites the experience of one new chief who "promptly abolished the precinct stations and centralized the entire department into one headquarters building . . ."

24. As Freeman (1973, p. 758) notes, "the more organizations seek to provide their core technologies with the stability necessary for a closed-system logic, the more administrative intensity they will display."

25. All of these structural modifications are based on direct effects, but the relationship between stability and structure may be affected by a set of indirect relationships from stability to technology to structure. This problem is similar to one described earlier in the Environmental Complexity section. Specifically, stable environments may produce routine technologies, which in turn produce complex and controlling structures. This is opposite to the predicted direct effects, and therefore may attenuate the magnitude of the direct effects.

26. History reveals one caveat to this thesis. As police organizations developed communications and transportation technologies, it became easier to control employees through impersonal means such as telephones, two-way radios, computers, and various types of tracking devices (such as electronic vehicle location systems). A number of researchers have demonstrated how technology permitted organizations to centralize spatially without a concomitant loss of organizational control. Hence, the effects of communications technologies may attenuate the relationship between dispersion and structure (Reiss, 1992; Reiss and Bordua, 1967).

27. Donaldson, an Australian, suggests that some of the dissensus can be blamed on the American academic establishment, which rewards new and unique perspectives more than it rewards incremental contributions and refinements to existing theories. According to Donaldson (1995, p. 1), "much of the academic work in the United States is scientifically wanting, lacking in theoretical coherence and often at odds with evidence from empirical studies of real organizations."

Chapter 6. Methodology and Descriptive Statistics

1. Smaller police agencies do exhibit some structural variation, therefore it would be useful to examine patterns of organizational structure in these agencies. Unfortunately, the data sources used in this study do not routinely collect information from the population of smaller agencies.

2. In 1992, there were 12,444 municipal police agencies in the United States serving 165,113,274 people and employing 349,647 sworn full-time police officers. Although the 432 largest municipal police agencies comprised only about 3% of all municipal police agencies, they served 48% of the total population covered by all municipal police agencies, and employed 57% of the police officers. The number of agencies in this size bracket increased from 432 in 1992 to 482 in 1998 (Maguire and Zhao, 2001).

3. Actually, the 1992 Directory Survey lists 435 large municipal police agencies, but the list contains three errors. First, there is one listing for "Bloomingdale Police Department" in Michigan with a population of 503 and 265 full-time sworn officers. There are two agencies of this name in Michigan, but after contacting them both I learned that one of them has only one officer. Second, there are two listings for "Joliet Police Department" in Illinois, one with 191 officers and the other with 189 officers. They are both the same agency, and this is a duplicate listing. Third, there are two listings for "Hamilton Township Police Department" in New Jersey, both with 171 officers. There are two agencies of this name in New Jersey, but after contacting them both I learned that one of them has approximately 40 officers. After dropping these three incorrect listings from the sample, 432 large municipal police agencies remain. These errors are characteristic of an overall quality control problem in the data used to count American police (e.g., Bayley, 1994; Maguire et al., 1997a). Fortunately, the Bureau of Justice Statistics has improved its level of quality control in subsequent studies.

4. One other data source is used as an element of the environmental capacity measure. Previous research has shown that the police accreditation process, through the Commission on Accreditation for Law Enforcement Agencies (CALEA), may have some impact on organizational structure—especially on formalization and specialization (Cordner and Williams, 1996). Accreditation data were collected directly from CALEA and merged with the remaining data sources. The accreditation information will be discussed in more detail later in the chapter.

5. In a previous analysis using some of the same data sets as this study, I found obvious sample selection bias between those who did and did not make into the final analysis using a merged database (Maguire, 1997). Fortunately for the present study, the source of the bias was the sampling strategy used in another survey that is not used in this study. Although selection bias could possibly be a problem in this study, the risk is minimized because all of the primary databases that are merged in this analysis are from surveys that used very simi-

lar sampling strategies. Nonetheless, I explore the possibility of sample selection bias further in chapter 7.

6. My understanding of the concept, definition, and measurement of a police department's age has benefitted greatly from discussions with Samuel Walker at the University of Nebraska at Omaha, and from a paper by, and ongoing correspondence with William King at Bowling Green State University (King, 1999).

7. Based on dozens of discussions with respondents to my supplemental survey, it seems that many U.S. police agencies have little sense of their own history. Respondents were generally frustrated by the age question, and often unable to locate resources within the department that would enable them to answer the question. Interestingly, many respondents who could not estimate the year their departments were established would consult or refer me to the department's unofficial "history buff." Although these people clearly knew a great deal about the department's evolution and could often recite a litany of early historical events, they were frequently unable to find documentation about the initial establishment of the agency.

8. Monkkonen (1981), for example, uses the ratio of nonpatrol to patrol officers as an indicator of "bureaucratization," which is clearly synonymous with structure.

9. Although I find some of Manning's arguments to be persuasive, his review is overly critical in some ways. One theme that is noticeably absent from the review, for instance, is whether the structural organization theory perspective that Langworthy applied to the police was appropriate and/or compelling.

10. In 1991, the National Institute of Justice awarded a research grant to the Police Foundation to conduct a national survey of community policing. After a variety of design stages including a formal pretest, the survey was mailed to a stratified random sample of over 2,000 police agencies in May of 1993. Responses were received from 1,606 agencies (Annan, 1994). All agencies with 100 or more sworn police officers were included in the sample, thus the sampling strategy was similar to that used in the other data sets in this study.

11. This construct is not a measure of community policing, it is a measure of task routineness. The assumption of this measure, as described in chapter 5, is that community policing tasks are nonroutine in comparison with other more traditional police tasks. If some of the police organizations (and their officers) in this sample have routinized community policing functions, then this measure of task routineness will contain measurement error. The best way to measure task routineness would be direct observation research, not agency level survey data.

12. For more information, call 1-800-368-3757, or write to: Commission on Accreditation for Law Enforcement Agencies, Inc., 10306 Eaton Place, Suite 320, Fairfax, VA 22030-2201.

13. For a simplistic explanation of the differences between cause and effect indicators, see Bollen (1989a). For a more in-depth explanation, see Bollen (1989b).

14. For the most part, the social environment of a municipal police organization is contained within the boundaries of a municipality. When I speak of environmental complexity in this study, I am referring to the complexity of the population within the municipality, or within the community. The word community has several meanings, but in this context I am referring to the jurisdiction served by the police agency. More generally, the concept of environmental complexity applies to many units of analysis both larger (countries) and smaller (neighborhoods) than communities.

15. The terms heterogeneity, complexity, and differentiation are all used interchangeably in this section.

16. This file was prepared specially by the Census Bureau so that the U.S. Department of Justice could access place-level demographic data on local police jurisdictions. The Census Bureau defines a "place" as any local jurisdiction that is either incorporated or otherwise designated by the Census Bureau as a place. While the definition of a place is problematic for small jurisdictions and areas with overlapping boundaries, place-boundaries coincide with city-boundaries in nearly all large municipalities.

17. If the income categories contained equal increments (e.g., each group represents an extra $5,000 dollars of income), then it would be possible to compute estimated standard deviations on income for each community by taking the middle value in each group ($27,500 in an income group of $25,000 to $30,000) and using it as the average deviation from the mean for each person in the group. Unfortunately the census income categories are not arranged in evenly sized increments, so using this technique to calculate a standard income deviation would not produce an accurate measure of differentiation.

18. For purposes of this study, the police chief executive is the person within a police department who holds the highest command authority. For most departments this is simply the police chief—the highest ranking sworn officer in the department. For some agencies however, a non-sworn (civilian) commissioner or superintendent is the police chief executive because the individual holding this office has command authority over all sworn personnel. Some municipalities have instituted a public safety director position to oversee all police, fire, and ambulance services. Since, in most cases, the public safety director is not located within the police organization, he or she is not considered the police chief executive.

19. Strictly speaking, we cannot calculate the average tenure of police chiefs from this data since the current chief is still in office. Thus, the 5-year figure should be considered a lower threshold.

20. The theoretically expected effects of area on structure should be moderated by the population-per-area, or the density of the jurisdiction. Thus theoretically, we are really interested in the concept of density, not raw population. However, when multiplying $(A \times D)$, the area terms cancel each other out: substituting $(P \div A)$ for D, the interaction term for area and density equals $(A \times P/A)$,

which reduces to P. Thus, to form the interaction term, I use A × P instead. The complex relationships between A, P, and D in large American cities have been explored in the past by urban sociologists (see Craig and Haskey, 1978), but many issues remain unsettled.

21. In their exploration of the structural covariates of city homicide rates, Land, McCall, and Cohen (1990, p. 943) explore another possible relationship between P and A. They use principle components analysis to develop a "population structure component" that consists of two variables: population size (P) and population density (P ÷ A), both in natural log form. However, they state that their use of principle components analysis to form a single composite from these variables "should be sharply distinguished from the specification of a latent-variable/ factor-analytic/ covariance-structure model. . . ." In other words, their analysis should not be interpreted to mean that P and A emerge from a single latent variable.

22. The decision whether to include or not include the components of an interaction term in regression models is controversial. Nearly all discussions of interaction terms assume the researcher will include the main effects together with the interaction effect in the model. I do not include the main effects of population and area here because they are not elements of the theoretical model, and because they would introduce multicollinearity problems into the model.

23. Many respondents that I spoke with struggled to understand the difference between ranks and levels of command.

24. Approximately 66 of the agencies that responded to the supplemental survey reported having a rank of corporal. The function of this rank in American police agencies is somewhat enigmatic. A handful of surveys were completed by corporals but the responses did not contain corporal as a formal rank. Corporal is generally listed in order of ranks between police officer and sergeant. I initially assumed that all corporals were first line supervisors, until some surveys were returned with a greater number of corporals than police officers. Since it makes no sense to have fewer subordinates than superordinates, I began to contact agencies with corporals to investigate further. The study was nearly completed by the time I began to examine the role of corporals, and therefore I was only able to confirm their function in about a dozen agencies. For the remaining agencies, I counted corporal as a command level if there were more of them than the next higher rank, and fewer of them than the next lower rank. About half of the 66 departments seem to assign corporals as first-line supervisors (32), and about half use this title to designate senior or accomplished police officers. Future surveys should attempt to clarify the role of corporals.

25. In Langworthy's (1986) study, size explained between 2% and 26% percent of the variance in height, depending upon the sample used. Crank and Wells (1991) found that size has a nonlinear effect on height—the effects of size on height are greater in smaller departments. The relationship between height and size will be explored further in chapter 7.

26. After this manuscript was submitted for publication, Wilson (2002) pointed out a flaw in my measure of vertical differentiation. Unlike the other variables for which I computed the Gibbs-Martin D, the number of command levels is not constant across organizations. This means that the potential range of values that D can assume varies by the number of command levels. Wilson (2002) proposes a standardized measure that adjusts the D-value for each agency by the maximum possible value of D. According to Wilson (2002), the correlation between his standardized measure and my original measure is .991 (p < .000), suggesting that the two are essentially interchangeable. Nonetheless, I caution future researchers to use Wilson's (2002) standardized measure.

27. Nearly all of the agencies with a small percentage of officers at the lowest rank have corporals as their second rank. As discussed earlier, it is unknown for many of these agencies whether corporals actually function in a command capacity or whether the title merely designates distinguished or experienced police officers.

28. Langworthy (1986) operationalizes occupational differentiation as the percentage of civilians employed by the agency. Although civilians in police organizations perform a variety of functions that are not necessarily specialized (e.g., Lutz and Morgan, 1974), they do represent a separate occupational category than sworn police officers.

29. Although functional differentiation (FD) has been measured a number of ways, this study follows the method suggested by Reimann (1973, p. 464), who operationalizes "functional specialization" as "the number of discrete, identifiable functions performed by at least one, full-time specialist." Subsequent analyses treating FD as an additive index comprised of indicators in which (0 = no unit, 1 = PT unit, 2 = FT unit) yielded similar results. However, the part-time category is a probable source of uncertainty in the FD construct because respondents may be unsure about what exactly constitutes a part-time special unit. Walker and Katz (1995) discovered a substantial degree of measurement error in one of the LEMAS questions regarding specialized units. Specifically, 37.5% of the departments who indicated in their LEMAS responses that they had a specialized unit for enforcing bias crime statutes, when contacted subsequently by researchers, reported that they never had such a unit. Presumably, similar problems would affect questions regarding other types of special units, which are combined to form the composite FD index in this study.

30. This is an imperfect measure of functional differentiation. Recall from our discussion of environmental complexity, that the level of differentiation in nominal variables is best measured using the Gibbs-Martin D formula. This formula not only takes into account the number of separate groups, but also the number of members in each group. This would be an ideal strategy for measuring functional differentiation, but unfortunately, until 1997, the LEMAS series only collected information on the presence or absence of special units, not on the number of personnel in each unit.

31. My understanding of spatial differentiation and the various sources of data for measuring this concept has benefitted greatly from conversations with Bob Langworthy at the Justice Center, University of Alaska at Anchorage.

32. Most police departments, even in this sample of large municipal agencies, have only one police station, thus it is necessary to use additional measures of spatial differentiation. The supplemental survey also collected information on "the number of fixed part-time police service facilities staffed by sworn police officers (mini-stations, kobans, police posts, storefronts, etc. . . . .)." Unfortunately, there were two problems with these counts. First, departments had some difficulty in distinguishing between these facilities and those staffed by volunteers (or not staffed on a regular basis at all), thus the measures probably have some validity problems. Second, the largest police agencies were not able to provide these counts, and since I did not want these agencies to drop out of the analysis due to missing data on this measure, I decided to just use full-time police stations and beats.

33. This information is from 1993. Since that time, according to the supplemental survey response, the NYPD has merged with the Transit Police and the Housing Authority Police. Due to the merger, the NYPD had more than 100 police stations as of 1996.

34. When speaking with early respondents to the supplemental survey, I learned that the phrase "patrol beat" has two different meanings for the police. Some define a beat as a patrol sector or a zone, and some define a beat as an individual patrol unit, whether an automobile, a bicycle, or a foot patrol officer. This study maintains the same definition as Langworthy (1986), in which a beat is an individual patrol unit. According to this definition, a two person patrol car would be a single beat, and two one-officer patrol cars would be two beats. The focus is on the deployment of patrol units across the jurisdiction's space. Once I discovered that "beats" has two meanings, I changed the wording of the beat questions.

35. There is some controversy in the organizational literature about the best way to measure administrative intensity. In addition to using the proportion of administrative personnel, studies of administrative intensity have used a number of other measures, including the A/P ratio, which is the ratio of administrative to production employees. Langworthy (1986, p. 53) argues that these different methods are robust and produce similar results.

36. This measure is the best available estimate of administrative personnel in large municipal police agencies, but it is not ideal. Police agencies are not accustomed to counting employees in ways that are useful to organizational researchers. Therefore, nonproduction employees in the patrol bureau probably get counted as patrol personnel. Production employees in an administrative division probably get counted as administrative personnel. The scope of measurement error in this variable is inestimable because it depends on how individual police agencies divide up their workers into divisions.

Chapter 7. Testing the Theory

1. In addition, linear structural equation models are often referred to as "LISREL" models, based on Jöreskog and Sörbom's popular LISREL computer program used to estimate SEM models (Alwin, 1988).

2. Causation cannot be established in recursive models estimated with cross-sectional survey data. Nevertheless, social scientists frequently employ the language of causation in path modeling, causal modeling, and/or structural modeling to describe the degree of change effected in an outcome variable by a unit change in a causal variable. However, when using cross-sectional data, there is no actual change in the causal variable, and therefore "the 'change' interpretation of the structural coefficient is an analogue" (Alwin, 1988, p. 77). While some researchers are fairly comfortable using causal language (Alwin, 1988, p. 77; Asher, 1983, pp. 11–12), others recommend strongly against this practice (Schumacker and Lomax, 1990, p. 90). Recognizing the limitations of cross-sectional models in establishing causation, I employ the language of causation to describe the effects of independent variables on dependent variables.

3. As opposed to cluster analysis, in which researchers explore relationships among sets of individual cases.

4. For a more comprehensive list of fields (including citations) that use structural equation models, see Hayduk (1987, p. xiii).

5. Schumacker and Lomax suggest an additional step between model specification and estimation: determining whether the model is "identified." In other words, does the model as specified contain sufficient information to calculate unique solutions for all of the unknowns? Given the ease with which researchers can specify structural equation models in today's SEM software packages, it is often tempting to allow the software to determine whether a model is identified. Nevertheless, it is important for the analyst using SEM to become familiar with the conditions of identification to make necessary adjustments when a model is not identified.

6. Unlike factor analysis, estimating a measurement model allows the researcher to test whether coefficients are significantly different from zero rather than arbitrarily dropping indicators with loadings less than (0.3). The loading for occupational differentiation was significant at the (0.05) level, but the loading was so small (0.19), that I decided to drop it from the model anyway.

7. Since latent variables have no natural unit of measurement, it is necessary to impose a metric. Throughout this study, I use the "reference indicator" approach, which forces the latent variable to assume the metric of one of its indicators by fixing the (unstandardized) loading with that indicator at one. In this case, since none of the indicators has an intuitively appealing unit of measurement, I arbitrarily chose D_{educ}.

8. If (a) equals the number of indicators, (b) equals the sum of the correlations between indicators, and $(\sum h\mu^2)$ equals the sum of squared factor loadings (the communalities), then omega is defined as follows:

$$\Omega = 1 - \left(\frac{a - \Sigma h\mu^2}{a + 2b}\right)$$

Omega is a moderate measure of the reliability of a composite; compared with other measures, it tends to produce reliability estimates that fall in the middle (Bacon, Sauer, and Young, 1995). Recent research shows that neither omega, nor the more popular alpha coefficient, should be used to make decisions about which items in the composite to retain (Bacon, Sauer, and Young, 1995). It is not used here for that purpose, merely to provide a reasonable estimate of the reliability of the composite measure.

9. According to the rules for using logarithms, $\ln (P \times A) = \ln (P) + \ln (A)$.

10. As described in chapter 6, there are two possible measures of concentration: the proportion of employees at the lowest command level (LowRank) and the Gibbs-Martin measure of differentiation applied to the rank data (D_{rank}). Both Langworthy (1986) and Crank and Wells (1991) used LowRank—nobody to my knowledge has used Drank to measure vertical differentiation. The two measures are almost perfectly correlated, though measured in opposite directions ($r = -0.96$). Although LowRank does not account for the distribution of personnel throughout the rank structure, it is probably a reasonable approximation in police organizations. In most large municipal police organizations, the structure of upper-level ranks more or less resembles the narrow end of a pyramid, and therefore it is the distribution of personnel at the lowest ranks (the base of the pyramid) that contributes most heavily to a measure of distribution throughout the various levels of the organization.

11. Recall from our discussion in chapter 6 that the maximum value of D is 1 minus the reciprocal of the number of groups, thus the maximum value approaches 1 as the number of groups increases toward infinity. For example, the maximum value of D_{rank} with 5 ranks is equal to 1 minus one-fifth, or (0.8), and for 8 ranks it is 1 minus one-eighth, or (0.875). Because the number of ranks is built into the computation of D_{rank}, we would expect these two variables to be correlated.

12. Crank and Wells (1991, p. 178) report a significant positive correlation between "height" and concentration ($r = 0.354$). Based on this finding, they suggest that "the greater the height of the organization, the greater the concentration of personnel at the lowest ranks." They operationalize height as the number of ranks, which is equivalent to the segmentation measure used in this study. I find a significant negative correlation ($r = -0.159$) between segmentation and concentration (using LowRank, or the percentage of officers at the lowest rank). The reason for this large discrepancy is probably that Crank and Wells misread their correlation matrix (Table 1, p. 178), which shows the actual correlation to be ($r = -0.029$). The ($r = 0.354$) figure that they relied on for the above quoted comment comes from elsewhere in the matrix. Combining this revised interpretation of the Crank and Wells study with the present findings suggests that the more segmented the police organization, the lower the concentration of personnel at the lowest command levels.

13. Inadmissible solutions in SEM frequently include negative error variances (known as "Heywood" cases) and out-of-range standardized regression and correlation coefficients (Bentler and Chou, 1987; Rindskopf, 1984; Wothke, 1993).

14. For correct models, this ratio should be close to 1. However, there is some disagreement among researchers about how large the ratio should be before concluding that the model does not fit the data (Arbuckle, 1997). According to Wheaton and his colleagues (1977), a ratio of 5 or less is fairly reasonable. Carmines and McIver (1981, p. 80) suggest that "χ^2 to degrees of freedom ratios in the range of 2 to 1 or 3 to 1 are indicative of an acceptable fit between the hypothetical model and the sample data." Byrne (1989), on the other hand, suggests that ratios larger than two represent a poor fit.

15. At the 0.05 level, if the absolute value of the critical ratio is greater than 1.96, the effect is statistically significantly different from 0.

16. "The ratio of sample size to the number of free parameters may be able to go as low as 5:1 under normal and elliptical theory, especially when there are many indicators of latent variables and the associated factor loadings are large . . . a ratio of 10:1 may be more appropriate for arbitrary distributions. These ratios need to be larger to obtain trustworthy z-tests of the significance of parameters, and still larger to yield correct model evaluation chi-square probabilities" (Bentler and Chou, 1987, p. 91).

17. When evaluating the fit of a single model, a nonsignificant chi-square test statistic implies that the model fits the data well. However, when comparing nested models using the hierarchical chi-square test, a significant reduction in chi-square suggests that the simpler model fits the data better than the more complex model.

18. Based on the idea that sample selection bias resulting from nonrandom sampling procedures "is proportional to the probability of exclusion" (Berk 1983, p. 392), researchers for many years have used statistical procedures to correct models for selection bias. The Heckman two-step procedure and other similar statistical corrections for selection bias use logit or probit models to estimate the predicted probability of nonresponse. They then introduce this probability as an independent variable into the main regression model, therefore "controlling" for nonresponse bias. However, Monte Carlo research by Stolzenberg and Relles (1987, p. 406) has demonstrated that in simulations, this time-worn technique "reduced the accuracy of coefficient estimates as often as it improved them." They recommend that such procedures should only play a "small and infrequent" role in correcting for sample selection bias.

19. Although I do not find evidence of nonresponse bias in this study, some researchers contend that organizational survey nonresponse may be systematic. Tomaskovic-Devey, Leiter, and Thompson (1994) develop a theory that links organizational survey nonresponse to various features of organizations and their environments. If this theory is valid, then organizations that do not respond

to surveys should, as a set, be different than organizations that do complete surveys. Organizations with poorly developed information-processing technologies,
for instance, may find it more difficult to fill out some surveys.

Chapter 8. Summary and Conclusions

1. There are a number of scattered references to this possibility in the
police literature. Guyot (1991, pp. 4–5), for instance, suggests that organizational age produces changes in the nature and scope of tasks that police agencies
perform. Ferdinand (1992) suggests that a common trajectory in the evolution
of a police agency may be from a service to a legalistic style, and that this trend
will be reflected in arrest statistics, agency structure, and patterns of leadership.
Wertsch (1992) notes a similar trend in his discussion of the Des Moines Police
Department's evolution throughout the twentieth century. Historical research is
clearly needed to determine how aging processes affect (or constrain) various
characteristics of large municipal police organizations.

2. For police organizations that do have a clear set of goals about agency
success, Oettmeier (1992) suggests that they need to match their structures to
their objectives. He implores police executives to achieve a tighter fit between
their organizations and changes in strategy and/or environment.

3. For example, Mohr (1971, p. 452) suggests that at least one contextual
variable—technology—might not affect structure in the absence of effectiveness
criteria: "[T]echnology may not actually force structure, but rather . . . organizations will be effective only insofar as their structures are consonant with, or
follow the dictates of, their technologies." The consonance hypothesis has
received qualitative support over the years from researchers noting how the "fit"
between technology and structure is integral to organizational effectiveness
(Burns and Stalker, 1961; Woodward, 1965; Mastrofski and Ritti, 1995).

4. While conventional wisdom in policing suggests that police organizations do not "go out of business" (Travis and Brann, 1997), recent work by
William King and his colleagues (King, Travis, and Langworthy, 1997) challenges this assumption. Based on a survey of county Sheriffs in Ohio, King and
his colleagues documented the death of 104 police agencies (and the birth of an
additional 15). They are now replicating this study in several other states. These
"dead" police agencies were quite small, however, and it is rare for larger municipal police departments like the ones in my sample to shut down. Sometimes
they may consolidate with other agencies to capitalize on economies of scale. In
general, however, police agencies have amazingly persistent life spans compared
with other types of organizations. For example, more than half of the agencies
in my sample are more than 90 years old, with a mean and median age of 93
years. A recent national study based on a random sample of organizations (of
many types) found a mean age of 39 years (Marsden, Cook, and Knoke, 1996).
Public organizations were the oldest, with a median age of more than 53 years.

5. Chapter 4 mentioned one exception to this assertion: the relationship between technology and structure. There are three allusions to this possibility in the literature, but none have been very well developed so far. First, researchers who study the determinants of innovation sometimes use structural features as independent variables. Since most innovations are technical or technological in nature, this line of research implies that structure may be antecedent to technology (King, 1998). Second, Manning (1992) has argued that in police organizations, technology and structure are intertwined in a complex simultaneous causal relationship (see chapter 4 for a discussion of Manning's hypothesis). His hypothesis was very general, however, and it was only mentioned in passing. Lastly, Glisson (1978) tested a theoretical model in which structure was exogenous to technology. As pointed out in chapter 3 however, this research contains some serious flaws. Nevertheless, Glisson (1978,1992) makes a logical case that structure may precede technology in causal order. In short, it is possible that structure may be antecedent to technology, and there are some fairly compelling theoretical reasons that this may be so, but to date there is no good research to demonstrate such an effect.

6. Prior to the 1997 LEMAS survey, the Bureau of Justice Statistics (BJS) sent a draft of the survey instrument to researchers who use the LEMAS data. Based on feedback from researchers, BJS modified the instrument in an effort to rectify the problems with the 1993 instrument. Using the 1997 data, researchers will now be able to construct better measures of spatial and functional differentiation. I am grateful to Brian Reaves and Andrew Goldberg at BJS for instituting these changes.

7. Why do centralization and formalization have such low levels of explained variance compared with administrative intensity? Administrative intensity is the one structural control and coordination factor that might be difficult for police managers to alter at will. This would involve hiring, firing, or transferring personnel to/from administrative positions. Formalization and centralization are easier to change: they might sway and shift in response to the culture of the staff, the tone of the organization, or the behavior of the leader. A new leader might change the level of centralization or formalization overnight with a swift command or memo. Centralization and formalization are easier to change than the other elements of structure in this study, and therefore they may be more random. In short, they may present fewer constraints.

8. For a review of structural changes that community policing reformers have recommended, see Cordner (1997), Maguire (1997), Mastrofski (1998), Mastrofski and Ritti (2000), or Redlinger (1994).

9. Although there do not appear to be any contextual constraints on these structural elements, there may be other types of constraints. For example, Wenger (1973) discusses the tendency of police organizations during civil disturbances to revert to a military model of command (e.g., formalized and centralized) to function effectively. It may be that although these modes of command are not effective in routine day-to-day police work (e.g., Bittner, 1973), there are some circumstances under which the military model is functional.

References

Aiken, M., & Hage, J. (1968). Organizational interdependence and intra-organizational structure. *American Sociological Review* 3(6): 912–931.

Aldrich, H. E. (1972a). Technology and organizational structure: A reexamination of the findings of the Aston Group. *Administrative Science Quarterly* 17:26–43.

Aldrich, H. E. (1972b). Reply to Hilton: Seduced and abandoned. *Administrative Science Quarterly* 17:55–57.

Aldrich, H. E. (1979). *Organizations and environments.* Englewood Cliffs, NJ: Prentice-Hall.

Aldrich, H. E. (1992). Incommensurable paradigms? Vital signs from three perspectives. In M. Reed & M. Hughes (eds.), *Rethinking organization: New directions in organization theory and analysis.* Newbury Park, CA: Sage Publications.

Allison, G. T. (1992). Public and private management: Are they fundamentally alike in all unimportant respects? In J. M. Shafritz & A. C. Hyde (eds.), *Classics of public administration* (pp. 457–475). Belmont, CA: Wadsworth Publishing.

Alwin, D. F. (1988). Structural equation models in research on human development and aging. In K. W. Schaie, R. T. Campbell, W. Meredith, & S. C. Rawlings (eds.), *Methodological Issues in Aging Research* (pp. 71–170). New York: Springer Publishing.

Anderson, T., & Warkov, S. (1961). Organizational size and functional complexity: A study of administration in hospitals. *American Sociological Review* 26:23–38.

Angell, J. E. (1971). Toward an alternative to the classic police organizational arrangements: A democratic model. *Criminology* 9:185–206.

Angell, J. E. (1975). The democratic model needs a fair trial: Angell's response. *Criminology* 12:379–384.

Annan, S. (1994). *Community policing strategies: A comprehensive analysis.* Methodology Report submitted to the National Institute of Justice. Washington, DC: Police Foundation.

Arbuckle, J. L. (1997). *Amos users guide version 3.6.* Chicago: Smallwaters.

Archambeault, W. G., & Wierman, C. L. (1983). Critically assessing the utility of police bureaucracies in the 1980s—Implications of management theory Z. *Journal of Police Science and Administration* 4:420–429.

Argyris, C. (1972). *The applicability of organizational sociology.* Cambridge: Cambridge University Press.

Asher, H. B. (1983). *Causal modeling.* Sage university paper series on quantitative applications in the social sciences, 07-003. Newbury Park, CA: Sage Publications.

Bacon, D. R., Sauer, P. L., & Young, M. (1995). Composite reliability in structural equations modeling. *Educational and Psychological Measurement* 55:394–406.

Bailey, J. (1996). Policing the force: The LAPD is treated to a business analysis and it comes up short. *Wall Street Journal,* Tuesday, June 11.

Baker, A. W., & Davis, R. C. (1954). *Ratios of staff to line employees and stages of differentiation of staff functions.* Columbus, Ohio: Bureau of Business Research, Ohio State University.

Banfield, E., & Wilson, J. Q. (1963). *City politics.* Cambridge, MA: Harvard University Press.

Baron, J. N., Mittman, B. S., & Newman, A. E. (1991). Targets of opportunity: Organizational and environmental determinants of gender integration within the California civil service, 1979–1985. *American Journal of Sociology* 96(6):1362–1401.

Bayley, D. H. (1985). *Patterns of policing.* New Brunswick, NJ: Rutgers University Press.

Bayley, D. H. (1992). Comparative organization of the police in English-speaking countries. In M. Tonry & N. Morris (eds.), *Modern policing.* Chicago: University of Chicago Press.

Bayley, D. H. (1994). *Police for the future.* New York: Oxford University Press.

Bendix, R. (1956). *Work and authority in industry.* New York: John Wiley & Sons.

Benson, J., & Fleischman, J. A. (1994). The robustness of maximum likelihood and distribution free estimators to non-normality in confirmatory factor analysis. *Quality and Quantity* 28(2):117–136.

Bentler, P. M. (1989). *EQS structural equations program manual.* Los Angeles: BMDP Statistical Software.

Bentler, P. M. (1997). Personal correspondence via electronic mail: January 9, 1997.

Bentler, P. M., & Chou, C. (1987). Practical issues in structural modeling. *Sociological Methods and Research* 16(1):78–117.

Berger, P. L., & Luckman, T. (1967). *The social construction of reality.* New York: Doubleday.

Berk, R. A. (1983). An introduction to sample selection bias in sociological data. *American Sociological Review* 48:386–98.

Bernard, T. J., & Snipes, J. B. (1996). Theoretical integration in criminology. In M. Tonry (ed.), *Crime and justice: A review of research*, Vol. 20 (pp. 301–348). Chicago: University of Chicago Press.

Berry, W. D., & Feldman, S. (1985). *Multiple regression in practice*. Sage university paper series on quantitative applications in the social sciences, 07–050. Newbury Park, CA: Sage Publications.

Beyer, J. M., & Trice, H. M. (1979). A reexamination of the relations between size and various components of organizational complexity. *Administrative Science Quarterly* 24:48–64.

Bittner, E. (1973). Quasi-military organization of the police. In T. J. Sweeney & W. Ellingsworth (eds.), *Issues in police patrol: A book of readings*. Washington, DC: Police Foundation.

Black, D. (1976). *The behavior of law*. New York: Academic Press.

Blackburn, R. S. (1982). Dimensions of structure: A review and reappraisal. *Academy of Management Review* 7(1):59–66.

Blau, P. M. (1955). *The dynamics of bureaucracy: A study of interpersonal relations in two government agencies*. Chicago: University of Chicago Press.

Blau, P. M. (1956). *Bureaucracy in modern society*. New York: Random House.

Blau, P. M. (1970). A formal theory of differentiation in organizations. *American Sociological Review* 35:201–218.

Blau, P. M. (1977). *Inequality and heterogeneity: A primitive theory of social structure*. New York: Free Press.

Blau, P. M. (1994). *The organization of academic work* (2nd ed.). New York: John Wiley & Sons.

Blau, P. M., Heyderbrand, W. V., & Stauffer, R. E. (1966). The structure of small bureaucracies. *American Sociological Review* 31:179–191.

Blau, P. M., & Schoenherr, R. A. (1971). *The structure of organizations*. New York: Basic Books.

Blau, P. M., & Scott, W. R. (1962). *Formal organizations*. San Francisco: Chandler.

Bollen, K. A. (1989a). "Cause" and "effect" indicators. In E. Babbie, *The practice of social research* (5th ed.) (p. 395). Belmont, CA: Wadsworth Publishing.

Bollen, K. A. (1989b). *Structural equations with latent variables*. New York: John Wiley & Sons.

Bollen, K. A. (1997). Posting to the SEMNet (Structural Equation Modeling Network) electronic discussion group: January 8, 1997.

Bollen, K. A., & Stine, R. A. (1993). Bootstrapping goodness-of-fit measures in structural equation models." In K. A. Bollen & J. S. Long (eds.), *Testing Structural Equation Models* (pp. 111–135). Newbury Park, CA: Sage Publications.

Bordua, D. J., & Reiss, A. J. (1966). Command, control and charisma: Reflections on police bureaucracy. *American Journal of Sociology* 72:68–76.

Borges, J. L. (1964). The moon. In J. L. Borges, *Dreamtigers* (pp. 64–66). (Mildred Boyer & Harold Morland, trans.). Austin, TX: University of Texas Press.

Braiden, C. (1986). Bank robberies and stolen bikes: Thoughts of a street cop. *Canadian Police College Journal* 10(1):1–14..

Bratton, W. J., with Knobler, P. (1998). *Turnaround: How America's top cop reversed the crime epidemic.* New York: Random House.

Brown, J. L., & Schneck, R. (1979). A structural comparison between Canadian and American industrial organizations. *Administrative Science Quarterly* 24(1):24–47.

Brown, M. K. (1981). *Working the street: Police discretion and the dilemmas of reform.* New York: Russell Sage Foundation.

Browne, M. W. (1984). Asymptotically distribution-free methods in the analysis of covariance structures. *British Journal of Mathematical and Statistical Psychology* 37:62–83.

Burns, T., & Stalker, G. M. (1961). *The management of innovation.* London: Tavistock.

Burrell, G., & Morgan, G. (1979). *Sociological paradigms and organizational analysis.* London: Heinemann.

Byrne, B. M. (1989). *A primer of LISREL: Basic applications and programming for confirmatory factor analytic models.* New York: Springer Publishing.

Carmines, E. G. (1986). The analysis of covariance structure models. In W. D. Berry & M. S. Lewis-Beck (eds.), *New tools for social scientists: Advances and applications in research methods* (pp. 23–56). Beverly Hills, CA: Sage Publications.

Carmines, E. G., & McIver, J. P. (1981). Analyzing models with unobserved variables. In G. W. Bohrnstedt & E. F. Borgatta (eds.), *Social measurement: Current issues.* Beverly Hills, CA: Sage.

Carroll, G. R., & Delacroix, J. (1982). Organizational mortality in the newspaper industries of Argentina and Ireland: An ecological approach. *Administrative Science Quarterly* 27:169–198.

Castrogiovanni, G. J. (1991). Environmental munificence: A theoretical assessment. *Academy of Management Review* 16(3):542–565.

Chan, W., Yung, Y., & Bentler, P. M. (1995). A note on using an unbiased weight matrix in the ADF test statistic. *Multivariate Behavioral Research* 30(4):453–459.

Child, J. (1972a). Organization structure and strategies of control: A replication of the Aston study. *Administrative Science Quarterly* 17:163–177.

Child, J. (1972b). Organizational structure, environment and performance: The role of strategic choice. *Sociology* 6:1–22.

Child, J. (1973). Predicting and understanding organization structure. *Administrative Science Quarterly* 18:168–185.

Child, J., & Mansfield, R. (1972). Technology, size, and organizational structure. *Sociology* 6(3):369–393.

Chou, C., Bentler, P. M., & Satorra, A. (1991). Scaled test statistics and robust standard errors for non-normal data in covariance structure analysis: A Monte Carlo study. *British Journal of Mathematical and Statistical Psychology* 44:347–357.

Clark, J. P., Hall, R. H., & Hutchinson, B. (1977). Interorganizational relationships and network properties as contextual variables in the study of police performance. In D. H. Bayley (ed.), *Police and society*. Beverly Hills, CA: Sage Publications.

Coleman, J. S. (1974). *Power and the structure of society*. New York: W.W. Norton.

Comstock, D., & Scott, W. R. (1977). Technology and the structure of subunits: Distinguishing individual and workgroup effects. *Administrative Science Quarterly* 22:177–202.

Cordner, G. W., & Williams, G. L. (1996). Community policing and accreditation: A content analysis of CALEA standards. In L. T. Hoover (ed.), *Quantifying quality in policing*. Washington, DC: Police Executive Research Forum.

Cordner, G. W. (1997). Community policing: Elements and effects. In G. Alpert & R. Dunham (eds.), *Critical issues in policing: Contemporary readings*. Prospect Heights, IL: Waveland Press.

Craig, J., & Haskey, J. (1977). The relationships between the population, area, and density of urban areas. *Urban Studies* 15:101–107.

Crank, J. P. (1989). Civilianization in small and medium police departments in Illinois, 1973–1986. *Journal of Criminal Justice* 17:167–177.

Crank, J. P. (1990). The influence of environmental and organizational factors on police style in urban and rural environments. *Journal of Research in Crime and Delinquency* 27(2):166–189.

Crank, J. P. (1994). Watchman and community: Myth and institutionalization in policing. *Law and Society Review* 28(2):325–351.

Crank, J. P., & Langworthy, R. (1992). An institutional perspective of policing. *Journal of Criminal Law and Criminology* 83(2):338–363.

Crank, J. P., & Wells, L. E. (1991). The effects of size and urbanism on structure among Illinois police departments. *Justice Quarterly* 8(2):170–185.

Curran, P. J., West, S. G., & Finch, J. F. (1996). The robustness of test statistics to nonnormality and specification error in confirmatory factor analysis. *Psychological Methods* 1(1):16–29.

Dalton, D. R., Todor, W. D., Spendolini, M. J., Fielding, G. J., & Porter, L. W. (1980). Organization structure and performance: A critical review. *Academy of Management Review* 5:49–64.

Dess, G. G., & Beard, D. W. (1984). Dimensions of organizational task environments. *Administrative Science Quarterly* 29:52–73.

Dewar, R., & Hage, J. (1978). Size, technology, complexity, and structural differentiation: Toward a theoretical synthesis. *Administrative Science Quarterly* 23(1):111–136.

Dimaggio, P., & Powell, W. W. (1983). The iron cage revisited: Institutional isomorphism and collective rationality in organizational fields. *American Sociological Review* 48:147–160.

Donaldson, L. (1995). *American anti-management theories of organization: A critique of paradigm proliferation.* Cambridge: Cambridge University Press.

Downs, A. (1967). *Inside bureaucracy.* Boston: Little, Brown.

Duffee, D. E. (1990). *Explaining criminal justice: Community theory and criminal justice reform.* Prospect Heights, IL: Waveland Press.

Duncan, O. D. (1966). Path analysis: Sociological examples. *American Journal of Sociology* 72:1–16.

Duncan, R. B. (1972). Characteristics of organizational environments and perceived environmental uncertainty. *Administrative Science Quarterly* 17:313–327.

Durkheim, É. (1949). *The division of labor in society* (George Simpson, trans.). Glencoe, IL: Free Press. (Original appeared in French as *De la division du travail swocial.* Paris: Alcan, 1893.)

Epstein, S. R., Russell, G., & Silvern, L. (1988). Structure and ideology of shelters for battered women. *American Journal of Community Psychology* 16(3):345–367.

Evers, F. T., Bohlen, J. M., & Warren, R. D. (1976). The relationships of selected size and structure indicators in economic organizations. *Administrative Science Quarterly* 21:326–342.

Ferdinand, T. N. (1992). From a service to a legalistic style police department: A case study. In E. H. Monkkonen (ed.), *Policing and crime control.* Munich: K. G. Saur.

Fisher, J. C., & Mason, R. L. (1981). The analysis of multicollinear data in criminology. In J. A. Fox (ed.), *Methods in quantitative criminology.* New York: Academic Press.

Flinn, J. J. (1973). *History of the Chicago police from the settlement of the community to the present time.* New York: AMS Press. (Original work published 1871.)

Fogelson, R. M. (1977). *Big city police.* Cambridge, MA: Harvard University Press.

Ford, J. D., & Slocum, J. (1977). Size, technology, environment, and the structure of organizations. *Academy of Management Review* 2:561–575.

Fowler, K., & Schmidt, D. (1989). Determinants of tender post-acquisition financial performance. *Strategic Management Journal* 10:339–350.

Franz, V., & Jones, D. M. (1987). Perceptions of organizational performance in suburban police departments—A critique of the military model. *Journal of Police Science and Administration* 2:153–161.

Freeman, J. H. (1973). Environment, technology, and the administrative intensity of manufacturing organizations. *American Sociological Review* 38:750–763.

Friedrich, R. J. (1980). Police use of force: Individuals, situations, and organizations. *Annals of the American Academy of Political and Social Science* 452:82–97.

Frisby, W. (1985). A conceptual framework for measuring the organizational structure and context of voluntary leisure service organizations. *Society and Leisure* 8(2):605–613.

Galbraith, J. (1973). *Designing complex organizations.* Reading, MA: Addison-Wesley.

Galbraith, J. (1977). *Organization design.* Reading, MA: Addison-Wesley.

Gerbing, D. W., & Andersen, J. C. (1993). Monte Carlo evaluations of goodness-of-fit indices for structural equation models. In K. A. Bollen & J. S. Long (eds.), *Testing structural equation models.* Newbury Park, CA: Sage Publications.

Gibbs, J., & Martin, W. T. (1962). Urbanization, technology, and the division of labor: International patterns. *American Sociological Review* 27:667–677.

Gillespie, D. F., & Mileti, D. S. (1977). Technology and the study of organizations: An overview and appraisal. *Academy of Management Review* 2(1):7–16.

Glisson, C. A. (1978). Dependence of technological routinization on structural variables in human service organizations. *Administrative Science Quarterly* 23(3):383–395.

Glisson, C. (1992). Structure and technology in human service organizations. In Y. Hasenfeld (ed.), *Human Services as Complex Organizations* (pp. 184–202). Newbury Park, CA: Sage Publications.

Glisson, C. A., & Martin, P. Y. (1980). Productivity and efficiency in human service organizations as related to structure, size, and age. *Academy of Management Journal* 23(1):21–37.

Goldstein, H. (1977). *Policing a free society.* Cambridge, MA: Ballinger.

Goldstein, H. (1990). *Problem-oriented policing.* New York: McGraw-Hill.

Gouldner, A. W. (1954). *Patterns of industrial bureaucracy.* Glencoe, IL: Free Press.

Greenberg, S. F. (1992). *On the dotted line: Police executive contracts.* Washington, DC: Police Executive Research Forum.

Gupta, P. P., Dirsmith, M. W., & Fogarty, T. J. (1994). Coordination and control in a government agency: Contingency and institutional theory perspectives on GAO audits. *Administrative Science Quarterly* 39:264–284.

Guyot, D. (1979). Bending granite: Attempts to change the rank structure of American police departments. *Journal of Police Science and Administration* 7(3):253–284.

Guyot, D. (1991). *Policing as though people matter.* Philadelphia: Temple University Press.

Hage, J. (1980). *Theories of organizations: Form, process, and transformation.* New York: John Wiley & Sons.

Hage, J., & Aiken, M. (1967a). Program change and organizational properties: A comparative analysis. *American Journal of Sociology* 72(5):503–519.

Hage, J., & Aiken, M. (1967b). Relationship of centralization to other structural properties. *Administrative Science Quarterly* 12(1):72–92.

Hage, J., & Aiken, M. (1969). Routine technology, social structure, and organization goals. *Administrative Science Quarterly* 14(3):366–377.

Hage, J., & Aiken, M. (1970). *Social change in complex organizations.* New York: Random House.

Hagle, T. (1995). *Basic math for social scientists: Concepts.* Sage university paper series on quantitative applications in the social sciences, 07-108. Thousand Oaks, CA: Sage Publications.

Haire, M. (1959). Biological models and empirical histories of the growth of organizations. In M. Haire (ed.), *Modern Organization Theory* (pp. 272–306). New York: John Wiley & Sons.

Hall, R. H., Haas, J. E., & Johnson, N. J. (1967). Organizational size, complexity, and formalization. *American Sociological Review* 32:903–912.

Hall, R. H. (1972). *Organization: Structure and process.* Englewood Cliffs, NJ: Prentice Hall.

Hall, R. H. (1991). *Organizations: Structures, processes, and outcomes* (5th ed.). Englewood Cliffs, NJ: Prentice Hall.

Hall, R. H. (1999). *Organizations: Structures, processes, and outcomes* (7th ed.). Upper Saddle River, NJ: Prentice Hall.

Harring, S. L., & McMullin, L. M. (1992). The Buffalo police 1872–1900: Labor unrest, political power and the creation of the police institution. In E. H. Monkkonen (ed.), *Policing and crime control*. Munich: K. G. Saur.

Harrison, F. (1975). Bureaucratization: Perceptions of role performance and organizational effectiveness. *Journal of Police Science and Administration* 3(3):319–326.

Harrison, F., & Pelletier, M. A. (1987). Perceptions of bureaucratization, role performance, and organizational effectiveness in a metropolitan police department. *Journal of Police Science and Administration* 15(4):262–270.

Harvey, E. (1968). Technology and the structure of organizations. *American Sociological Review* 33:247–259.

Hasenfeld, Y. (1972). People processing organizations: An exchange approach. *American Sociological Review* 37:256–263.

Hasenfeld, Y. (1992a). The nature of human service organizations. In Y. Hasenfeld (ed.), *Human services as complex organizations* (pp. 3–23). Newbury Park, CA: Sage Publications.

Hasenfeld, Y. (1992b). Theoretical approaches to human service organizations. In Y. Hasenfeld (ed.), *Human services as complex organizations* (pp. 24–44). Newbury Park, CA: Sage Publications.

Hassell, K. (2000). *Police-probation partnerships: One city's response to serious habitual juvenile offending.* Unpublished master's thesis, University of Nebraska at Omaha.

Hayduk, L. A. (1987). *Structural equation modeling with LISREL: Essentials and advances.* Baltimore: Johns Hopkins University Press.

Heise, D. R. (1972). How do I know my data? Let me count the ways. *Administrative Science Quarterly* 17:58–61.

Heise, D. R., & Bohrnstedt, G. W. (1970). Validity, invalidity, and reliability. In E. F. Borgatta and G. W. Bohrnstedt (eds.), *Sociological Methodology.* San Francisco: Jossey-Bass.

Henly, S. J. (1993). Robustness of some estimators for the analysis of covariance structures. *British Journal of Mathematical and Statistical Psychology* 46:313–338.

Herbert, S. (1997). *Policing space: Territoriality and the Los Angeles police department.* Minneapolis: University of Minnesota Press.

Heydebrand, W. (1973a). *Hospital bureaucracy: A comparative study of organizations.* New York: Dunellen.

Heydebrand, W. (1973b). General introduction. In W. V. Heydebrand (ed.), *Comparative organizations: The results of empirical research.* Englewood Cliffs, NJ: Prentice Hall.

Hickson, D. J., & McMillan, C. J. (eds.) (1981). *Organization and nation: The Aston programme IV.* Aldershot: Gower Publishing.

Hickson, D. J., Pugh, D. S., & Pheysey, D. C. (1969). Operations technology and organization structure: An empirical reappraisal. *Administrative Science Quarterly* 14(3):378–397.

Hilton, G. (1972). Causal inference analysis: A seductive process. *Administrative Science Quarterly* 17(1):44–61.

Holdaway, E. A., & Blowers, T. A. (1971). Administrative ratios and organizational size: A longitudinal examination. *American Sociological Review* 36:278–286.

Hsu, C., Marsh, R. M., & Mannari, H. (1983). An examination of the determinants of organizational structure. *American Journal of Sociology* 88(5):975–996.

Huff, C. R. (1987). Organizational structure and innovation in urban police departments. *Public Administration Review* 47(6):508–509.

Hunt, R. G., & Mageneau, J. M. (1993). *Power and the police chief: An institutional and organizational analysis.* Newbury Park, CA: Sage Publications.

Indik, B. P. (1964). The relationship between organization size and supervision ratio. *Administrative Science Quarterly* 9(3):301–312.

Inkson, J. H. K., Pugh, D. S., & Hickson, D. J. (1970). Organization context and structure: An abbreviated replication. *Administrative Science Quarterly* 15(3):318–329.

Jaccard, J., Turrisi, R., & Wan, C. K. (1990). *Interaction effects in multiple regression.* Sage University Paper series on Quantitative Applications in the Social Sciences, 07-072. Newbury Park, CA: Sage Publications.

Jermier, J. (1979). Review of "Police work: The social organization of policing" by P. K. Manning. *Administrative Science Quarterly* 24:688–692.

Jöreskog, K. G., & Sörbom, D. (1989). *LISREL 7: A guide to the program and applications* (2nd ed.). Chicago: SPSS.

Jurkovich, R. (1974). A core typology of organizational environments. *Administrative Science Quarterly* 18(3):380–394.

Kalleberg, A. L., & Leicht, K. T. (1991). Gender and organizational performance: Determinants of small business survival and success. *Academy of Management Journal* 34(1):136–161.

Kalleberg, A. L., Knoke, D., Marsden, P. V., & Spaeth. J. L. (eds.) (1996). *Organizations in America: Analyzing their structures and human resource practices.* Thousand Oaks, CA: Sage Publications.

Kaplan, D. (1991). The behaviour of three weighted least squares estimators for structured means analysis with non-normal likert variables. *British Journal of Mathematical and Statistical Psychology* 44:333–346.

Kasarda, J. D. (1974). The structural implications of social system size: A three-level analysis. *American Sociological Review* 39:19–28.

Katz, C., Maguire, E. R., & Roncek, D. W. (2001). The formation of specialized police gang units: A test of three competing theories. Unpublished manuscript, Arizona State University West.

Kaufman, H., & Seidman, D. (1970). The morphology of organizations. *Administrative Science Quarterly* 15(4):439–451.

Kelling, G., & Bratton, W. (1993). Implementing community policing: The administrative problem. *Perspectives on Policing*, no. 4. Washington DC: National Institute of Justice.

Kelling, G. L., Pate, T., Dieckman, D., & Brown, C. (1974). *The Kansas City preventive patrol experiment: A summary report*. Washington, DC: Police Foundation.

Khandwalla, P. N. (1977). *The design of organizations*. New York: Harcourt Brace Jovanovich.

Kimberly, J. R. (1975). Environmental constraints and organizational structure: A comparative analysis of rehabilitation organizations. *Administrative Science Quarterly* 20(1):1–9.

Kimberly, J. R. (1976). Organizational size and the structuralist perspective: A review, critique, and proposal. *Administrative Science Quarterly* 21: 571–597.

King, W. R. (1998). *Innovativeness in American municipal police organizations*. Unpublished Ph.D. dissertation, University of Cincinnati, Cincinnati, Ohio.

King, W. R. (1999). Time, constancy, and change in American municipal police organizations. *Police Quarterly* 2(3):338–364.

King, W. R., Travis, L.F. III, & Langworthy, R. H. (1997, November). Police organizational death. Presented at the annual meeting of the American Society of Criminology, San Diego, CA.

Klatzky, S. R. (1970). Relationship of organizational size to complexity and coordination. *Administrative Science Quarterly* 15(4):428–438.

Kraska, P. B., & Kappeler, V. E. (1997). Militarizing American police: The rise and normalization of paramilitary units. *Social Problems* 44(1):1–16.

Kriesburg, L. (1973). Organizations and international cooperation. In W. V. Heydebrand (ed.), *Comparative organizations: The results of empirical research*. Englewood Cliffs, NJ: Prentice Hall.

Kriesburg, L. (1976). Centralization and differentiation in international non-governmental organizations. *Sociology and Social Research* 61(1):1–23.

Kuykendall, J., & Roberg, R. (1982). Mapping police organizational change: From a mechanistic toward an organic model. *Criminology* 20:241–256.

Lammers, C. J. (1974). The state of organizational sociology in the United States: Travel impressions by a Dutch cousin [Letter to the Editor]. *Administrative Science Quarterly* 19:422–430.

Lammers, C. J., & Hickson, D. J. (eds.) (1975). *Organizations alike and unlike: International and inter-institutional studies in the sociology of organizations*. Boston: Routledge & Kegan Paul.

Land, K. C., McCall, P. L., & Cohen, L. E. (1990). Structural covariates of homicide rates: Are there any invariances across time and social space? *American Journal of Sociology* 95(4):922–963.

Lane, R. (1992). Urban police and crime in nineteenth century America. In M. Tonry & N. Morris (eds.), *Modern policing*. Chicago: University of Chicago Press.

Langworthy, R. (1983a). The effects of police agency size on the use of police employees: A re-examination of Ostrom, Parks and Whitaker. *Police Studies* 5:11–19.

Langworthy, R. H. (1983b). *The formal structure of municipal police organizations*. Unpublished doctoral diss., State University of New York at Albany.

Langworthy, R. H. (1985a). Police department size and agency structure. *Journal of Criminal Justice* 13:15–27.

Langworthy, R. H. (1985b). Administrative overhead in municipal police departments. *American Journal of Police* 4:20–37.

Langworthy, R. H. (1985c). Wilson's theory of police behavior: A replication of the constraint theory. *Justice Quarterly* 2:89–98.

Langworthy, R. H. (1986). *The structure of police organizations*. New York: Praeger.

Langworthy, R. H. (1992). Organizational structure. In *What works in policing?*, eds. G. W. Cordner & D. C. Hale. Cincinnati, OH: Anderson Publishing.

Langworthy, R. H. (1994). Personal communication, Ann Arbor, MI.

Langworthy, R. H. (1996). Personal communication, Washington, DC.

Langworthy, R. H., & Chamlin, M. B. (1997, March). Types of police organization. Presented at the annual meeting of the Academy of Criminal Justice Sciences, Louisville, KY.

Langworthy, R. H., & LeBeau, J. (1992). Spatial distribution of sting targets. *Journal of Criminal Justice* 20(6):541–551.

Lawrence, P. R., & Lorsch, J. W. (1967). Differentiation and integration in complex organizations. *Administrative Science Quarterly* 12(1):1–47.

Lipsky, M. (1980). *Street-level bureaucracy: Dilemmas of the individual in public services*. New York: Russell Sage Foundation.

Loehlin, J. C. (1992). *Latent variable models: An introduction to factor, path, and structural analysis* (2nd ed.). Hillsdale, NJ: Lawrence Erlbaum Associates.

Lunden, W. A. (1958). The mobility of chiefs of police. *Journal of Criminal Law, Criminology, and Police Science* 49(2):178–183.

Lundman, R. J. (1994). Demeanor or crime? The midwest city police-citizen encounters study. *Criminology* 32(4):631–656.

Lutz, C., & Morgan, J. (1974). Jobs and rank. In O. G. Stahl & R. A. Staufenberger (eds.), *Police personnel administration.* Washington, DC: Police Foundation.

MacFarlane, R. I., & Morris, A. S. (1981). *A synthesis of research affecting police administration.* McLean, VA: Public Administration Service.

Maguire, B. (1990). The police in the 1800s: A three-city analysis. *Journal of Crime and Justice* 13(1):103–132.

Maguire, E. R. (1994, April). Police organizational structure and child sexual abuse case resolution patterns. Presented at the Academy of Criminal Justice Sciences meeting, Chicago, IL.

Maguire, E. R. (1997). Structural change in large municipal police organizations during the community policing era. *Justice Quarterly* 14(3):701–730.

Maguire, E. R., Kuhns, J. B., Uchida, C. D., & Cox, S. (1997a). Patterns of community policing in non-urban America. *Journal of Research in Crime and Delinquency* 34(3):368–394.

Maguire, E. R., Snipes, J. B., Uchida, C. D., & Townsend, M. (1997b). Counting cops: Estimating the number of police officers and police agencies in the United States. *Policing: An international journal of police strategies and management* 21(1):97–120.

Maguire, E. R., & Mastrofski, S. D. (2000). Patterns of community policing in the United States. *Police Quarterly* 3(1):4–45.

Maguire, E. R., & Zhao, J. (2001). *The structure of large municipal police organizations in the community policing era.* Unpublished report, George Mason University, Manassas, VA.

Mannheim, B. F., & Moskovits, N. (1979). Contextual variables and bureaucratic types of Israeli service organizations. In Cornelis J. Lammers and David J. Hickson (eds.), *Organizations alike and unlike: International and inter-institutional studies in the sociology of organizations.* Boston: Routledge & Kegan Paul.

Manning, P. K. (1971). The police: Mandate, strategies, and appearances. In J. D. Douglas (ed.), *Crime and Justice in American Society.* New York: Macmillan.

Manning, P. K. (1977). *Police work: The social organization of policing.* Cambridge, MA: MIT Press.

Manning, P. K. (1988a). Review of *The structure of police organizations* by Robert Langworthy. *Administrative Science Quarterly* June, vol. 33: 323–327.

Manning, P. K. (1988b). *Symbolic communication: Signifying calls and the police response.* Cambridge, MA: MIT Press.

Manning, P. K. (1989). Community policing. In *Critical issues in policing: Contemporary readings*, eds. R. G. Dunham & G. P Alpert. Prospect Heights, IL: Waveland Press.

Manning, P. K. (1992). Information technologies and the police. In M. Tonry & N. Morris (eds.), *Modern policing* (pp. 51–98). Chicago: University of Chicago Press.

Mansfield, R. (1973). Bureaucracy and centralization: An examination of organizational structure. *Administrative Science Quarterly* 18:477–488.

March, J. G., & Simon, H. A. (1958). *Organizations.* New York: John Wiley & Sons.

Mardia, K. V. (1970). Measures of multivariate skewness and kurtosis with applications. *Biometrika* 57:519–530.

Marsden, P. V., Cook, C. R., & Kalleberg, A. L. (1994). Organizational structures: Coordination and control. *American Behavioral Scientist* 37(7):911–929.

Marsden, P. V., Cook, C. R., & Knoke, D. (1996). American organizations and their environments. In A. L. Kalleberg, D. Knoke, P. V. Marsden, & J. L. Spaeth (eds.), *Organizations in America: Analyzing their structures and human resource practices* (pp. 45–66). Thousand Oaks, CA: Sage Publications.

Marsh, R. M., & Mannari, H. (1981). Technology and size as determinants of the organizational structure of Japanese factories. *Administrative Science Quarterly* 26(1):33–57.

Mastrofski, S. D. (1981). Policing the beat: The impact of organizational scale on patrol officer behavior in urban residential neighborhoods. *Journal of Criminal Justice* 9:343–358.

Mastrofski, S. D. (1988). Varieties of police governance in metropolitan America. *Politics and policy* 8:12–31.

Mastrofski, S. D. (1995). Personal communication.

Mastrofski, S. D. (1997). Personal communication.

Mastrofski, S. D. (1998). Community policing and police organization structure. In J.-P. Brodeur, *How to recognize good policing: Problems and issues* (pp. 161–189). Newbury Park, CA: Sage Publications.

Mastrofski, S. D. (2001). The romance of police leadership. In E. Waring, D. Weisburd, & L. Sherman (eds.), *Theoretical advances in criminology* (pp. 153–196). New Brunswick, NJ: Rutgers University Press.

Mastrofski, S. D., & Ritti, R. R. (1995, November). Making sense of community policing: A theory-based analysis. Presented at the American Society of Criminology meeting, Boston, MA.

Mastrofski, S. D., & Ritti, R. R. (1996). Police training and the effects of organization on drunk driving enforcement. *Justice Quarterly* 13(2):291–320.

Mastrofski, S. D., & Ritti, R. R. (2000). Making sense of community policing: A theory-based analysis. *Police Practice* 1(2):183–210.

Mastrofski, S. D. Ritti, R. R., & Hoffmaster, D. (1987). Organizational determinants of police discretion: The case of drinking-driving. *Journal of Criminal Justice* 15:387–402.

Mastrofski, S. D., & Uchida, C. D. (1993). Transforming the police. *Journal of Research in Crime and Delinquency* 30(3):330–358.

McCoy, C. (1993). *Politics and plea bargaining*. Philadelphia: University of Pennsylvania Press.

McDowall, D., & Loftin, C. (1986). Fiscal politics and the police: Detroit, 1928–1976. *Social Forces* 65(1):162–176.

Melman, S. (1951). The rise of administrative overhead in the manufacturing industries of the United States 1899–1947. *Oxford Economic Papers* 3:62–112.

Merton, R. K., Gray, A. P., Hockey, B., & Selvin, H. C. (eds.) (1952). *Reader in bureaucracy*. Glencoe, IL: Free Press.

Meyer, A. D. (1982). Adapting to environmental jolts. *Administrative Science Quarterly* 27:515–537.

Meyer, J., & Rowan, B. (1977). Institutionalized organizations: Formal structure as myth and ceremony. *American Journal of Sociology* 83(2):340–363

Meyer, M. W. (1968a). Automation and bureaucratic structure. *American Journal of Sociology* 74(3):256–264.

Meyer, M. W. (1968b). The two authority structures of bureaucratic organizations. *Administrative Science Quarterly* 13(2):211–228.

Meyer, M. W. (1972a). *Bureaucratic structure and authority: Coordination and control in 254 government agencies*. New York: Harper & Row.

Meyer, M. W. (1972b). Size and the structure of organizations: A causal analysis. *American Sociological Review* 37(4):434–440.

Meyer, M. W. (1979). *Change in public bureaucracies*. Cambridge: Cambridge University Press.

Meyer, M. W., & Brown, M. C. (1978). The process of bureaucratization. In M. W. Meyer & Associates (eds.), *Environments and Organizations* (pp. 51–77). San Francisco: Jossey-Bass.

Meyer, M. W., & Zucker, L. G. (1989). *Permanently failing organizations*. Newbury Park, CA: Sage Publications.

Mills, P. K., & Moberg, D. J. (1982). Perspectives on the technology of service organizations. *Academy of Management Review* 7(3):467–478.

Mintzberg, H. (1979). *The structure of organizations*. Englewood Cliffs, NJ: Prentice-Hall.

Mohr, L. (1971). Organizational technology and organizational structure. *Administrative Science Quarterly* 16(4):444–451.

Monkkonen, E. H. (1981). *Police in urban America*. New York: Cambridge University Press.

Moore, M. H. (1992). Problem solving and community policing. In M. Tonry & N. Morris (eds.), *Modern policing*. Chicago: University of Chicago Press.

Moore, M. H., & Stephens, D. (1992). Organization and management. In W. A. Geller (ed.), *Local government police management*. Washington, DC: International City Managers Association.

Murphy, C. J. (1986). *The social and formal organization of small town policing: A comparative analysis of RCMP and municipal policing*. Unpublished Ph.D. dissertation, University of Toronto, Canada.

Muthén, B., & Kaplan, D. (1992). A comparison of some methodologies for the factor analysis of non-normal likert variables: A note on the size of the model. *British Journal of Mathematical and Statistical Psychology* 45:19–30.

Muthén, L. K., & Muthén, B. (1998). *Mplus: The comprehensive modeling program for applied researchers, user's guide*. Los Angeles: Muthén and Muthén.

National Criminal Information Center (1989). Originating agency identifier (ORI) file. In *NCIC Operating Manual*, chapter 13. Washington, DC: Federal Bureau of Investigation.

Oettmeier, T. N. (1992). Matching structure to objectives. In L. T. Hoover (ed.), *Police management: Issues and perspectives* (pp. 31–60). Washington, DC: Police Executive Research Forum.

Ostrom, E. (1973). On the meaning and measurement of output and efficiency in the provision of urban police services. *Journal of Criminal Justice* 1:93–112.

Ostrom, E., Parks, R. B., & Whitaker, G. P. (1978a). *Patterns of metropolitan policing*. Cambridge, MA: Ballinger.

Ostrom, E., Parks, R. B., & Whitaker, G. P. (1978b). Police agency size: Some evidence on its effects. *Police studies* March, vol. 1, issue 1:34–46.

Ostrom, E., Parks, R. B., Whitaker, G. P., & Percy, S. L. (1979). The public service production process. In R. Baker & F. A. Meyer, Jr. (eds.), *Evaluating alternative law enforcement policies*. Lexington, MA: Lexington Books.

Ostrom, E., & Smith, D. C. (1976). On the fate of "Lilliputs" in metropolitan policing. *Public Administration Review* 36(2):192–200.

Parsons, T. (1947). Introduction. In M. Weber, *The theory of social and economic organization* (pp. 3–86). Glencoe, IL: Free Press.

Perrow, C. (1967). A framework for the comparative analysis of organizations. *American Sociological Review* 32:194–208.

Perrow, C. (1986). *Complex organizations: A critical essay* (3rd ed.). Glenview, IL: Scott, Foresman.

Pfeffer, J. (1978). The micropolitics of organizations. In M. W. Meyer & Associates (eds.), *Environments and organizations* (pp. 29–50). San Francisco: Jossey-Bass.

Pfeffer, J., & Salancik, G. R. (1978). *The external control of organizations.* New York: Harper and Row.

Prottas, J. M. (1978). The power of the street-level bureaucrat in public service bureaucracies. *Urban Affairs Quarterly* 13:285–312.

Pugh, D. S. (1973). The measurement of organization structures: Does context determine form? *Organizational Dynamics* Spring:19–34.

Pugh, D. S., & Hickson, D. J. (1976). *Organizational structure in its context: The Aston Programme I.* Aldershot: Gower.

Pugh, D. S., & Hickson, D. J. (1989). *Writers on organizations* (4th ed.). Newbury Park, CA: Sage Publications.

Pugh, D. S., Hickson, D. J., & Hinings, C. R. (1969). An empirical taxonomy of structures of work organizations. *Administrative Science Quarterly* 14(1):115–126.

Pugh, D. S., Hickson, D. J., Hinings, C. R., Macdonald, K. M., Turner, C., & Lupton, T. (1963). A conceptual scheme for organizational analysis. *Administrative Science Quarterly* 8(3):289–315.

Pugh, D. S., Hickson, D. J., Hinings, C. R., & Turner, C. (1968). Dimensions of organization structure. *Administrative Science Quarterly* 13:65–105.

Pugh, D. S., Hickson, D. J., Hinings, C. R., & Turner, C. (1969). The context of organization structures. *Administrative Science Quarterly* 14:91–114.

Pugh, D. S., & Hinings, C. R. (eds.) (1976). *Organizational structure extensions and replications: The Aston Programme II.* Aldershot: Gower.

Pugh, D. S., & Payne, R. L. (eds.) (1977). *Organizational behaviour in its context: The Aston Programme III.* Aldershot: Gower.

Punch, M. (ed.) (1983). *Control in the police organization.* Cambridge, MA: MIT Press.

Reaves, B. (1993). *Census of state and local law enforcement agencies, 1992.* Washington, DC: Bureau of Justice Statistics.

Redlinger, L. (1994). Community policing and changes in the organizational structure. *Journal of Contemporary Criminal Justice* 10(1):36–58.

Reimann, B. C. (1973). On the dimensions of bureaucratic structure: An empirical reappraisal. *Administrative Science Quarterly* 18(4):462–476.

Reiss, A. J., Jr. (1992). Police organization in the twentieth century. In M. Tonry & N. Morris (eds.), *Modern Policing* (pp. 51–98). Chicago: University of Chicago Press.

Reiss, A. J., Jr., & Bordua, D. J. (1967). Environment and organization: A perspective on the police. In D. J. Bordua (ed.), *The police: Six sociological essays*. New York: John Wiley and Sons.

Richardson, J. F. (1992). The struggle to establish a London-style police force for New York City. In E. H. Monkkonen (ed.), *Policing and crime control*. Munich: K. G. Saur.

Riksheim, E., & Chermak, S. (1993). Causes of police behavior revisited. *Journal of Criminal Justice* 21:353–382.

Rindskopf, D. (1984). Structural equation models: Empirical identification, Heywood cases, and related problems. *Sociological Methods and Research* 13(1):109–119.

Robbins, S. P. (1987). *Organization theory: Structure, design, and applications*(2nd ed.). Englewood Cliffs, NJ: Prentice Hall.

Roberg, R. (1994). Can today's police organizations effectively implement community policing? In D. P. Rosenbaum (ed.), *The challenge of community policing*. Thousand Oaks, CA: Sage Publications.

Rosengren, W. R. (1967). Structure, policy, and style: Strategies of organizational control. *Administrative Science Quarterly* 12:140–164.

Rushing, W. A. (1966). Organizational size and administration. *Pacific Sociological Review* 9 (Fall):100–108.

Rushing, W. A. (1967). The effect of industry size and division of labor on administration. *Administrative Science Quarterly* 12:271–295.

Rushing, W. A. (1968). Hardness of material as an external constraint on the division of labor in manufacturing industries. *Administrative Science Quarterly* 10:423–443.

Rushing, W. A. (1976). Profit and nonprofit orientations and the differentiations-coordination hypothesis for organizations: A study of small general hospitals. *American Sociological Review* 41:676–691.

Samuel, Y., & Mannheim, B. F. (1970). A multidimensional approach toward a typology of bureaucracy. *Administrative Science Quarterly* 15:216–229.

SAS Institute. (1990). *SAS/STAT user's guide* (4th ed.). Cary, NC: SAS Institute.

Scheingold, S. A. (1991). *The politics of street crime*. Philadelphia: Temple University Press.

Schumacker, R. E., & Lomax, R. G. (1996). *A beginner's guide to structural equation modeling*. Mahwah, NJ: Lawrence Erlbaum Associates.

Scott, W. R. (1992). *Organizations: Rational, natural, and open systems* (3rd ed.). Englewood Cliffs, NJ: Prentice Hall.

Selznick, P. (1948). Foundations on the theory of organization. *American Sociological Review* 13:25–35.

Selznick, P. (1949). *TVA and the grass roots.* Berkeley & Los Angeles: University of California Press.

Selznick, P. (1957). *Leadership in administration.* New York: Harper & Row.

Sherman, L. W. (1980). Causes of police behavior: The current state of quantitative research. *Journal of Research in Crime and Delinquency* 17:69–100.

Skolnick, J. H., & Bayley, D. H. (1986). *The new blue line: Police innovation in six American cities.* New York: Free Press.

Skolnick, J. H., & Bayley, D. H. (1988). Theme and variation in community policing. In M. Tonry & N. Morris (eds.), *Crime and justice: A review of the research,* Vol. 10. Chicago: University of Chicago Press.

Slovak, J. (1986). *Styles of urban policing: Organization, environment, and police styles in selected American cities.* New York: New York University Press.

Smith, D. A. (1984). The organizational context of legal control. *Criminology* 22:19–38.

Smith, D. A., & Klein, J. R. (1983). Police agency characteristics and arrest decisions. In G. P. Whitaker & C. D. Phillips (eds.), *Evaluating performance of criminal justice agencies.* Beverly Hills, CA: Sage Publications.

Smith, D. A., & Klein, J. R. (1984). Police control of interpersonal disputes. *Social Problems* 31:468–481.

Smith, D. A., Visher, C. A., & Davidson, L. A. (1984). Equity and discretionary justice: The influence of race on police arrest decisions. *Journal of Criminal Law and Criminology* 75(1):234–249.

Snipes, J. B., & Worden, A. P. (1993). The relationship between police chief values and local legal community ethos: An exchange perspective. Unpublished paper, State University of New York at Albany.

Sparrow, M., Moore, M., & Kennedy, D. (1990). *Beyond 911: A new era for policing.* New York: Basic Books.

Stanfield, G. G. (1976). Technology and organization structure as theoretical categories. *Administrative Science Quarterly* 21:489–493.

Starbuck, W. (1976). Organizations and their environments. In M. D. Dunnette (ed.), *Handbook of industrial and organizational psychology* (pp. 1069–1123). Chicago: Rand McNally.

Stinchcombe, A. L. (1965). Social structure and organization. In J. G. March (ed.), *Handbook of organizations.* Chicago: Rand McNally.

Stinchcombe, J. B. (1980). Beyond bureaucracy—A reconsideration of the "professional" police. *Police studies* 3(1):49–61.

Stolzenburg, R. M., & Relles, D. A. (1990) Theory testing in a world of constrained research design: The significance of Heckman's censored sampling bias correction for nonexperimental research. *Sociological Methods and Research* 18(4):395–415.

Sudnow, D. (1965). Normal crimes: Sociological features of the penal code in a public defender's office. *Social Problems* 12:255–276.

Sutton, J. R. (1988). *Stubborn children.* Berkeley & Los Angeles: University of California Press.

Swanson, C. (1978). The influence of organization and environment on arrest practices in major U.S. cities. *Policy Studies Journal* 7:390–398.

Swanstrom, T. (1985). *The crisis of growth politics: Cleveland, Kucinich, and the challenge of urban populism.* Philadelphia: Temple University Press.

Terrien, F. W., & Mills, D. L. (1955). The effect of changing size upon the internal structure of organizations. *American Sociological Review* 29:11–13.

Thompson, J. D. (1967). *Organizations in action.* New York: McGraw-Hill.

Thompson, J. D., & Bates, F. E. (1957). Technology, organization and administration. *Administrative Science Quarterly* 2:323–343.

Tolbert, P. S. (1985). Institutional environments and resource dependence: Sources of administrative structure in institutions of higher education. *Administrative Science Quarterly* 30:1–13.

Tomaskovic-Devey, D., Leiter, J., & Thompson, S. (1994). Organizational survey nonresponse. *Administrative Science Quarterly* 39:439–457.

Travis, J., & Brann, J. E. (1997). Introduction. In *Measuring what matters, part two: Developing measures of what the police do.* Research in Action, Washington, DC: U.S. Department of Justice, National Institute of Justice.

Tsouderos, J. E. (1955). Organizational change in terms of a series of selected variables. *American Sociological Review* 20:206–210.

United States Census Bureau (1990). *1990 decennial census, summary tape file extract 3A* [electronic data tape]. Washington, DC: U.S. Census Bureau.

Van de Ven, A. H., & Delbecq, A. L. (1974). A task contingent model of work-unit structure. *Administrative Science Quarterly* 18(2):183–197.

Van de Ven, A. H., Delbecq, A. L., & Koenig, R. Jr. (1976). Determinants of coordination modes within organizations. *American Sociological Review* 41:322–338.

Van Maanen, J. (1978). The asshole. In P. K. Manning & J. Van Maanen (eds.), *Policing: A view from the street* (pp. 221–238). Santa Monica, CA: Goodyear.

Virtanen, K. (1979). A comparison of the historical development of police organization in Finland as compared to the other Scandinavian countries. In J.

Knutsson, E. Kuhlhorn, & A. Reiss, Jr. (eds.), *Police and the social order.* Stockholm: National Swedish Council for Crime Prevention.

Waegel, W. B. (1981). Case routinization in investigative police work. *Social Problems* 28(3):263–275.

Walker, S. (1980). *Popular justice.* New York: Oxford University Press.

Walker, S. (1992). The police and the community: Scranton, Pennsylvania 1866–1884, a test case. In E. H. Monkkonen (ed.), *Policing and crime control.* Munich: K. G. Saur.

Walker, S. (1993). Does anyone remember team policing? Lessons of the team policing experience for community policing. *American Journal of Police* 12(1):33–55.

Walker, S. (1998). *Popular justice* (2nd ed.). New York: Oxford University Press.

Walker, S., & Katz, C. (1995). Less than meets the eye: Police department bias-crime units. *American Journal of Police* XIV(1):29–48.

Walker, S., & Kreisel, B. W. (1996). Varieties of citizen review: The implications of organizational features of complaint review procedures for accountability of the police. *American Journal of Police* 15(3):65–88.

Watts, E. J. (1992a). St. Louis police recruits in the twentieth century. In E. H. Monkkonen (ed.), *Policing and crime control.* Munich: K. G. Saur.

Watts, E. J. (1992b). The police in Atlanta, 1890–1905. In E. H. Monkkonen (ed.), *Policing and crime control.* Munich: K. G. Saur.

Weber, M. (1947). *The theory of social and economic organization.* (A. M. Henderson & T. Parsons, Trans.) New York: Oxford University Press.

Weed (1982). Patterns of growth in welfare bureaucracies. *Sociological Quarterly* 23(3):391–401.

Weick, K. E. (1969). *The social psychology of organizing.* Reading, MA: Addison-Wesley.

Weick, K. E. (1976). Educational organizations as loosely coupled systems. *Administrative Science Quarterly* 21:1–19.

Weiss, A. (1992). *The innovation process in public organizations: Patterns of diffusion and adoption in American policing.* Ann Arbor, MI: UMI Dissertation Service.

Weiss, A. (1997). The communication of innovation in American policing. *Policing* 20(2):292–310.

Wells, L. E., & Falcone, D. N. (1992). Organizational variations in vehicle pursuits by police: The impact of policy on practice. *Criminal Justice Policy Review* 6(4):311–333.

Wenger, D. E. (1973). The reluctant army: The functioning of police departments during civil disturbances. *American Behavioral Scientist* 16(3): 326–342.

Wertsch, D. (1992). The evolution of the Des Moines police department: Professionalization and the decline of public disorder arrests in the twentieth century. In E. H. Monkkonen (ed.), *Policing and crime control*. Munich: K. G. Saur.

Wheaton, B., Muthen, B., Alwin, D. F., & Summers, G. F. (1977). Assessing reliability and stability in panel models. In D. R. Heise (ed.), *Sociological methodology 1977* (pp. 84–136). San Francisco: Jossey-Bass.

Williamson, O. E. (1985). *The economic institutions of capitalism*. New York: Free Press.

Wilson, J. M. (2002). Complexity and control: Testing a measurement model of police organizational structure. Unpublished paper. Columbus, OH: Ohio State University.

Wilson, J. Q. (1968). *Varieties of police behavior: The management of law and order in eight communities*. Cambridge, MA: Harvard University Press.

Wilson, J. Q. (1989). *Bureaucracy: What government agencies do and why they do it*. New York: Basic Books.

Wilson, J. Q., & Kelling, G. L. (1982). Broken windows: The police and neighborhood safety. *Atlantic Monthly* 249:29–38.

Woods, G. (1993). *The police in Los Angeles*. New York: Garland Publishing.

Woodward, J. (1965). *Industrial organization: Theory and practice*. Oxford: Oxford University Press.

Worden, R. E. (1989). Situational and attitudinal explanations of police behavior: A theoretical reappraisal and empirical assessment. *Law and Society Review* 23:667–711.

Worden, R. E. (1994). The "causes" of police brutality: Theory and evidence on police use of force. In W. A. Geller & H. Toch (eds.), *And justice for all: A national agenda for understanding and controlling police abuse of force* (pp. 33–60). Washington, DC: Police Executive Research Forum.

Worden, R. E., & Shepard, R. L. (1996). Demeanor, crime, and police behavior: A reexamination of the police services study data. *Criminology* 34(1):83–106.

Wothke, W. (1993). Nonpositive definite matrices in structural modeling. In K. A. Bollen & J. S. Long (eds.), *Testing structural equation models* (pp. 256–293). Newbury Park, CA: Sage Publications.

Wright, S. (1934). The method of path coefficients. *Annals of Mathematical Statistics* 5:161–215.

Wycoff, M. A. (1994). *Community policing strategies*. Unpublished report. Washington, DC: Police Foundation.

Young, R. C. (1988). Is population ecology a useful paradigm for the study of organizations? *American Journal of Sociology* 94(1):1–24.

Zhao, J. (1996). *Why police organizations change: A study of community-oriented policing.* Washington, DC: Police Executive Research Forum.

Zhao, J., & Lovrich, N. (1997). Collective bargaining and the police: What consequences for supplemental compensation policies in large agencies? Paper presented at the annual meeting of the Academy of Criminal Justice Sciences, Louisville, KY, March 12.

Name Index

273

Subject Index

279